# STOCK PHOTOGRAPHY

## THE COMPLETE GUIDE

# STOCK PHOTOGRAPHY

## THE COMPLETE GUIDE

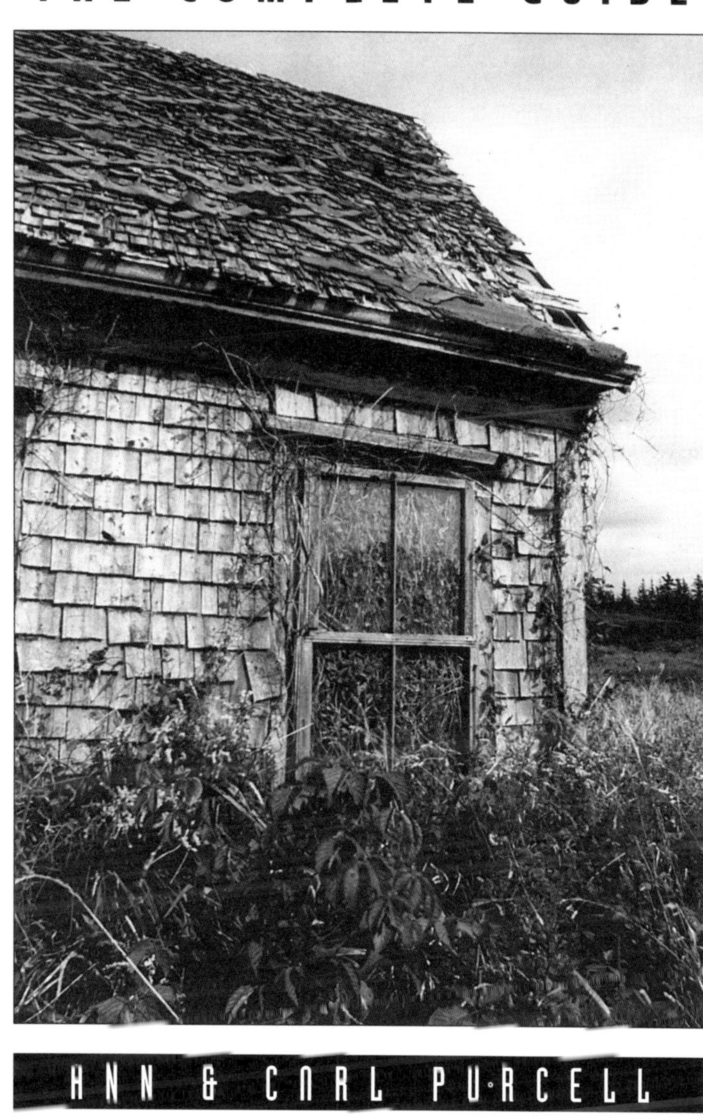

ANN & CARL PURCELL

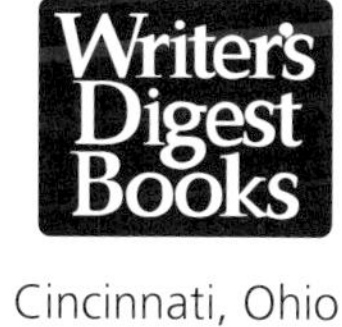


Cincinnati, Ohio

*Preceding page:* This weather-beaten house in Canada made an interesting photograph and was a welcome addition to our stock file. It is also a generic Nova Scotia countryside study.

 Published by Writer's Digest Books, an imprint of F&W Publications, Inc., 1507 Dana Avenue, Cincinnati, Ohio 45207. 1-800-289-0963.
First edition.
Printed and bound in Mexico.

97 96 95 94 93 5 4 3 2 1

**Library of Congress Cataloging in Publication Data**

Purcell, Ann.
Stock photography : the complete guide / Ann & Carl Purcell. — 1st ed.
p. cm.
ISBN 0-89879-552-4
1. Stock photography—Handbooks, manuals, etc. 2. Photographs—Marketing—Handbooks, manuals, etc. I. Purcell, Carl. II. Title.
TR690.6.P87 1993
770'.68—dc20 92-37710
CIP

Edited by Mark Garvey
Designed by Sandy Conopeotis

# DEDICATION

This book is dedicated to each other

and

to our brothers and sisters,

unsung heros who have greatly influenced our lives.

Love and thanks to:

Blair and Margot Purcell

Jim and Elizabeth Frederick

Elizabeth Frederick Derringer

Alice Purcell Pugh

Dick and Jeanne Houck

# TABLE OF CONTENTS

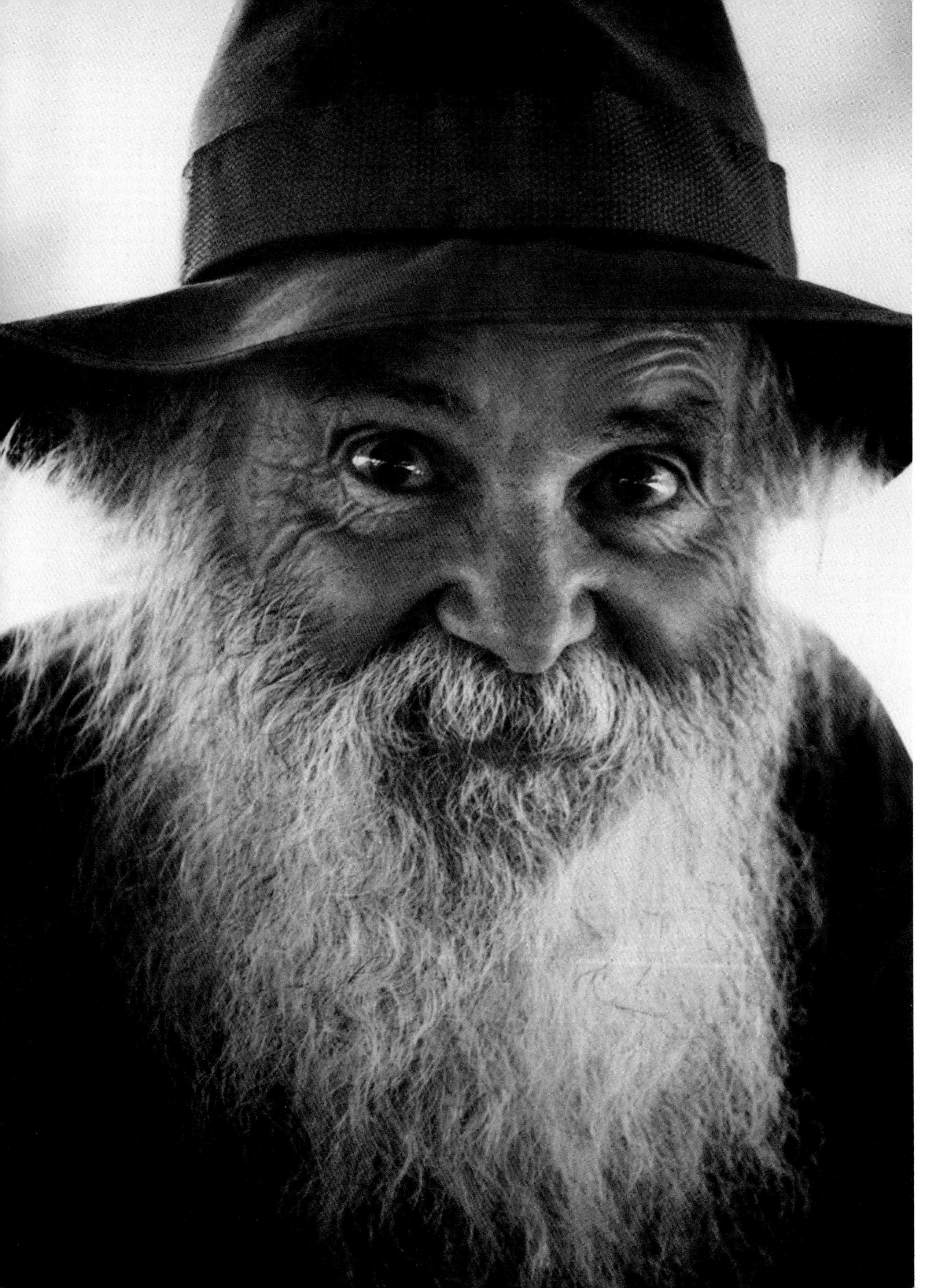

# INTRODUCTION

Serious amateurs take pictures mainly for their own satisfaction, but for whatever purpose the pictures were taken, they can have a long-term commercial value. Pictures that stay in your files or on your shelf in yellow boxes may be worth thousands upon thousands of dollars. The tricks are being well organized enough to find the needed image or subject, making yourself familiar to potential editors or art buyers, knowing how to get the pictures to the editors or art buyers who want to buy them, and negotiating a fair price for the use of the photos. In essence, that's what this book is all about. We will provide you with the guidelines on how to take good stock pictures, how to successfully market them, and how to either create your own stock photography business, supplement your present income by joining one or more stock agencies, or both.

We are perfect examples of what's possible. As travel writers and photographers, we shoot approximately 6,000 color slides every month. We shoot many of these on assignment for various magazines, book publishers, public relations companies and advertising agencies. We are well paid for what we do and our clients purchase the specific rights they want or need.

In almost all cases, we retain the rights to our pictures; the original slides, including the ones used by the client, come back to our files. We take great care to caption all slides and file them under the correct heading or category for easy location.

A big part of our job is finding out who needs what we have in our files and when. That is not as simple as it sounds. Quality is important for your reputation, but even quality won't matter if you can't put your hands on the right subject and get it to the editor or buyer in time to meet the deadline. Most picture editors learn what is wanted on Monday, and need to have the perfect picture on their light table by Wednesday. Some even need it by Tuesday. Close proximity of potential clients is not the key to success if you can't use simple marketing tools. Even if that editor works in New York and you also live in New York, that editor may never know that you have the ideal picture to fit his needs.

Fortunately for us, some important editors know that we have over 650,000 color slides from 94 countries in our home. Thanks to telephones and fax machines, we often learn about the photo needs almost as quickly as the picture editors do. It is literally possible for us to respond within minutes, and in the stock business a fast response can result in a sale. When *Travel & Leisure* needs slides of Montreal, we can make a pull and have it shipped by Federal Express or UPS the same day.

If necessary, the editor can view the slides the next morning. We fill four or five such requests every day and, if we did not thoroughly enjoy our field work, could probably earn a living from our existing stock file for the rest of our lives without ever taking another picture.

What kind of money can a competent photographer expect to make from stock sales? Of course, this varies according to the skill and time invested. Our sales for advertising have been as high as $10,000 for a single picture. However, we often sell reproduction rights for as low as $75 when the buyer is using twenty-five or more pictures at one time. We will turn down a possible sale when we feel the buyer is not meeting a fair industry standard that covers at least more than the cost of film, processing and considerable overhead. It is important that you sell your pictures to make a profit and not for the satisfaction of seeing them in print. Ironically, picture editors have more respect for photographers who place a fair market value on their pictures than those who sell out for anything they can get. In the long run, a good editor wants quality and is willing to pay for it.

In this book, we will define good stock pictures and provide specific suggestions for shooting for stock. We will explain model releases, their wording and their value, along with submission forms and holding fees. We will discuss the difference between editorial and advertising style and will show how pictures are composed to allow space for magazine logos and type.

Naturally, we will also talk about equipment, comparing the various formats and new features available on cameras. We will cover lighting, including both strobes and hot lights, and discuss their relative merits. We will talk about film and explain why we consider color-slide film the universal emulsion for publication, color prints, and black-and-white prints. In addition, we will show you various options for filing your slides, including plastic sleeves and metal cabinets. We will tell you how we edit our slides, caption them and organize them into categories. We will discuss self-promotion, advertising and pricing. We will provide information on projectors, viewers and light tables.

The stock photography business, like many others, is being inundated by new technology. Although you can get your business started without using fancy tools, we will show how modern equipment can make your work easier. Our book will provide vital information on computers, slide-labeling programs, databases, videodisks, CD-ROM, slide duping in various formats and digital imagery. We will discuss the selection of picture agencies and electronic networks that list photo requests. We will cover the procedure to copyright your work and make suggestions on how to keep your photographs from being used without your permission or without payment.

Clearly, a talented photographer can make a good living from stock photography. You should understand that it takes time to build your reputation, make the necessary contacts, caption and copyright all slides, organize your picture files, send out indexes or lists of subjects, and ultimately make sales. It has taken us a number of years to achieve our level of success, but it has been worth the effort. You can do the same, but you should know from the start that stock photography is a time-consuming, labor-intensive, highly competitive business.

As in any other field, there are no substitutes for excellence, talent and hard work. This book will teach you the ropes of the stock photography business and what to be shooting the next time you go out with your camera. We will say, however, without hesitation that, if you take good pictures and have a considerable number of them available and organized, your photos can create a substantial income for you. Don't let your slides sit unused on your shelf, freeloaders gathering dust. Put those babies to work! They can earn a living for you.

*Chapter 1*

# AN OVERVIEW OF THE STOCK BUSINESS

There is hidden treasure in your drawers and closets, possibly still in little yellow boxes. This book will tell you how to convert your color and black-and-white pictures into hard cash. We're talking about the business of stock photography, a subject with which we are very familiar.

A large portion of our income is derived from stock sales. Every good picture has the potential of generating substantial income over many years, but too often these hidden treasures get put back into those cardboard boxes, negative sleeves or file folders and accumulate nothing but dust.

Almost everyone has taken some photographs, usually to preserve special moments or to celebrate special people. Occasionally, you will notice a sight or photograph a scene that is separate from your personal life because it amuses you or intrigues you. From time to time, you might even see a scene that seems like a setup for an advertisement. You snap the photo and joke with your friends about how much Coca-Cola Incorporated or Bell Atlantic would pay for a picture like that.

Then there are stock photographers who look for photographs in all three situations, and set them up if the situation doesn't happen spontaneously. When we see a winner, we'll photograph it vertically (cover shot), horizontally (slide show or wraparound cover), with filters, without filters, and we'll bracket our shots to be sure that we have at least one with perfect exposure.

It is important to realize that you don't sell a picture; you sell the one-time right to use or publish a picture. That image still belongs to you and your copyright should be on it. Hopefully a good picture will be used many times over the years. As an example, we sold the right to print seventeen pictures of Laos to a book publisher for $2,500 several years ago. Yesterday's mail brought us a purchase order for $1,350 from the publisher because they were using twelve of those pictures in another book.

## THE BASICS

Both professional photographers and serious amateurs have many good pictures that can be sold if they know how to reach the right markets. If you're interested in such sales, this book has been written for you. There are some basic steps for getting started:

1. Locate and edit your potential stock pictures.
2. Caption them neatly and accurately.
3. File them in appropriate categories.
4. Create and mail a picture index to potential buyers.
5. Show your work to picture editors and art directors.
6. Get your pictures to the people who need them, when they need them.

Of course this list is simplistic, but the basic principles of the stock business are simple. A stock operation gets more complicated once you're up and running, and we will provide all the technical and organizational details you'll need to be successful in later chapters. The first four points in the preceding list can be done by any photographer; the amount of time and effort depends on how many pictures are involved. Item five is a matter of salesmanship. Direct mail promotion can be useful, but the best results come from personal contact with the people who buy pictures. Item six is much more complex. You must decide whether to deal with art directors and photo editors directly, to work through picture agencies, or a combination of both.

## THE 35MM COLOR SLIDE ADVANTAGE

Photographers shoot with various types of cameras in different sizes of film formats. They shoot color and black and white, depending on their needs and desires, for an assignment or picture-taking session. While any good pictures can be used for stock, we believe there are compelling reasons to use 35mm color transparency film (also called "slide" film) when shooting with stock in mind. Larger film formats used to be preferred by printers for reproduction, but better lenses and improved film emulsions have made 35mm slides quite acceptable for most

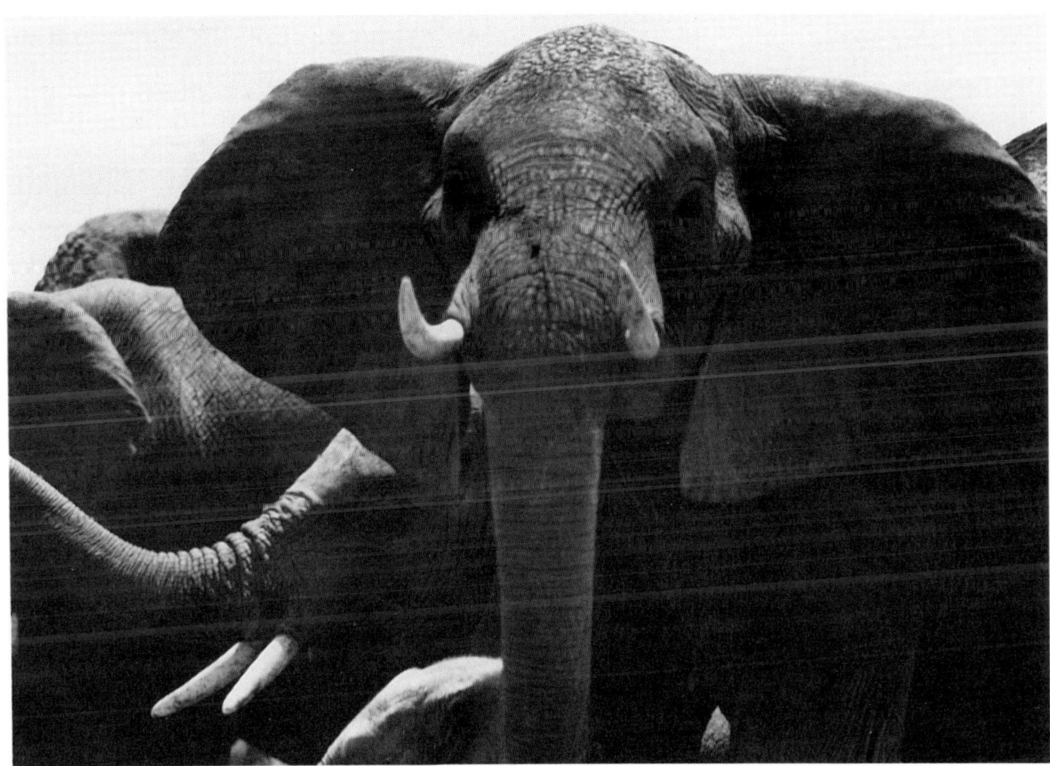

Elephants symbolize strength and an outstanding picture of this massive mammal is a valuable image for any stock file. Our extensive collection of slides of African animals has earned us many thousands of dollars.

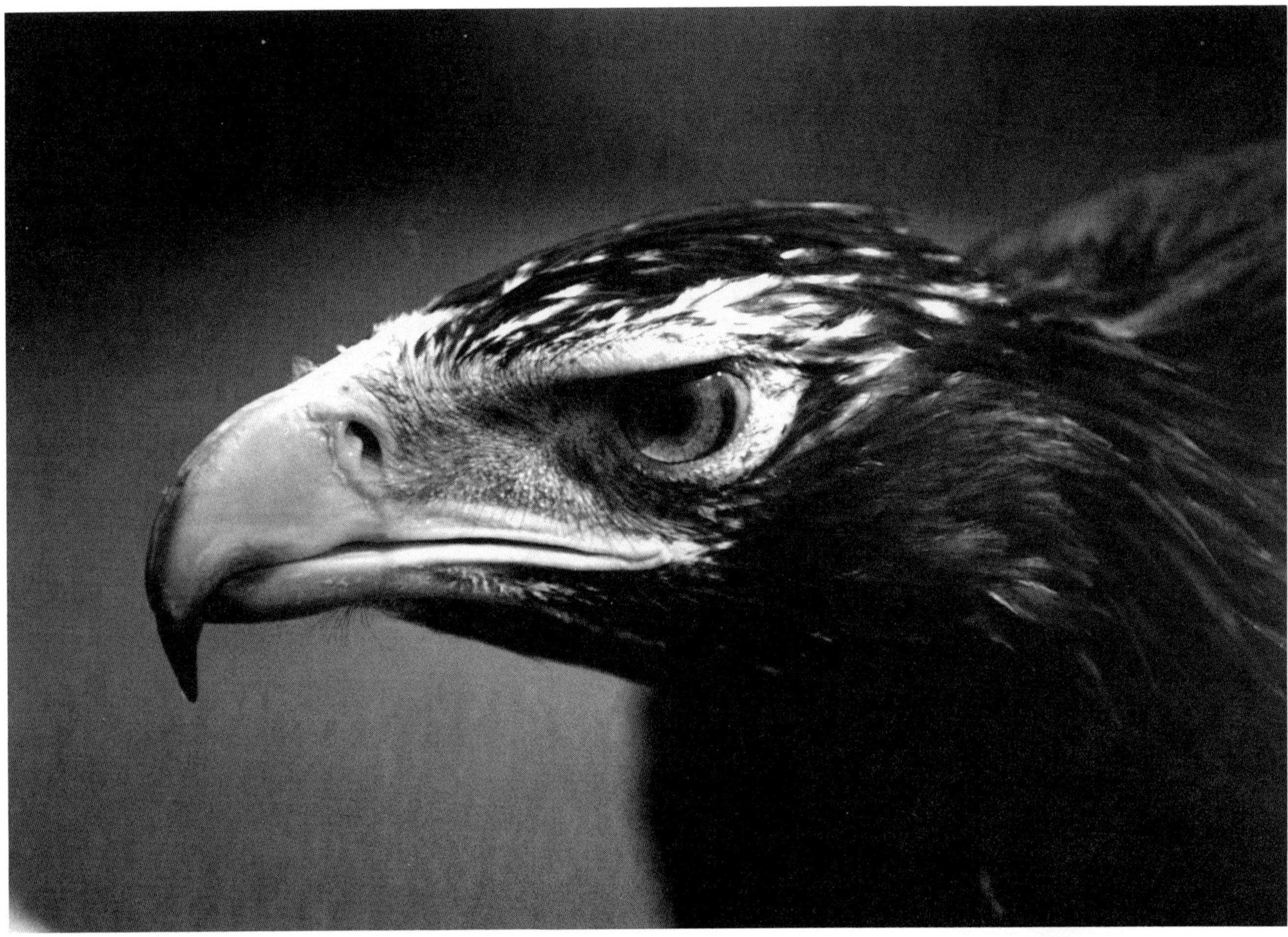

Wildlife shots are forever popular. This wedge-tailed eagle is an excellent example of a wildlife stock picture. We often shoot wildlife in the wild, but don't overlook the fact that you can get outstanding pictures of birds and animals in a zoo or wildlife park. This particular picture was taken in the Singapore Jurong Bird Park.

needs. The files at picture agencies have usually been set up for 35mm and slides are easy to insert into plastic sleeves (twenty to a page) and ship to clients. In addition, high-quality color prints and black-and-white prints can be obtained from slide film, making it an almost universal emulsion.

Color slides, color prints and black-and-white prints can also be made from color negative film, but the quality of slides and black-and-white prints converted from color negative film is not the best. In this book we will encourage photographers interested in stock sales to shoot most pictures with 35mm color slide film. The obvious advantage is not having to shoot every scene or situation with two cameras, one for color and one for black and white. This saves time and money and allows you to carry less camera equipment on location.

There are advantages to using 35mm cameras with interchangeable lenses for shooting stock. Such camera systems are compact, lightweight, and have the most advanced features, such as multimode automatic exposure, autofocus, dedicated flash and zoom lenses. Being portable, these camera systems are ideal for shooting stock on location. As many as three camera bodies, seven lenses and two electronic flash units can be carried in a single case. Obviously, we follow these recommendations on film and equipment ourselves, whether shooting on assignment or speculation. It has paid off very well in our case.

## RECORD KEEPING

When shooting for stock, it is important to get a model release for any people who appear prominently in the picture. We will discuss model releases and give examples in chapter three.

Another vitally important aspect of stock photography is keeping track of the pictures that you have submitted to a client. This is most often done in a client record book, a simple method of recording the number of slides submitted and logging them back in when they are returned. This sounds easy, but with many clients, multiple submissions and multiple returns, it can be very complex. We have devised a way to photocopy a sheet of slides, which provides us with a legible record of the captions and a recognizable black-and-white image of the slide; we will explain this in chapter four. Such a record allows us to specifically identify a slide if it is not returned by a client. Identification of a lost slide can be extremely important since the American Society of Media Photographers (ASMP) recommends that the value of an original slide be set at $1,500. If ten slides are lost, this could result in up to $15,000 compensation. You probably don't want to lose ten top-quality slides, but that amount could buy you a new sports car. In one case it did for us, and driving that car with the top down made us feel much better about the loss.

To protect yourself from loss or damage, it is necessary to have a submission form or delivery memo to send with your slides. This form should be printed and clearly state your terms of submission, including the value you place on each original slide. We discuss submission forms and provide an example of the one we use in chapter four.

The procedure for submitting to picture agencies is somewhat different, but it is still important to keep accurate records. A photo agency does not normally buy pictures from photographers, but takes them on consignment for their files and pays a commission (about 50 percent) to the photographers when a picture is published and payment is received. At first glance the agency's portion may seem high, but an agency has the cost of overhead, staff salaries and often spends considerable money to promote the pictures in their files. Many photographers prefer to spend most of their time taking pictures and let one or more agencies sell their images. A picture agency will not accept responsibility for your slides themselves, but if one of their clients loses or damages one of your slides, the agency will try to collect and then split the proceeds with you. Accordingly, you would not send an agency the standard delivery memo, but would make a careful record of what they keep.

## STOCK SALES

What is the potential for stock sales? There is no doubt that there is a huge market for stock photography in publishing, advertising, public relations, television and audiovisual. Tapping that potential requires talent, organization, perseverance and, to some degree, pure luck. Marketing stock is highly competitive and labor intensive. Years ago we decided that investing time and film into the stock business would eventually pay back our efforts many times over. Today, we are beginning to reap the benefits. Some photographers in the stock business guard their business secrets with jealousy, but we are pleased to lend others a helping hand. The hard lessons we have learned, the joyous discoveries, and the types of markets to which we sell are contained in this book. By following the blueprints we provide, you can turn stock sales into a big business.

It is important to know that while some photographers sell stock as a spin-off to their assignments or amateur endeavors, others work full time at the stock business and often do very well at it. Such photographers carefully analyze the market, decide what is needed, and then go out and shoot it. To shoot and market stock full time requires a unique dedication and self-discipline. It requires establishing your own market outlets and affiliating with one or more picture agencies. Agencies are like hungry animals; they have to be fed on a regular basis.

We specialize in travel and provide pictures for travel and geographic destinations throughout the world. Some photographers envy us, quite sure that they could become successful if only they could afford a trip around the world. Ironically, the best stock pictures can be shot right in your own hometown, even in your own backyard. The most sought-after stock pictures are family shots: mothers and fathers with their children, a little boy blowing out the candles on his birthday cake, a little girl playing with a kitten, or a grandfather sitting in a rocker on the front porch. One of our pictures that sells again and again is an older gentleman sitting under a tree with his granddaughter. Carl saw this charming pair in our neighborhood as he was driving to the supermarket. He called Ann from the grocery store and said, "I have a gift for you!" Ann turned off the stove and grabbed her cameras. The man and his granddaughter were still under the tree when Ann arrived and they were glad to pose for pictures, particularly when they heard that they were a "gift" from husband to wife. Naturally, we later had a large color print made and presented it to the proud grandfather. That picture sells more often than our stunning shots of the Taj Mahal in India.

The stock shooters we know study the picture requests and trends of the market carefully. They recognize the need for subjects, such as computers, minorities, soldiers in training, mailmen, school buses, household items, etc. We cannot count the times we have been asked to show a housewife doing the laundry. We constantly get requests for pictures to illustrate the problem of teens and drugs. These full-time stock photographers often hire models to meet their perceived needs. In looking through the files of a colleague, we saw many pictures of black families. He had hired black models purely for a stock shoot, knowing that within a year his investment would be more than paid back. That photographer understood the market.

We would not urge all would-be stock photographers to hire models. You can often get your relatives and friends to pose and sign model releases in exchange for color prints. Recently we traveled to Hawaii where we made arrangements for three professional models to spend half a day with us on a shoot at a mountain waterfall. They agreed to pose in exchange for large color prints to add to their portfolios.

The most profitable stock sales usually come when you can make multiple sales to a client at one time. In some instances your files will contain everything a client needs for a particular project. There are some countries we have covered that—to say the least—are off the beaten track. If we have a good selection on such a country, we often can sell many pictures from that file to a client who needs comprehensive coverage. In other instances, a customer will be looking for a number of pictures to illustrate major cities of the world and, since we have them available, the picture editor may use our pictures as a matter of convenience or one-stop shopping. We will also be able to negotiate a lower price per picture if the client is taking thirty instead of one.

Couples are always in demand to meet both editorial and advertising needs. Shoot attractive couples whenever possible and be sure to get model releases.

The big bucks are in advertising and one good sale for an international ad can buy a lot of hamburger. The trick is having an image that fits the concept in an art director's mind and somehow letting that art director know you have it and getting it to him to meet his deadline. Some picture agencies push advertising sales. Our agency in Japan sold a picture we had taken of storm-blown palm trees on the island of Moorea to the Nissan Motor Company. The ad said "Our engineers study the wind when they design cars." That sale was for $9,000; the picture was not one of our best, but it fit the concept.

Stock photography is an incredibly complex business. In doing this book, we felt it was important to interview Richard Weisgrau, executive director of the American Society of Media Photographers, an association that is invaluable to professional photographers throughout the United States. If you only belong to one photography association, this would be the one you should choose. Many ASMP members are involved in stock sales and Dick Weisgrau has been a leader in helping to set standards and guidelines in the business and addressing problems that have developed between photographers and agencies over the past few years. He was generous with his time and gave us some thoughtful answers.

## RICHARD WEISGRAU, EXECUTIVE DIRECTOR OF THE AMERICAN SOCIETY OF MEDIA PHOTOGRAPHERS

**Q:** ***What is ASMP's role in the stock industry?***

**A:** ASMP's role in the stock industry is the same as it is in all the other segments of the professional publication photographer's world. The Society was founded to protect and promote the interests of such photographers. Generally it impacts the stock photography segment by educating photographers on the conduct of their stock photo business, and about their relationship with their agents. We also maintain a dialogue with the Stock Agencies' Association. This dialogue resulted recently in the joint ASMP/PACA statement of principle that defines the minimal rights a photographer should have in a stock contract. Of course, when education and dialogue fails, we have a stronger means of advocacy, such as the courts.

**Q:** ***What impact do you feel that CD-ROM disks and clip art will have on stock prices and how soon will this impact be felt? (CD-ROM technology is discussed in chapter eight.) We are interested in finding out what you actually think* will *happen rather than what you think* ought to *happen.***

**A:** CD-ROM and CD-Clip Art will eventually drive the price of stock photography down. That will be a result of the reduced cost of distribution. However, that won't necessarily effect profitability if properly managed. Of course, if CD-Clip Art proliferates *without restrictions on use*, the price of stock will deteriorate and profitability will decrease. I don't think this is likely to happen. Additionally, as ease of distribution increases, the supply will increase. If demand increases, the supply/demand equation stays in balance and profitability can be maintained. I expect this will happen. Finally, the emergence of CD-ROM as an education and entertainment media will further increase demand, but with lower fees per use. Again, the supply/demand equation will dictate. All things considered, I'm convinced that stock photography has good income potential in this new era.

**Q:** ***Will picture agencies be able to survive in the age of electronic images?***

**A:** Yes, definitely. Their role might change, probably will, but they will be around. There has to be a filter/quality gate, distributor of the image. That is an agency in one form or another. The new technology will make it more difficult for the independent photographer to keep his/her work in the mainstream without an agency, since most publishers will be looking to lower transactional costs in negotiations over content rights. They will seek to deal with one agent of many photographers rather than with many individual photographers.

**Q:** ***What efforts is ASMP making to insure that stock agencies deal honestly with their photographers and pay them in a timely manner?***

**A:** ASMP is continuing to monitor the practices of agencies and it follows up on complaints about agencies from its members. We have audited, negotiated and battled with agencies. We have contributed legal assistance to members involved in legal actions against agencies. We are amassing a database of members' agency affiliations to set up an early warning/communications network. The most effective thing out of all of this is that most agencies know ASMP is concerned, observing and ready to act. Ultimately, we cannot force timely payment. If an agency has no cash, ASMP cannot change that. All we can do is to warn people.

**Q:** ***Do you feel that publications are tending to use more stock as opposed to giving assignments?***

**A:** Yes. Assignment photography is expensive when compared to stock. Publications are businesses and will save whenever they can. This trend will continue as the supply of available stock grows in size and diversity. Assignments seem destined to be employed to illustrate unique concepts or report on events or unique situations. That will always be the same. But when generic will suffice, cost will dictate.

**Q:** ***How will copyright be determined on composite electronic pictures made from several images taken by different photographers? (This is discussed in chapter eight.)***

**A:** There are two ways. First, by agreement of the parties involved, through a contractual relationship, to the division, if any, of copyright ownership. Second, by contest (perhaps legal), determining the degree of copyrightable contribution of each party to the whole. The composite electronic image will often be joint copyright, or a derivative work depending upon the facts of each case. Therein lies the problem of failing to contractually agree to copyright ownership before a work is created. After the fact, it requires sorting out the facts, which are not always as clear as one would like. That usually means lawyers, courts and money.

## GETTING STARTED

We have many letters and telephone calls from people who have read our books or heard us talk about our stock photography business and who have questions. We have even had people come for dinner in our house in Alexandria, Virginia, from as far away as Philadelphia, Pennsylvania, in order to ask our advice.

While this book is intended to give you a foot up—the benefit of hard and tried experience without having had to live through it yourself—and although we know that you can make a success of your stock photography business if you follow the advice we have given, we do wish to caution you. Even if you have decided that you want to make stock photography your permanent and sole business, do not leave your current job tomorrow. It takes time for people to know that they can come to you for the pictures they want. Art directors need to see your work several times before they will think of you when there is a photo assignment pending. It takes agencies almost an entire year from the time they receive your slides to start making money for you from those photos. You will need several months, at least, to set up and integrate all the parts of your stock business.

Our advice has always been to wait until you are making an equivalent of 50 percent of your regular salary in your spare time from your stock business before you leave your current full-time job. If you are making at least 50 percent of your final goal income just on weekends and vacations, you can consider leaving your job and probably make a decent living as a stock photographer. You may eat beans for the first few months, but you will prob-

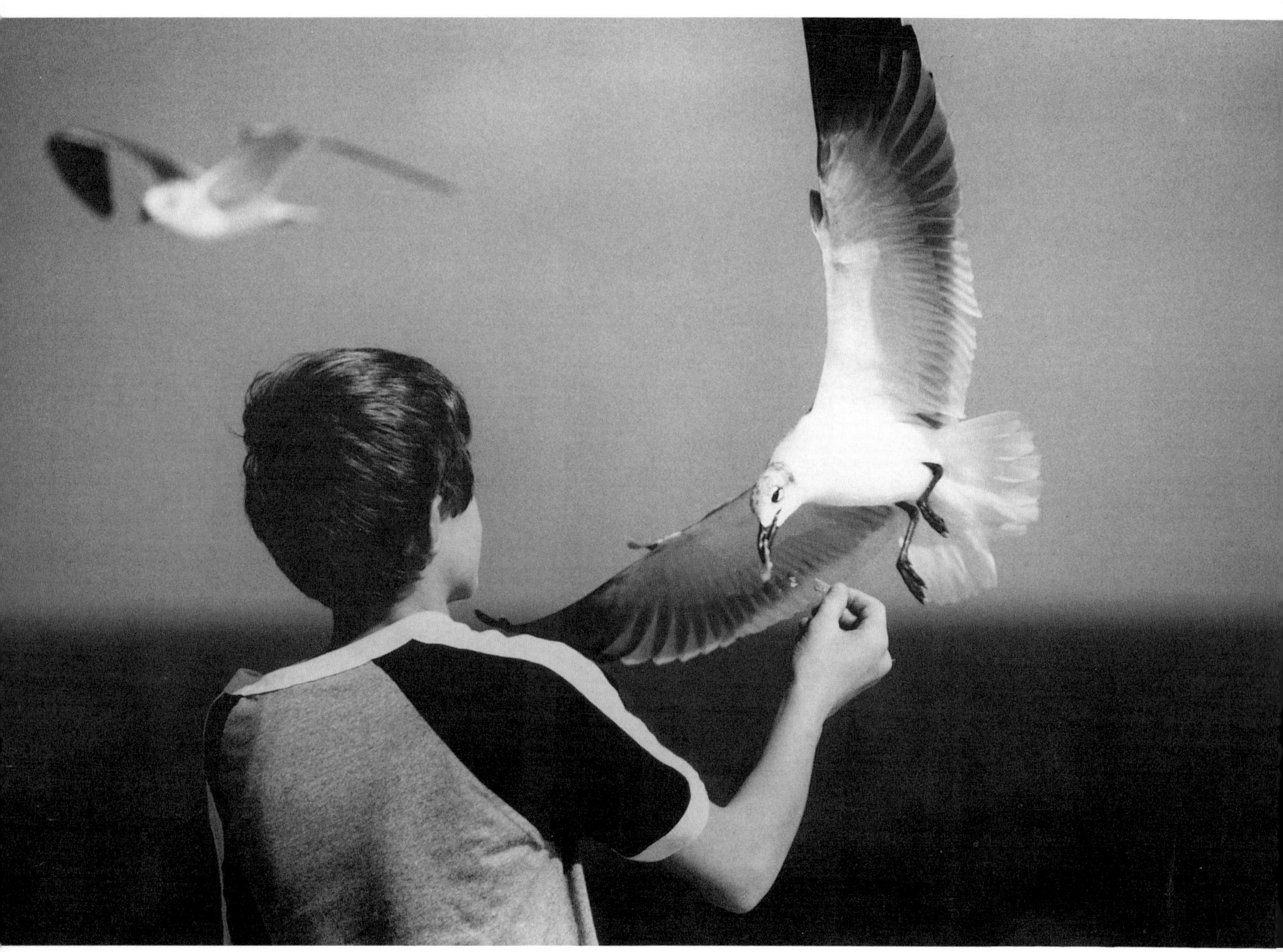

A child interacting with wildlife is a popular subject for stock files. Here a boy feeds a sea gull from the deck of a fishing boat in Florida.

ably make it, particularly if you follow all the advice we have given you.

If you decide that you want to set up a stock photography business just part-time or only when you are retired, the time to start is now. By the time you retire, you want your photographs already to be earning a nice amount of money for you. In the meantime, it certainly won't hurt to have an auxiliary income, which increases nicely each year, coming in from your photography.

When you first consider starting your stock photography business, it might seem like a lot of trouble. As you get more familiar with the various steps you must take for filing, marketing and tracking slides, you will find that the business side of the business becomes less confusing. The joy and freedom of being your own boss and doing exciting creative work will be extremely rewarding.

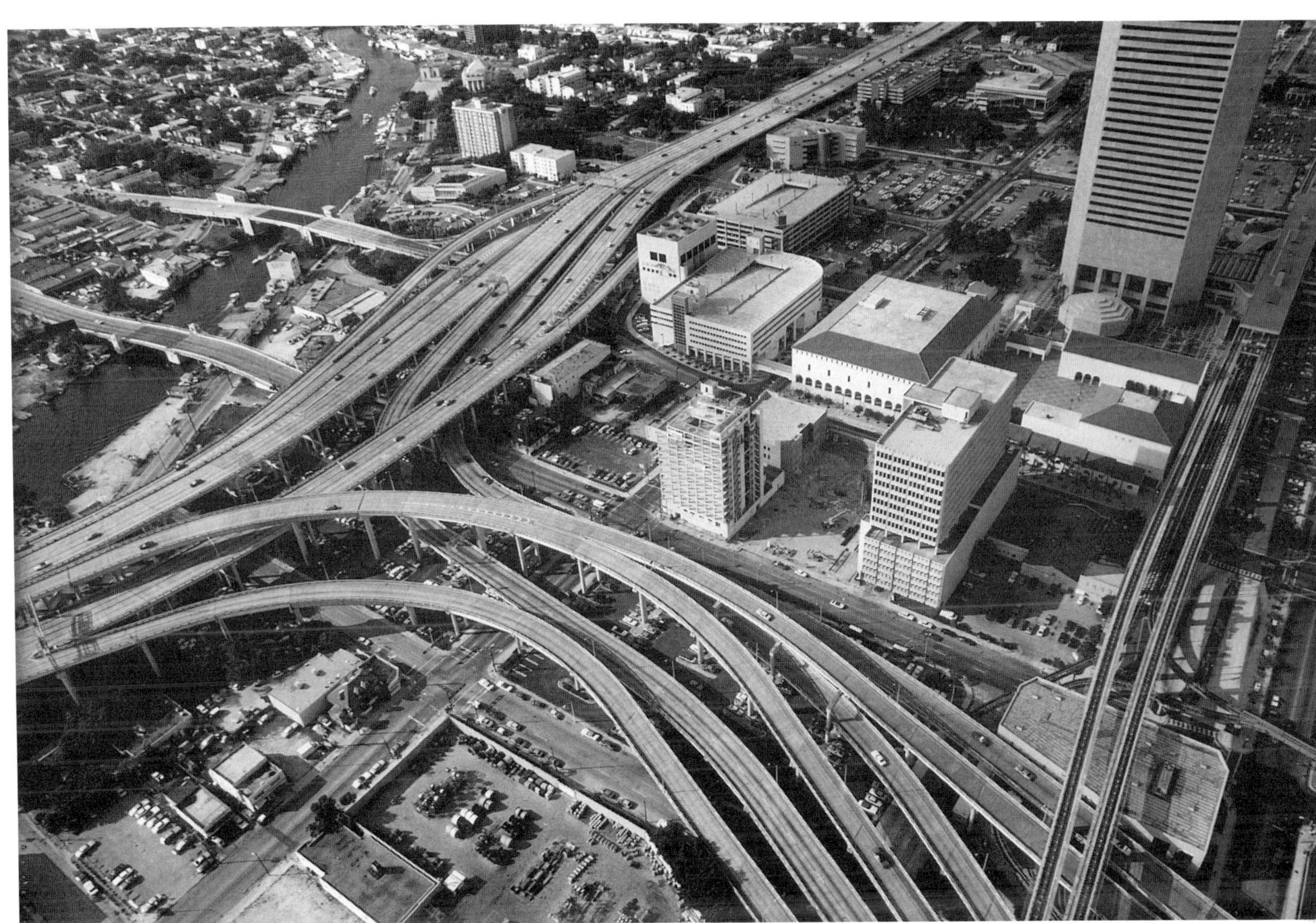

An aerial view of downtown Miami shows the complex freeway system in this city. Such an image can be used to illustrate urban growth and traffic problems

*Chapter 2*

# CREATIVE STOCK PHOTOS

By definition, creative stock photos are photos that sell. In a business enterprise, that has to be the bottom line. Of course, we all want at least some of our photography to have those often elusive qualities which can make photography art, but for stock pictures we need images that meet the commercial needs of picture editors and art directors. These needs can be as ethereal as an illustration to symbolize the coming of spring or as mundane as a picture to sell dog food, not that such a picture needs to be mundane, as the photo on page 25 shows.

## THE ROLE OF PICTURES

Pictures play a very important role in our visually oriented society. They convey information, they impart feelings, and they work to support words. We are bombarded by strong visual images in our lives. Movies, television, billboards, advertisements in magazines and newspapers, cereal boxes, postcards and books all use pictures to command our attention and hopefully to motivate our actions. Most of these pictures come from stock sources and understandably stock photography is big business. Pictures are essential to effective marketing of products and services and marketing is the keystone of our economy. The cover pictures on magazines were chosen to get the public to buy the magazine. The editorial photos accompanying each article inside the magazine have been picked to create a curiosity about the article, hopefully great enough that the person flipping through the magazine would take time to read the article.

Most photographers use stock sales, either through agencies or directly to clients, as a way to supplement their assignment income. They put their outtakes from assignments into categories in their personal file or send them to a picture agency. The theory is to put these perfectly good and useable pictures to work generating income.

For the photographer who creates his or her own file, stock sales are often slow at the beginning. It takes time for picture buyers to recognize your name and come to you for stock photos. To start you may have only a few subjects to offer. Over time, as your name becomes better known and you add more subjects to your file, the telephone will ring more often and you, or possibly someone who works for you, need to be ready to fill those requests. In addition, you must keep track of who has received how many pictures, invoice a client when a sale is made, and carefully refile the pictures in the correct categories when they are returned. This is painstaking detail work, but it is just as important to your success as taking a good picture in the first place.

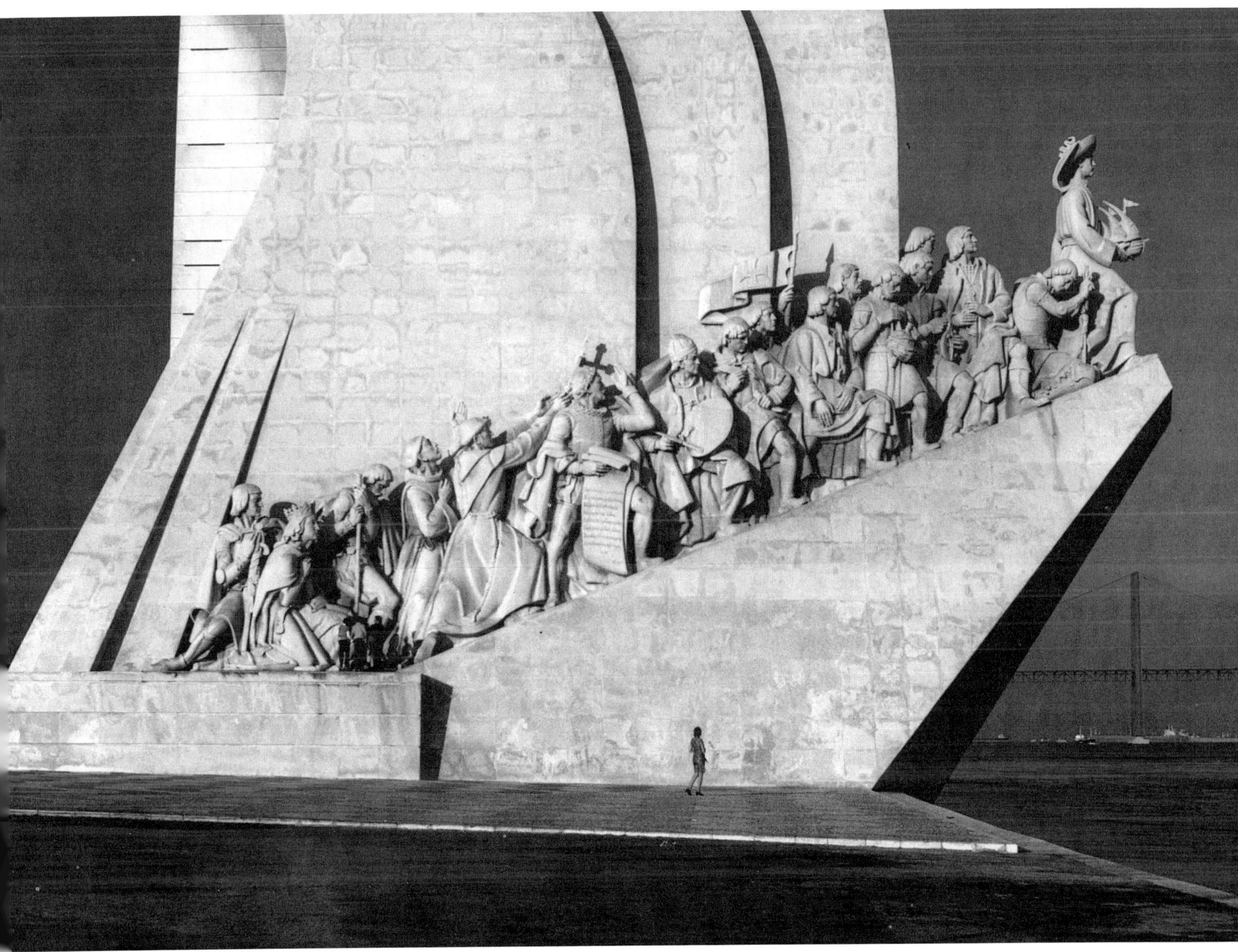

The Monument to Henry the Navigator in Lisbon, Portugal, is a massive stone sculpture. It is necessary to include a human figure in the picture to indicate its size. Use of a person is often necessary in scenes or landscapes, which cannot convey scale in any other way. With a person, this picture becomes much more valuable for stock.

## WHAT TO SHOOT?

To start any photographer needs to have a sense of what type of picture sells. Some photographers assume that it is the exotic, unusual picture taken in some remote part of the world that will bring big money, but in fact it is usually a warm, ordinary family picture with a father, mother and children that sells better than anything else. This is because such a subject has a universal appeal. The viewer can identify with this type of picture. Such a photograph can illustrate an advertisement for insurance, new homes, backyard barbecue grills or blue jeans.

When taking this type of family picture, try a variety of angles and variations. Shoot one with the whole family, try another with the father and son, another with the mother and daughter and still another with just the husband and wife together. Have them involved in different activities such as mowing the lawn, drinking lemonade, resting in a hammock or cutting flowers from the garden. Look for the interplay that takes place between family members and record it with your camera. Like any picture-taking session, you hopefully will get many useable shots, a few really good ones and maybe one or two real winners. Carry your camera when your child goes to the pediatrician or dentist. Photograph a friend or relative getting an electrocardiogram. Catch your neighbors having a picnic. Ask your bank teller to pose behind his grill. Snap your favorite gas station attendant at work. Ask if you can go with your niece to her ballet class or piano lesson.

It is important to get model releases (see chapter four for wording) at the time the pictures are taken. While the good pictures will sell from time to time, the real winners should sell again and again. When you are taking pictures of pets interacting with people or with other pets, use your model release, with just an alteration of title, as a property release. You will also need a property release if you are taking photographs of any house that is not your own.

We have found that the best-sellers are those pictures that show different generations interacting. Show a little boy trying to act grown-up by wearing his father's hat, a grandmother holding her daughter's new baby, or a grandfather taking his grandson for a walk along a tree-shaded path in the fall. Other pictures that are also "hot" sellers show the older generation staying fit. Our population consists of a larger percentage of older people than it used to, so advertisers and marketers frequently try to pitch their advertisements to people over fifty. Attractive older couples, young couples starting their married life and couples with young children are used again and again for ads touting health insurance, life insurance, credit cards, bank loans, new cars, travel services and real estate developments.

Remember to follow all the basic rules of good photography. Keep your pictures simple. Make sure that the background is not cluttered. If you cannot get the photo except with a cluttered background, throw the background out of focus. Let color be a graphic tool. Focus on people and don't forget that closer is better. If there is a product in your photo, try to take a few generic views in which you cannot see the brand name. A salable stock photo, for example, is a grandmother, mother and child in a Honda, obviously enjoying themselves and the child firmly locked into a Century car seat. A better stock photo is slightly closer up, so that you see the grandmother, mother and child in a car (brand unidentifiable) with the child firmly locked into a car seat (brand unidentifiable).

The diversity of stock subjects is as broad as the world, as far-reaching as outer space, and as intimate as a drop of water on a rose petal. As a stock photographer your goal is to create stunning images with a universal appeal for as many markets as possible. Your only limit for new subjects is your imagination. As travel photographers, we strive to interpret the destination in a memorable way, but we have learned that a travel stock picture needs to say, for instance, "This is Paris" in a clear and unmistakable way. You want to use a subject or a landmark that is obviously Paris. If an editor or art director is only going to use one picture, there are strong reasons that it should be a subject like the Eiffel Tower, the Arc de Triomphe or Notre Dame. When it is possible to use three or four pictures in a layout, other subjects, such as people, sidewalk cafés, museums, parks, etc., can be used. Often editors will use generic photos that are identified with the destination. In the case of Paris, it might be a picture of a wine bottle, a round of cheese and a loaf of French bread on a checkered tablecloth.

## FORMAT OR FILM SIZE

Beginning photographers getting into stock often wonder which is the best film format. They have heard that some art directors insist on a large format such as 2¼-by-2¼ inches or 4-by-5 inches, but in fact the 35mm color slide has become the most widely accepted size for stock. Those who insist on the larger formats are living in the past. Improvements in color film and camera lenses make 35mm the best choice. It is easy to shoot, easy to process, easy to file, easy to ship, and makes high-quality color separations for reproduction. Obviously 2-by-2 inch 35mm slides are easier to store and take up less space than bigger formats, but the primary advantage is in the compact size and sophistication of the 35mm single lens reflex (SLR) camera. Most stock photography is shot in the field and carrying one camera bag and a selection of zoom lenses for each picture situation is far more convenient than lugging around a suitcase with a view camera and tripod. The smaller camera also allows you to catch those elusive candid pictures that happen quickly and cannot be posed or re-created. With some pictures, there can never be a second chance. Your equipment does not have to be fancy. Many of the newer "point-and-shoot" cameras take excellent professional-quality photographs. The most important component of any photograph is the photographer's eye. If you see a good photo, take it and never mind whether your camera cost $150 or $1,500. The picture will sell if it is good.

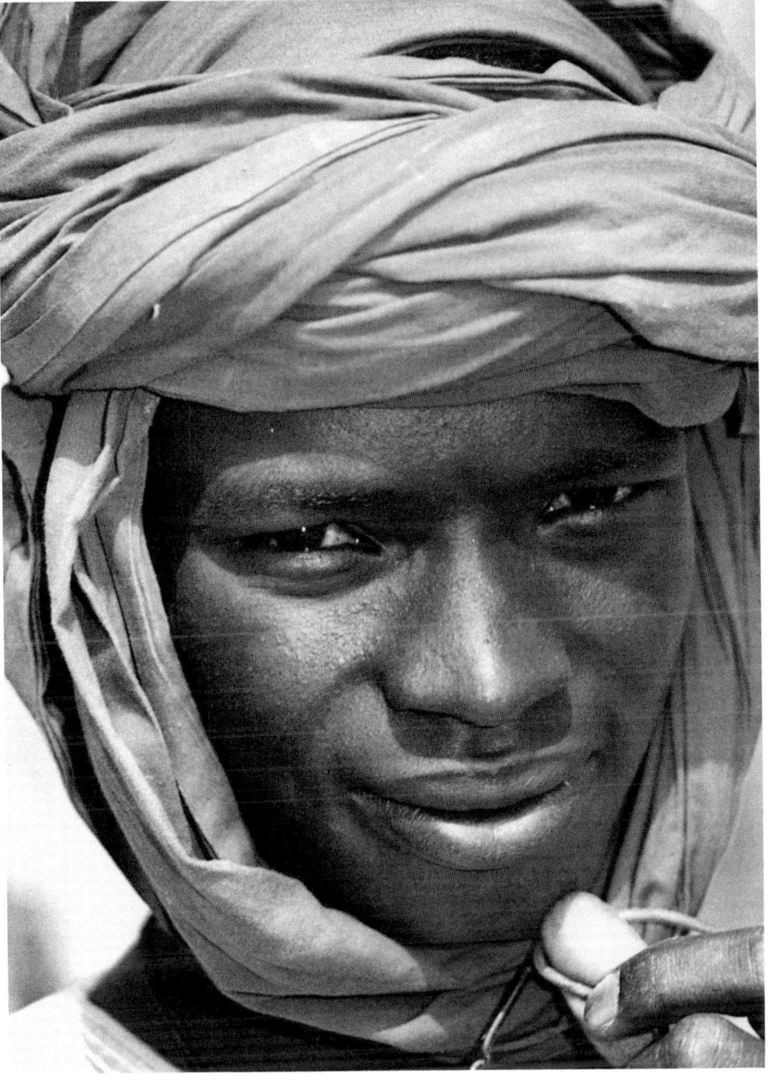

Textbooks frequently need pictures of specific African tribes. Having good shots of Masai, Samburu, Zulu or Kikuyu can often result in repeated sales. This shot of a turbaned Taureg from Senegal is an example of a tribal face. If, like ourselves, you have accumulated an extensive collection of ethnic or tribal faces from any part of the world, it is to your advantage to let picture researchers and editors know about your collection.

## STOCK CATEGORIES

Our own stock files are organized alphabetically and broken down into both generic and geographic categories. A stock photographer usually receives photo requests with a brief description of the needed picture. A generic request may ask for beaches, clouds or palm trees without a requirement for a specific location. Obviously, clouds can be seen anywhere in the world and it doesn't make any difference if a cloud picture was taken in Florida or the South Pacific. On the other hand, if an editor needs a beach in Hawaii, it is essential that the photo shows a beach in that island group. The palm trees from a beach in South America may be a different variety than those found in Hawaii. If the request is for a specific beach in Hawaii, it is important that the picture you send is of that specific beach. Your reputation depends on your accuracy and honesty.

## People Photography

Broadly speaking, stock falls into three categories: people, places and things. Under people, subcategories might be babies, children, men, women and seniors. Since we take so many shots of the same subject and travel so widely, we divide our people pictures between generic and geographic categories. Under Nepal, we will have a category labeled "People of Nepal," but a few slides of Nepalese people will also be placed in the generic category. For example, one of these "generics" might be found under "Man with Beard." Another might be put in "Families" and a third, of a monk, might find itself filed under "Religion."

Of course, people pictures can be close-ups of faces, head-and-shoulder shots, full body pictures, small groups and even crowds. Some people pictures, especially those made with a wide angle lens, can be environmental portraits showing the subject in relationship to his or her environment. The people category can include shots of people engaged in various activities such as their work or participating in sports. We have a big generic file of "People with Pets" that is in demand almost as often as the "People at a Computer" file.

## Place Photography

The photography of places should emphasize the location, whether that is a city, a mountain range or an island. We put most of our "place" pictures into geographic categories, since this is the way most picture buyers will request them. When we get a call for the Matterhorn mountain in Switzerland, we look for it under the Switzerland category. Within Switzerland, we may have a subcategory labeled "Matterhorn," but we initially look for it in the country where it is located.

In addition to filing shots of the Matterhorn under Switzerland, we will probably file a few under the generic category of "Mountains." This holds true for most subjects that might be requested under their generic listing. We would not, however, file pictures of Paris under a generic heading of cities. If a picture buyer requested city shots without specifying a particular city, we know enough to look under the major cities and our staff people would do the same. Setting up a slide file is largely a matter of common sense and the alphabet.

We keep a cross-reference card file for generics. If, for example, we get a call for "mountain," we can look in the card file for "Mountain" and find a list of mountains, in which there will be the heading "Switzerland—Matterhorn." The advantage of this card file is particularly apparent when we (and our memories) are out on a trip. Our office staff can be asked for a subject like "water buffalo." Without being able to ask us, they can refer to the cross-reference card file and find the fifteen countries in which we have water buffalo.

## Country Files

In creating a country file, we would logically divide it into regions, provinces or states and within these broad categories list the major cities. Within the cities, we set up subheadings. New York might have subheadings for Central Park, Fifth Avenue, Grand Central Station, Lower Manhattan, Statue of Liberty, Times Square, United Nations, etc. Each subheading, filed alphabetically within the city, makes it easier and faster to find a particular picture.

## Inanimate Objects

The photography of things can include diamonds to sports cars and literally anything in between. It is surprising how often picture buyers seek images of common objects. They are finding that it is often less expensive to obtain such a picture from stock than to assign a photographer to shoot it. What are appropriate subjects for stock in the world around us? Try shooting items such as computers, telephones, books, world globes, clocks, kitchen utensils, pencils, musical instruments, umbrellas, etc. Obviously the list is endless. Such objects should be clearly defined and easy to recognize. Many photographers prefer a plain roll-paper background for taking this type of picture. Sometimes a totally plain subject will make a good stock image. We once sold a picture of nothing more than blue-green water, taken looking down from the deck of a ship, for $500. The art director used it for a background and superimposed type against it.

## Plants and Animals

Among living things, other than people, are the important categories of flora and fauna, more commonly known as plants and animals. Animals represent a major stock category. Editors, art directors and picture buyers are constantly looking for appealing pictures of domestic animals to meet a variety of needs. Appealing images of puppies and kittens are always in demand. Horses are also popular subjects.

There is also a growing interest in wildlife. We lead photographic safaris to East Africa every year and, over a period of twelve years, have created an outstanding file on African birds and animals. These have been sold to *National Geographic*, *International Wildlife* and numerous other publications. We have just finished the production of a CD-ROM disk containing hundreds of our wildlife pictures. (Details on CD-ROM will be found in chapter eight.) As always, accurate caption information is vitally important.

Some photographers have devoted their lives to taking close-up pictures of flowers and other plants. In fact there is a serious market for flower pictures, both in botany textbooks and seed catalogs. It is very important to caption your flower pictures accurately with both the common and Latin names. It is often difficult to get this information on a field trip and we turn to reference books at home or in our local library to get accurate caption information. On occasion, we have called

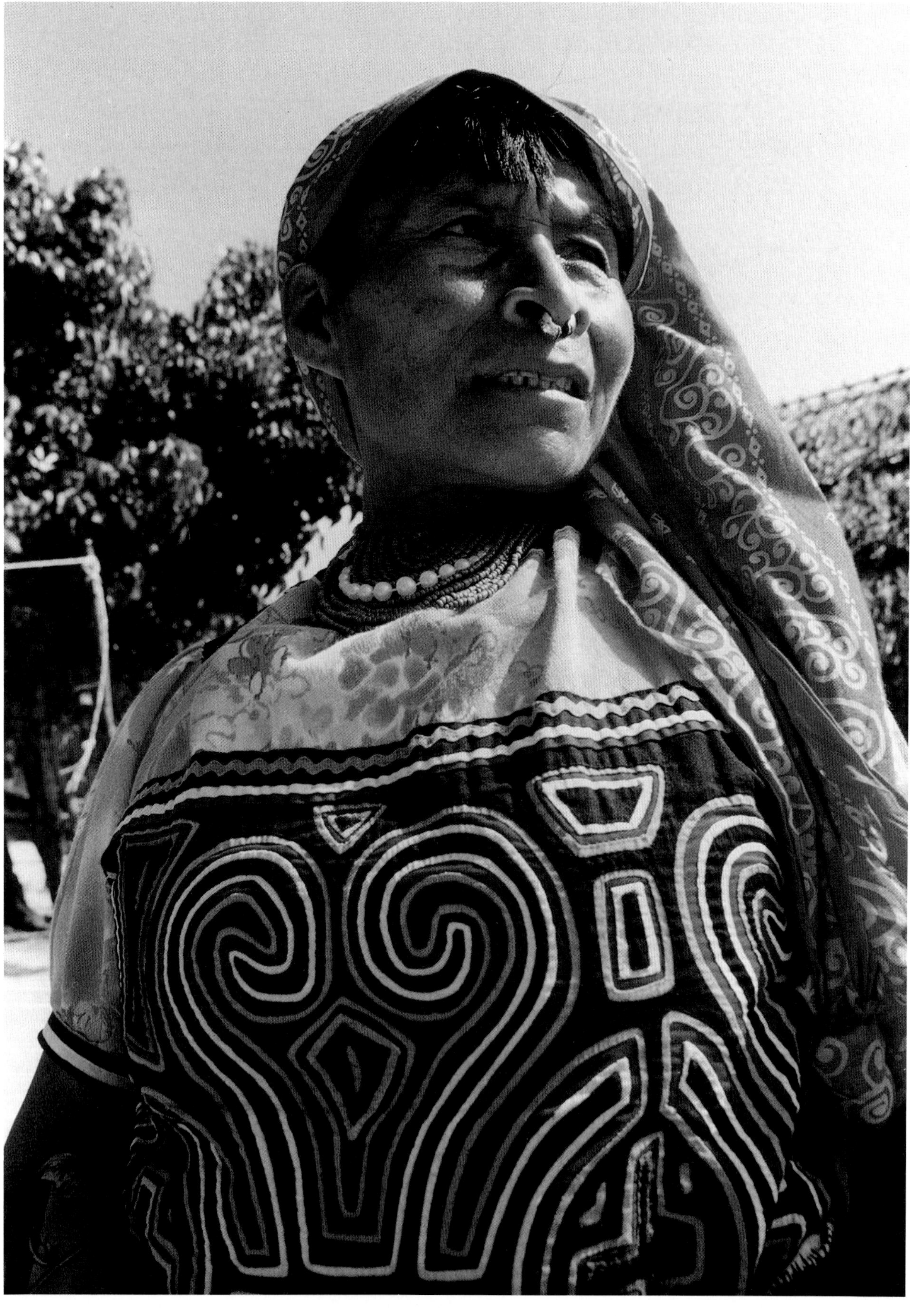

one of the colleges in our area, and even the Library of Congress, to get information for our captions. We have found librarians to be accurate, painstaking and endlessly patient.

Vegetables also make good stock pictures. These are often used to illustrate food and health articles. From time to time we go to the supermarket and shop for vegetables such as red and green peppers, eggplant, radishes and squash. Then we go to the fruit section for oranges, apples, cherries, grapes and bananas. We take these home to shoot in our studio or sometimes on the back porch, arranging artistic still lifes. (We always consider the outdoors the best studio with the finest lighting in the world.) When finished, we have been known to eat our subjects.

Other food shots can be made in your kitchen, in the garden or on the farm. An ever popular subject is a spacious field of wheat with blue skies and white clouds. It goes without saying that there are many photo opportunities in restaurants and sidewalk cafés and this is another case where, for filing purposes, you may want to divide your "take" between the geographic setting or place and the generic category of food. An editor may call you and ask for a picture of a plateful of crawfish. Will you look under generic "Food—Prepared" or under "Louisiana"? The caption of the crawfish slides in the generic file may pinpoint three other destinations where you shot crawfish. Your cross-reference file might list two more.

## COMPOSITION

Composition is a creative skill that is difficult to define. Some photographers develop an "eye" for good pictures, but there are no hard-and-fast rules. Some stock photos require special composition that allows for magazine logos at the top or large areas for the placement of reverse type. The preferred format for television use or slide shows is horizontal. Magazine covers are usually vertical.

A photographer who shoots for stock will shoot a subject in a variety of ways, always keeping in mind the different requirements for publication design, television or audiovisual presentation. Take advantage of a really strong subject in ideal light. It is a good idea to shift the focal point or main subject to the left and to the right; frame the picture both horizontal and vertical; leave space at the top, at the bottom; and even shoot the picture with a wraparound cover in mind, meaning that you should have the strong focal point of the photo positioned on the far right-hand side of the horizontal format.

## DESIGN AND COLOR

Design and color work hand in hand, but these important elements are as difficult to define as composition. Bright, bold colors work well for stock since they tend to catch the eye. Color can be used as a graphic tool. *Caribbean Travel & Life* is a magazine that consistently uses cover photographs with a strong sense of design and composition, and most of the color pictures are pulled from stock files. These cover pictures are often beach and water scenes with broad belts of sand, water and sky accented by models in colorful swimsuits or beach umbrellas. The name of the magazine, frequently in bright red or white, is superimposed on the top of the photograph. A few subjects covered

The Cuna Indians on the San Blas Islands of Panama are glad to pose for the visitor's camera for a small consideration (about twenty-five cents). Such ethnic pictures are useful as illustrations in travel brochures, textbooks and encyclopedias.

in the magazine are listed in smaller type, also superimposed, and the subjects are always brief and simple so that the type does not fight with the photograph. Some editors are tempted to jam as much information onto the cover as possible, but in such a case the design doesn't always work well.

Our photographic colleague Lisl Dennis has a superb sense of design and her images sell very well through the Image Bank stock agency. In fact, Lisl subjugates the subject matter to the design. She will sometime cut off a person's head if she thinks doing so will enhance the visual impact of her picture. We don't suggest using Lisl's approach for most stock pictures, but for some clients it works very well.

In our generic files we have a category called "Art & Abstract" and it contains many of our favorite pictures. Some of these are bright red barns, yellow brick walls and out-of-focus Christmas lights at night. An art director likes to play with such images to create a visual message. Your file should contain all the building blocks an art buyer might need to convey a concept and not all building blocks are conventional subjects shot in a conventional way. What's more, electronic imagery opens the door to combining various elements of different pictures into one. Ideally, a photographer supplies a single creative image and the art director places it in a layout and combines it with type to achieve the desired effect.

## UNIVERSAL APPEAL

Some of the best stock images have universal appeal. There are certain key subjects that have a broader appeal than others. Children, cute animals, family groups and pretty girls are all in this category. The degree of appeal, however, depends to a large degree on the skill of the photographer. He or she must catch the split second when the puppy licks the little boy's face or when a baby takes his first steps into his mother's arms. Such subjects have universal appeal, but the photographer transforms the moment in time into a preserved memory. Outstanding stock images can be used to symbolize virtues and human qualities and the art director for an advertising agency will take a picture to illustrate feelings of friendship, security, happiness, hope, strength and trust. The picture and the concept can be used to illustrate an article or to sell a product.

One of the best places to learn about stock photography is in the pages of major magazines. Study the illustrations and advertisements carefully. These are pictures that have sold, many of them from stock files, and most of them for big money. We are not suggesting that you go out to shoot identical pictures. (That's plagiarism!) We are suggesting that you look at the concepts, style and lighting. If you can shoot similar subjects in a similar style, those pictures should work well for stock until you find your own photographer's eye, angle and style. Look carefully at pictures on billboards, in store windows, in brochures and in books. Some art director paid good money to use those pictures. They could be yours and, without much doubt, some of your pictures are probably better than the ones used. In part, this book was written to show you how to recognize your good stock pictures and the best way to get them into

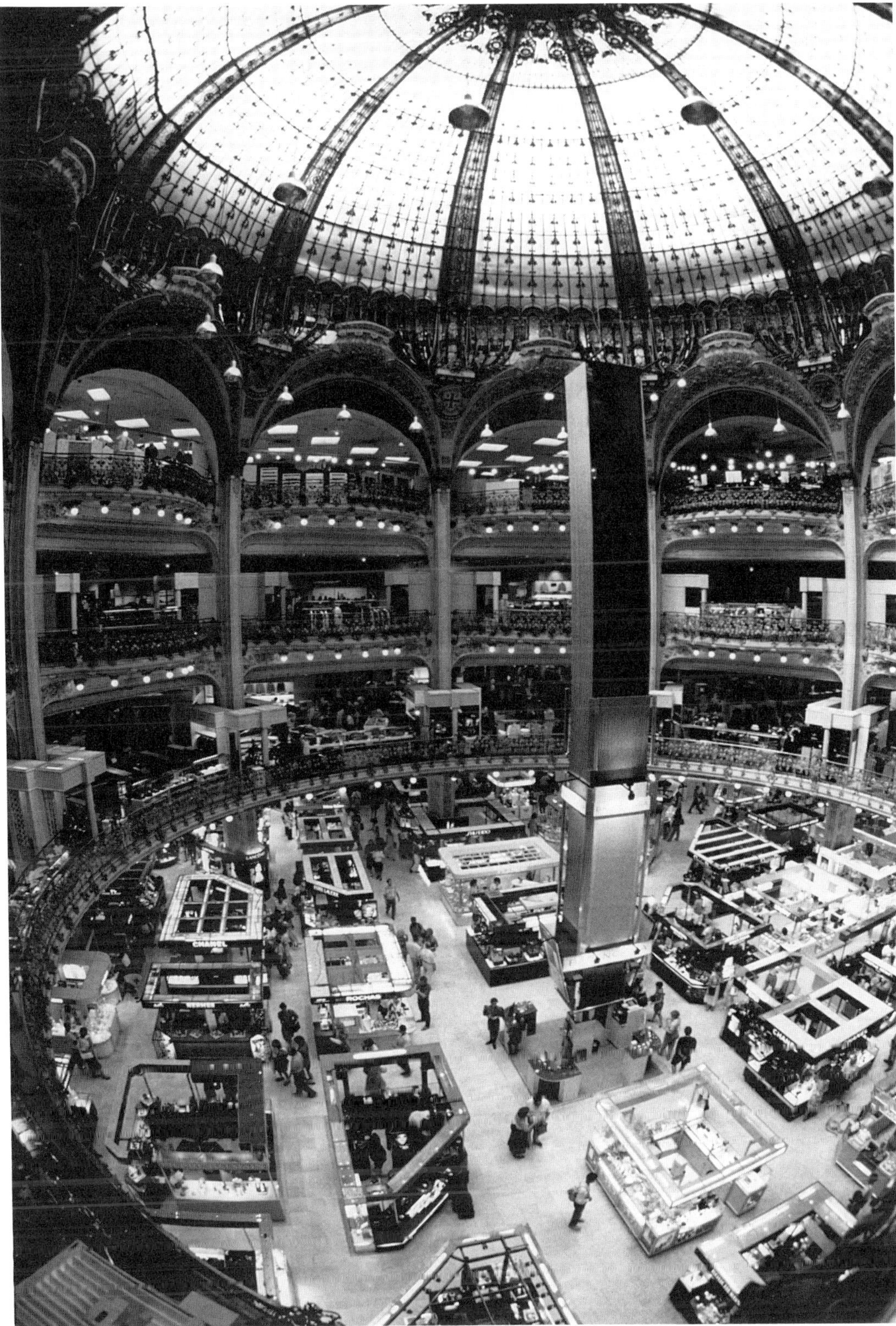

The atrium in the *Galleries Lafayette*, one of the leading department stores in Paris, is an ideal subject for a wide-angle lens. This shot was taken from the third floor balcony.

the hands of the right art director at the right time.

Our artistic friends are shocked when they see some of the subjects we shoot for stock. They correctly say, "Those pictures are clichés" and we reply, "That's right, but clichés help pay our bills." Every artist or photographer from Michelangelo to Steichen had to create images that would pay the bills, buy the film or purchase the oil paints and canvases. Like other artists, we shoot pictures both to pay the bills and to satisfy our creative urges. Sometimes we take pictures that sell often as stock images and also satisfy our desire to create serious and meaningful or artful photographs.

The stock photography field is very broad. Without having ever met you, we can assure you that if you have purchased this book, you have probably already taken enough pictures to get started in stock photography. If you have taken pictures of your newest grandson or your oldest child when she graduated from college or your father laughing at your mother when she decorated your brother's sixteenth birthday cake, you have useable stock. All of those are "hot" stock photos. To repeat, you have a treasure of stock shots lying unused in those little yellow boxes. Put those lazy slides to work!

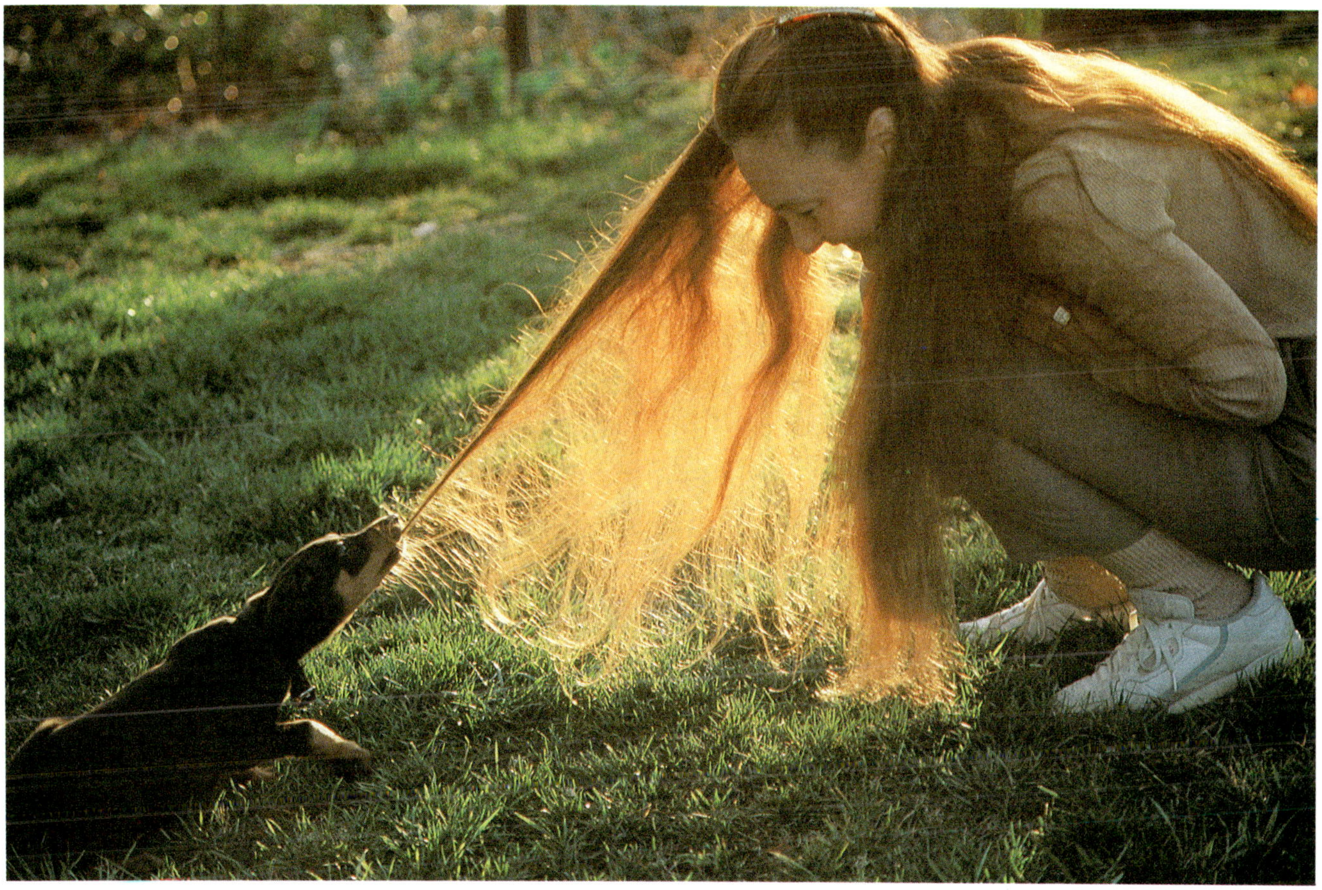

Some of the best stock pictures can be taken in your own backyard. This picture of a puppy tugging on Ann Purcell's hair would make an excellent image to illustrate a major ad for dog food or to be included with an article about training puppies in a magazine on pets. The sun coming through the red hair rim-lights the figure in an interesting way.

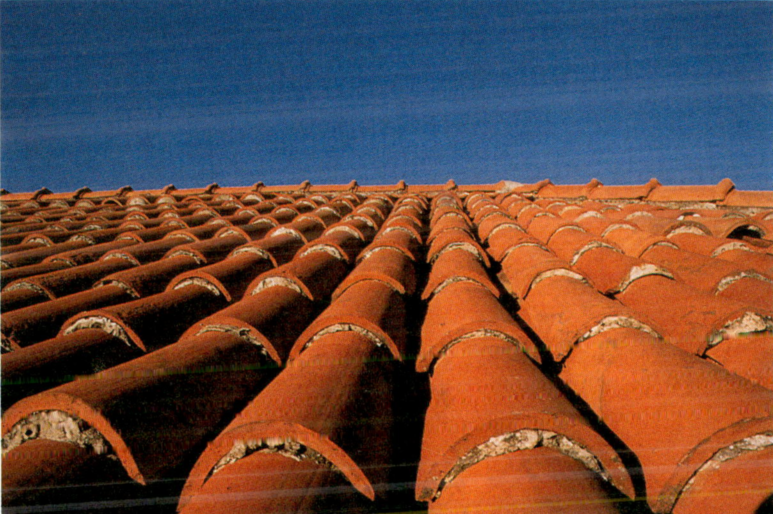

Stock pictures, whenever possible, should have many potential uses. This image of a red tile roof has strong color and graphic design suitable for many editorial and advertising needs. The fact that it was taken in Dubrovnik, Yugoslavia, a city that has been ravaged by civil war, makes it newsworthy within a certain time frame. Red tile roofs are typical of many Mediterranean countries and, in that sense, this picture is generic and could be representative of Spain, France or Italy as well as Yugoslavia. It is an image that offers opportunities for electronic manipulation with a computer. We plan to superimpose a black cat walking across the top of the roof, silhouetted against the blue sky.

This picture of a cruise ship in Hong Kong was used in a calendar, but it has also been used in a cruise brochure and as an illustration in travel magazines. This shot was taken over fifteen years ago, which proves the old adage that good old stock pictures never die, they just get sold over and over again.

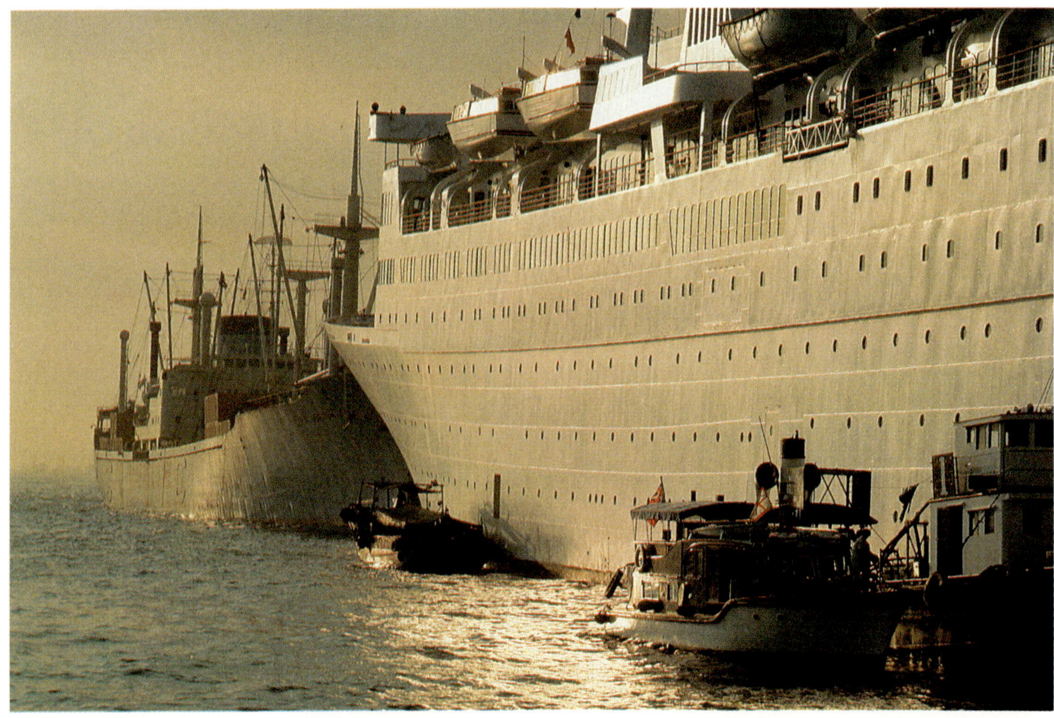

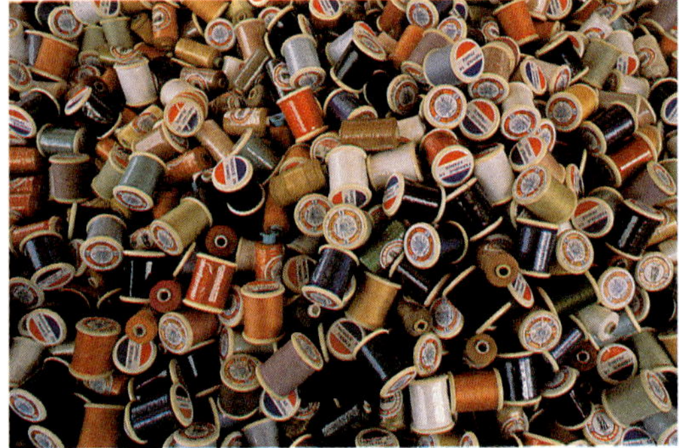

(Above) Common objects photographed with a good eye will often make salable stock pictures. This shot of a display counter of spools of colored thread could be sold to a sewing magazine. It could also be used as a background for a sewing accessory advertisement.

(Right) This picture of seafood, attractively displayed, was taken at the Pike Street Market in Seattle. Such photographs are often needed to illustrate food articles in travel and homemaking magazines. A trade publication called *Seafood Leader* has used a number of our pictures of fresh seafood from markets around the world. Although they themselves do not pay high rates, their clients use their publication as a seafood photo catalog. We have received numerous calls from seafood companies wishing to use our photos for advertisement.

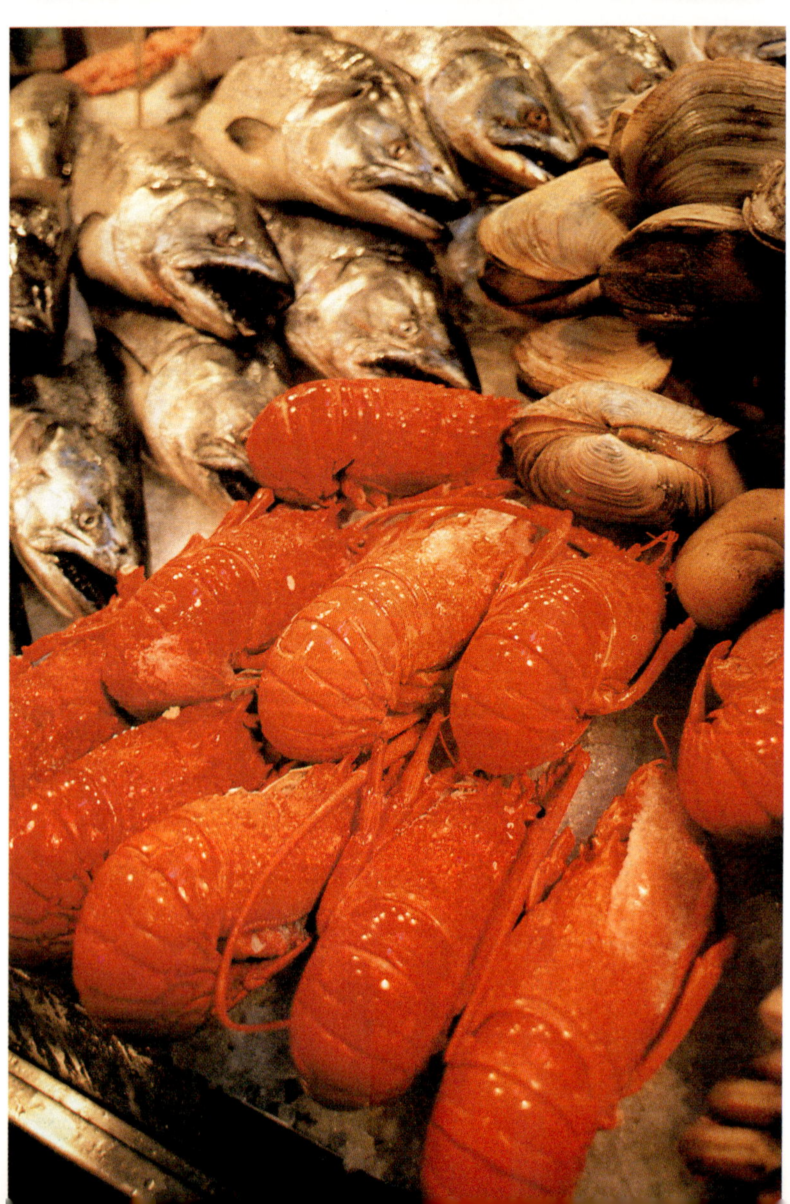

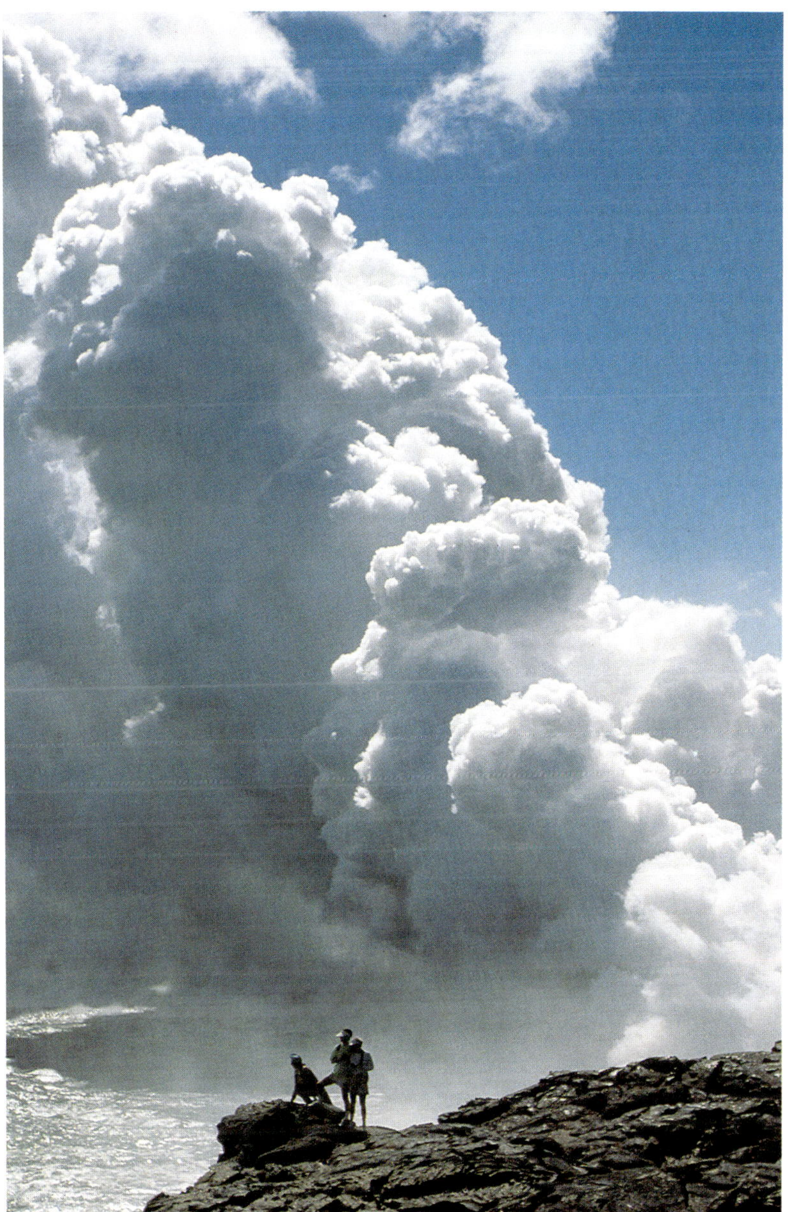

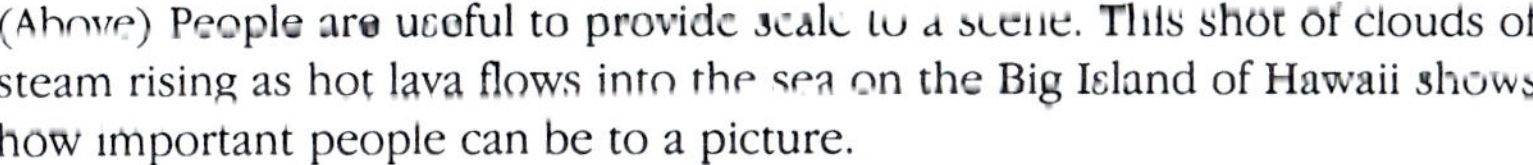

(Above) People are useful to provide scale to a scene. This shot of clouds of steam rising as hot lava flows into the sea on the Big Island of Hawaii shows how important people can be to a picture.

(Right) Finding a spiderweb adorned with the morning dew is like coming across a diamond among beach pebbles. This one was nearly perfect, but required a dark raincoat to be held behind it to bring out the droplets of water. If you find a spiderweb without the dew, it is even permissible to create your own dew with a spray bottle filled with water. A spray bottle is just one of the tools of the trade.

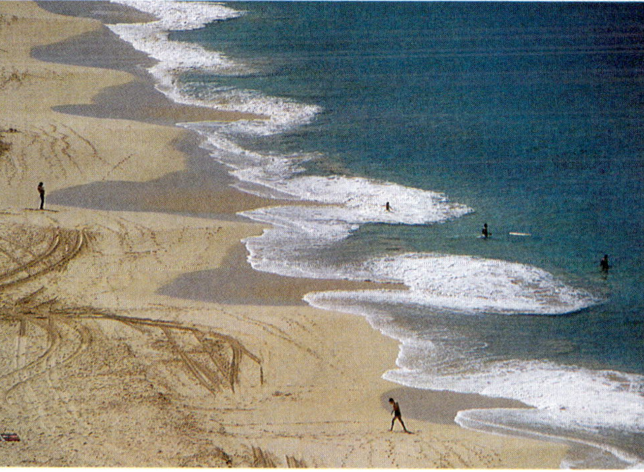

Beaches are always a popular stock subject, probably because most people would rather be lying on a beach than sitting at a desk. While long shots of a beach, such as this one on the island of Maui in Hawaii, are often requested, it is also productive to shoot close-ups of couples and families enjoying the beach at the water's edge. (Don't forget to get model releases.)

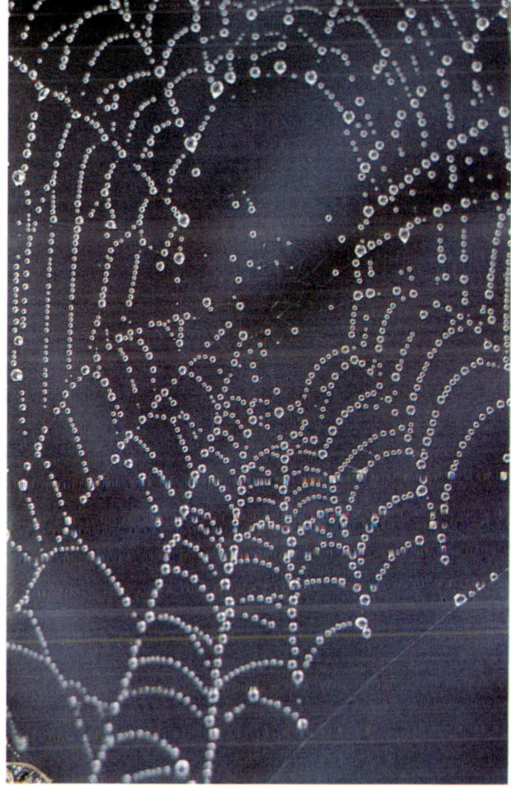

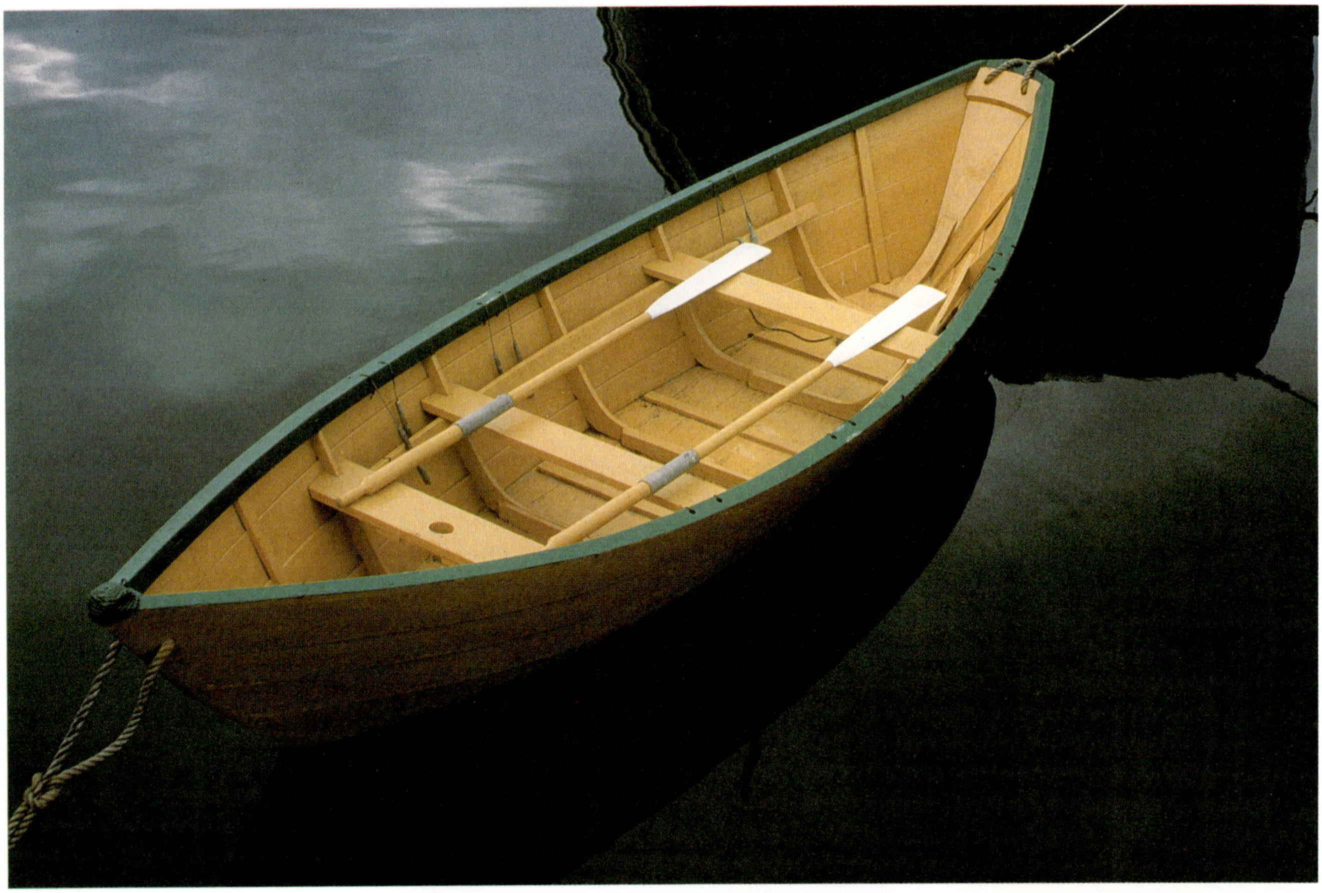

(Above) It is important to keep your pictures simple. This shot of a dory in Nova Scotia has a simplicity in both color and composition. The dark background allows space for reverse type if needed.

(Right) We caught this lion on the Masai Mara in Kenya with two hot air balloons from Governor's Camp in the background. Such a picture might not have wide application for stock, but it could be used to promote the hot air balloon rides over the Mara or to depict the exotic.

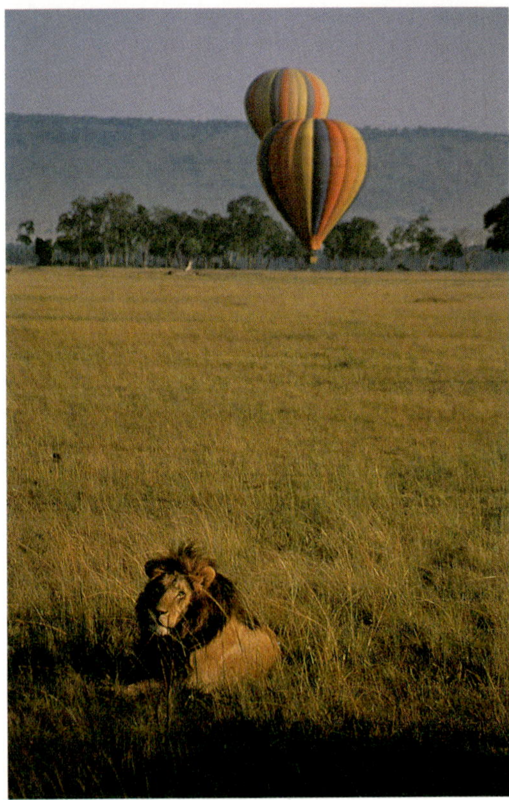

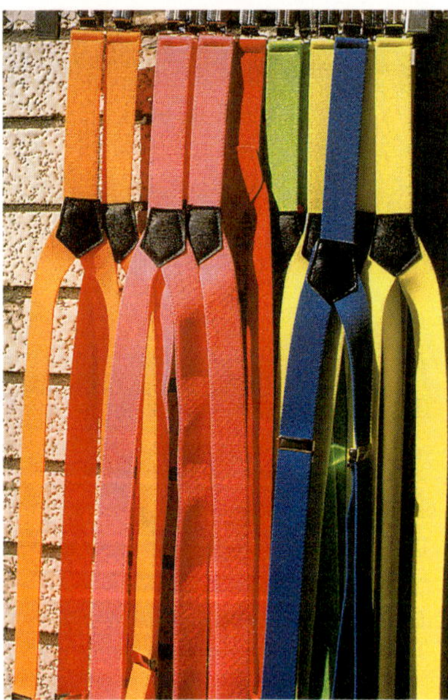

Simple color images can make valuable stock pictures. These colorful suspenders in an outdoor market in Montreal could be used to spark a layout on fashion or to promote house paint. Many editors get tired of the ordinary scenic travel photo. Be sure to include the unusual in your coverage.

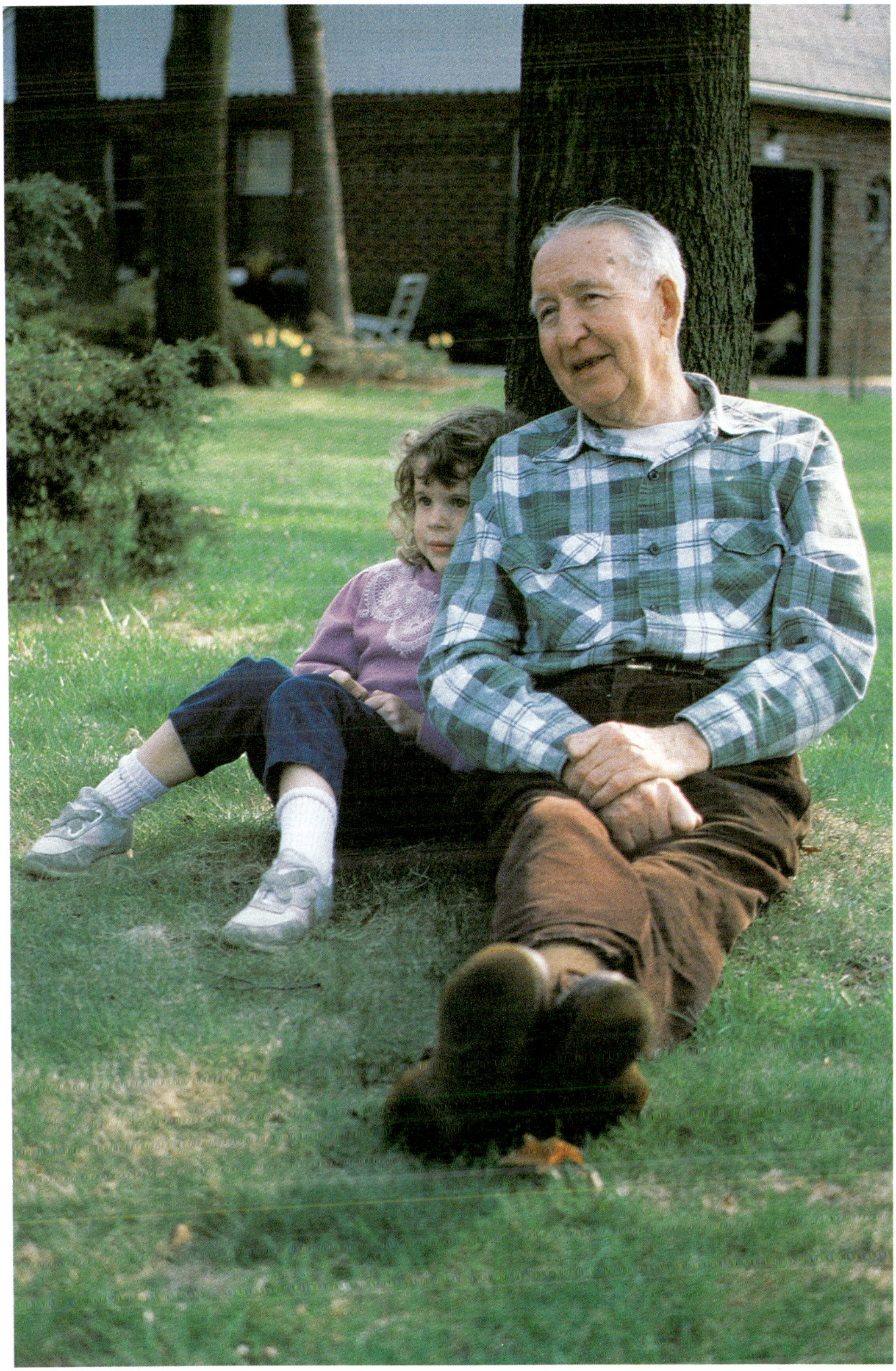

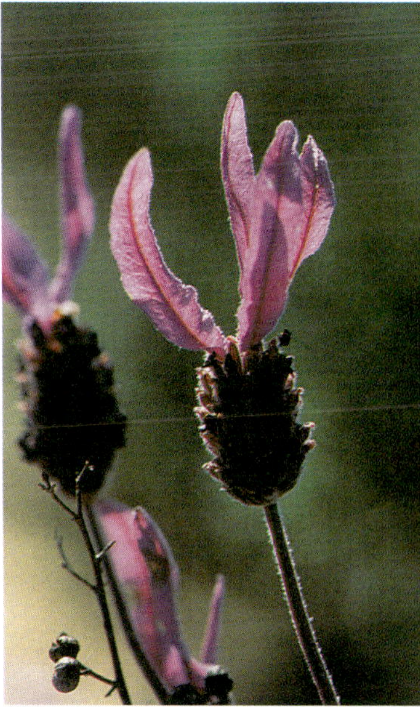

Flowers will often sell well as a colorful stock shot but for educational textbooks it is necessary to include in the caption both the common and Latin names for a particular flower. This Spanish wildflower is called a lavanda, but we were unable to find the Latin name in our botanical reference books. If anyone knows it, please drop us a note.

We often give each other photographic gifts. Carl saw this gentleman with his granddaughter sitting in the front yard of his house as he was driving to the grocery store. From the store he called Ann and told her where to find this heartwarming picture. Ann grabbed her camera and ran over to get the shot. Needless to say, she also got a model release. The shot has been used in numerous publications throughout the United States.

Holidays offer many opportunities for stock pictures. We carved these jack-o'-lanterns and invited some neighbor children over on Halloween to inspect them. We used a white Christmas tree light on an extension cord to provide the light inside the pumpkins. (Candles would have been too dim.) We shot at dusk to show some detail in the rest of the picture. Prints were made for the parents and we got model releases.

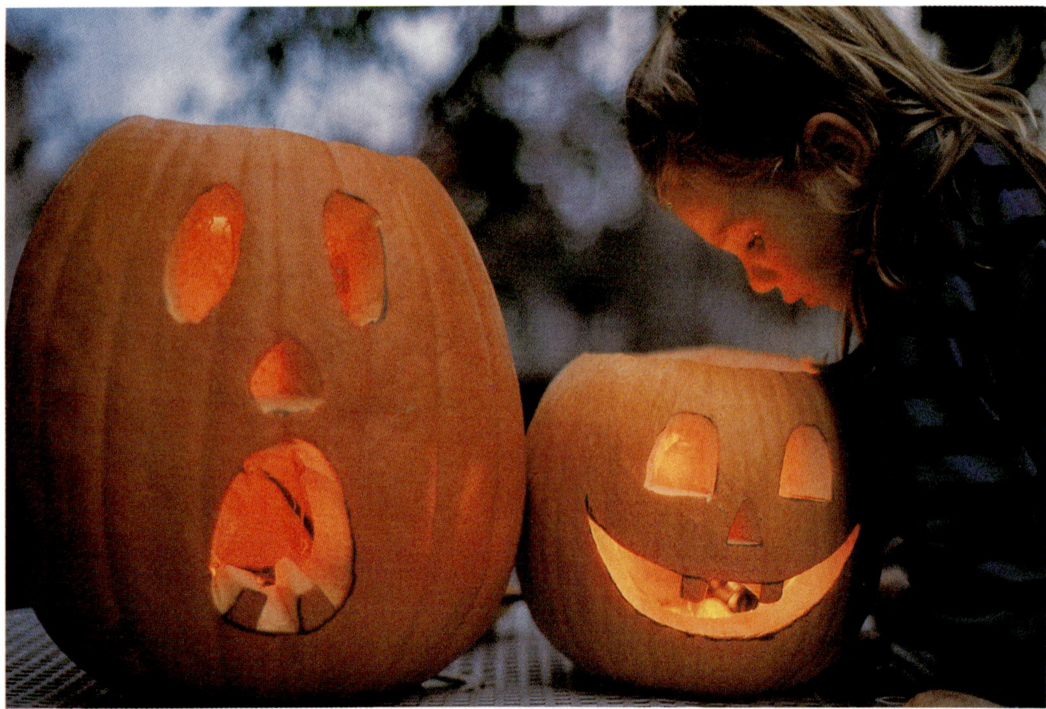

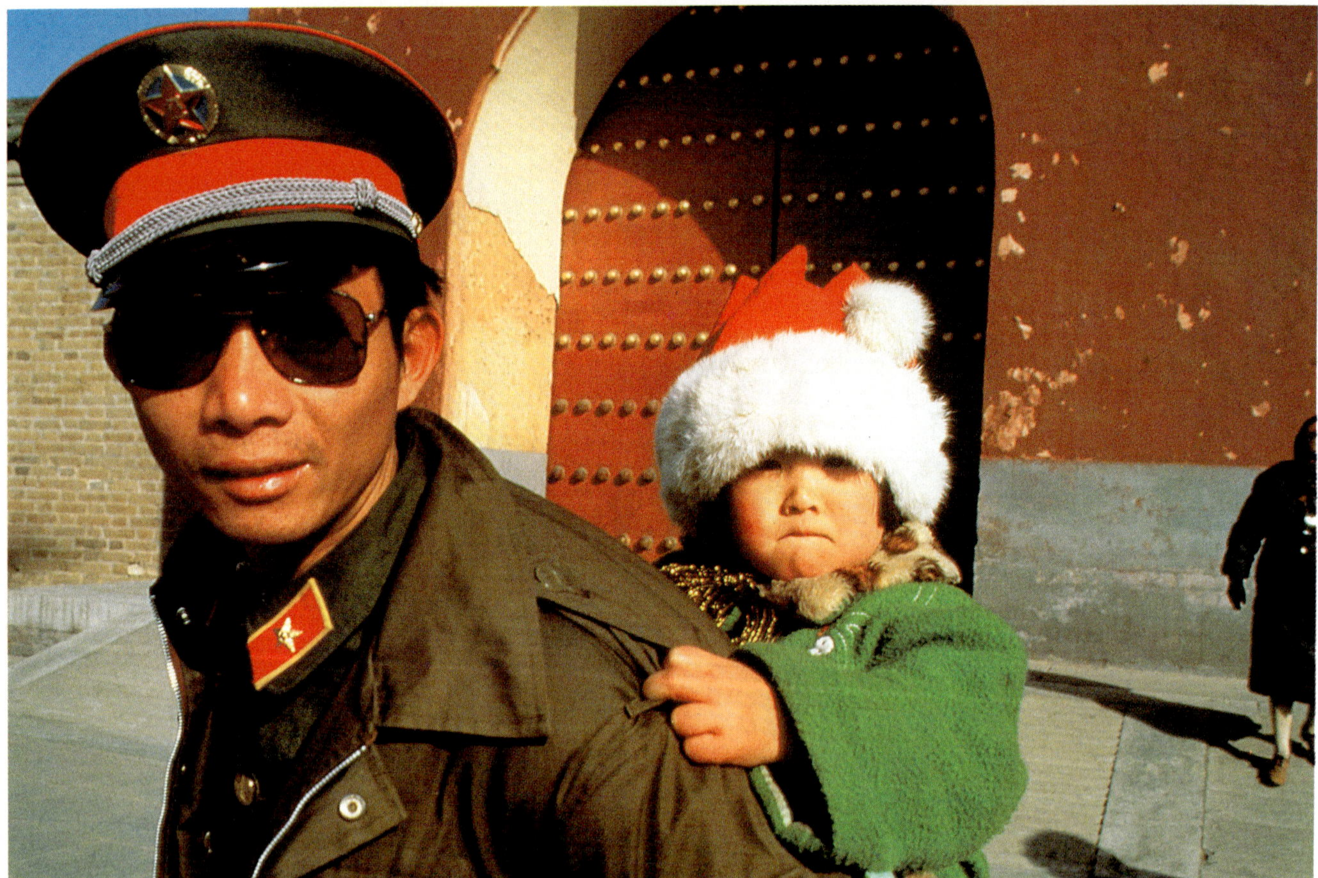

Our coverage from four trips to China has resulted in countless stock sales. When human rights problems in China came to a head after Tian'amen Square, sales declined. We were favorably impressed by the friendliness of the Chinese people and their willingness to be photographed. It is a country where you can get particularly good views of several generations interacting—shots that will be good sellers in your stock file.

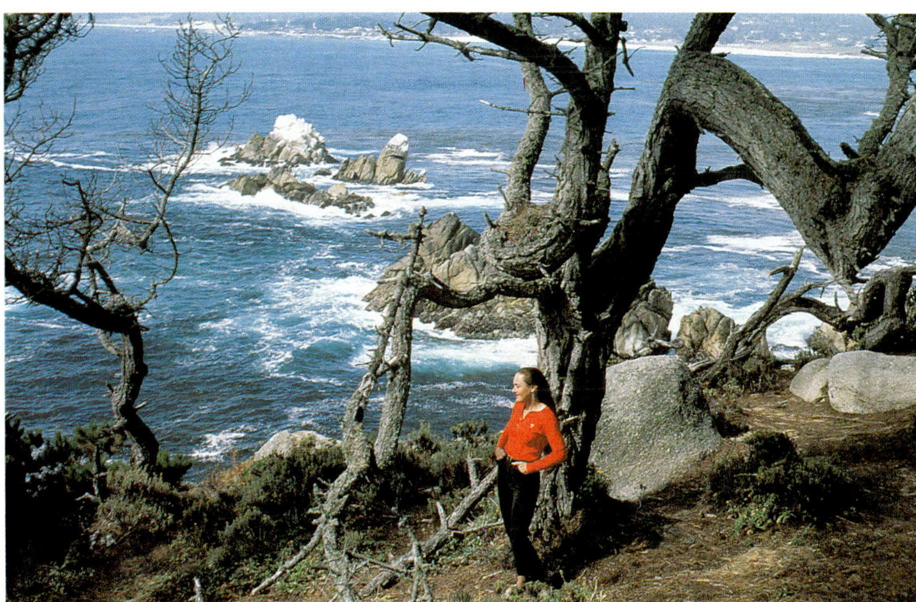

Point Lobos in California was the site of many famous black-and-white photographs by the late art photographer Edward Weston. We were also impressed by the beauty of Point Lobos, but shot it in color for stock. We shoot all our film ½ stop underexposed for better color saturation. (For example, we shoot Kodachrome 64 at ASA 80, and we shoot Fujichrome 100 at ASA 125.) We then have the film processed normally.

Nature offers many graphic contrasts for the photographer. This scene in Finland shows a field of yellow flowers contrasted against the dark clouds of an approaching rainstorm. Such an image, with large areas of flat color, permits the use of type or reverse type by an imaginative art director. This shot has been a best-seller for several years.

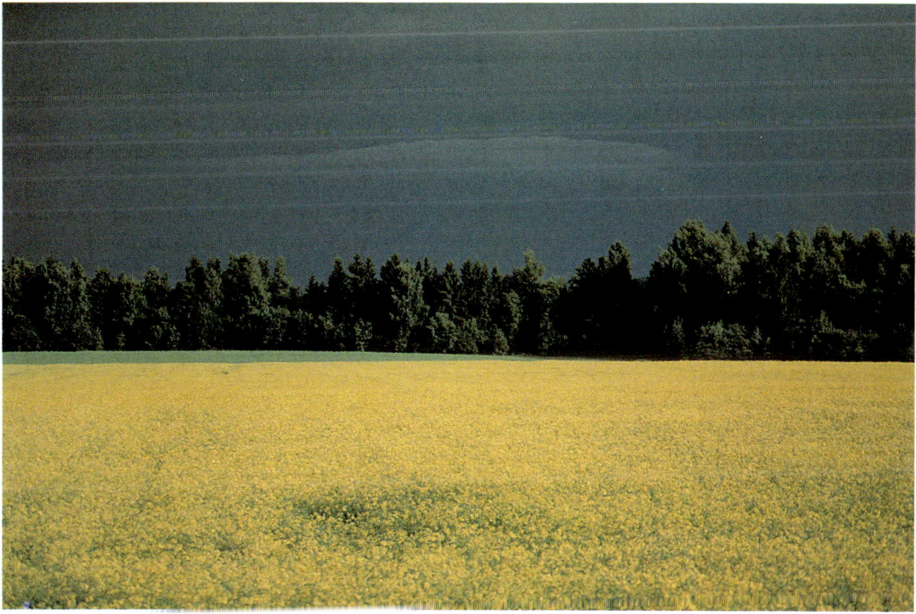

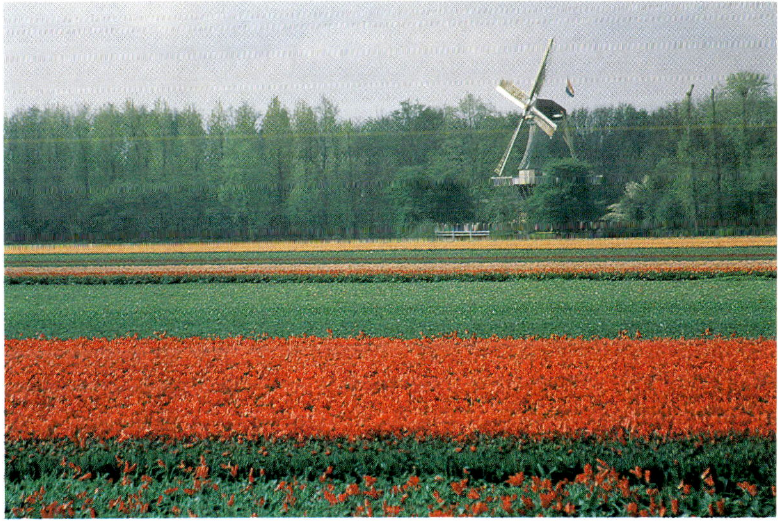

The location of these fields of brilliant tulips is quickly made clear by the windmill in the distance. Effective travel pictures utilize such national icons to identify the country. This photo, taken in the Netherlands, can be cropped horizontally, square or vertically and type can be laid over the image. (Knowing, however, that this was a useful shot, we took it both horizontally and vertically.) It is an "evergreen" ageless shot, and is still useful years after it was taken.

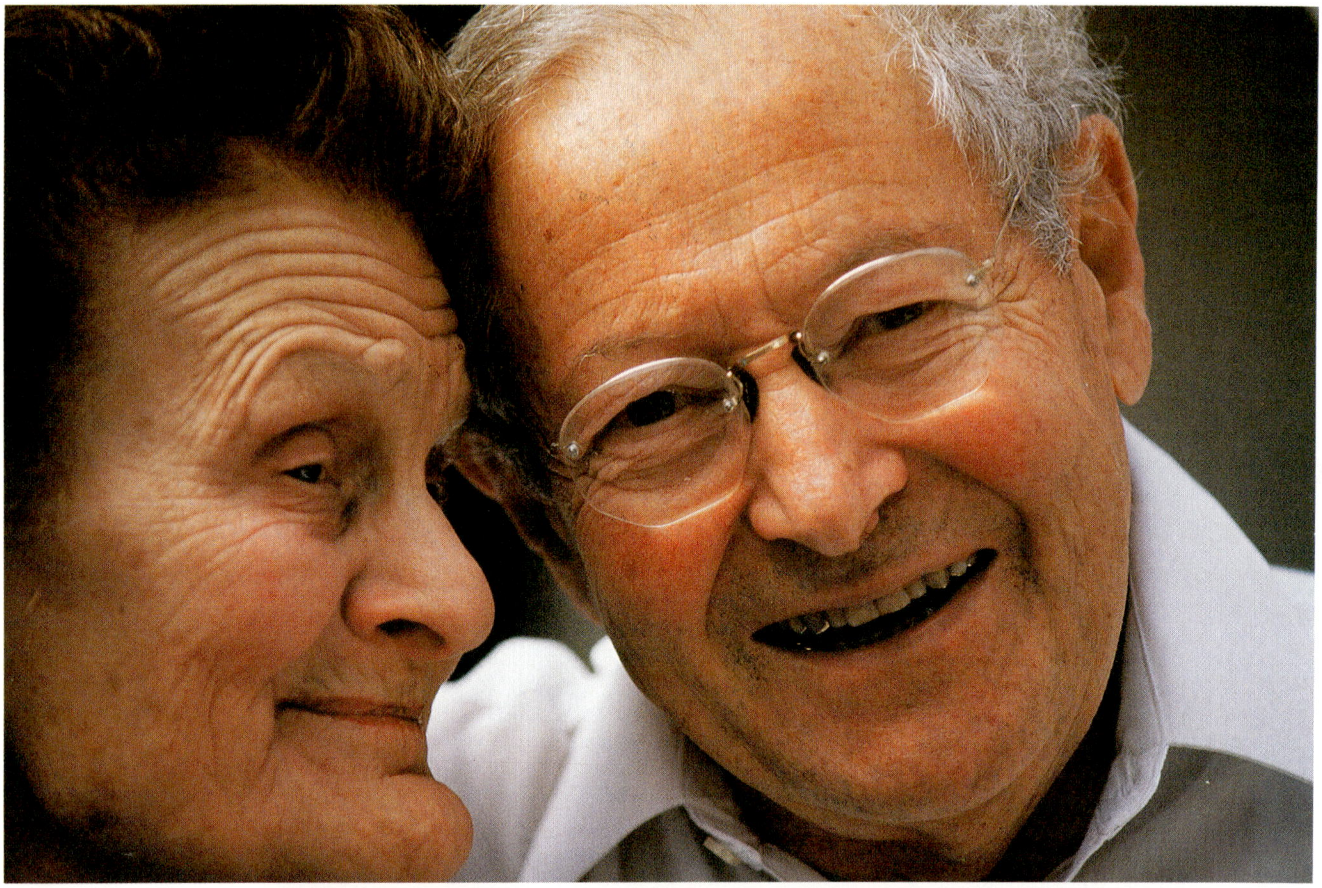

Recruit family members to pose for your pictures. Ann Purcell's parents were delighted to pose for her on their golden anniversary. Naturally, Ann promised them a print and asked for a model release. This kind of photograph is very useful for advertisements. An insurance company would talk about planning for your old age; a jeweler might remind the viewer that diamonds are permanent; a health club could infer that you will still be enjoying each other in your golden years only if you use their services.

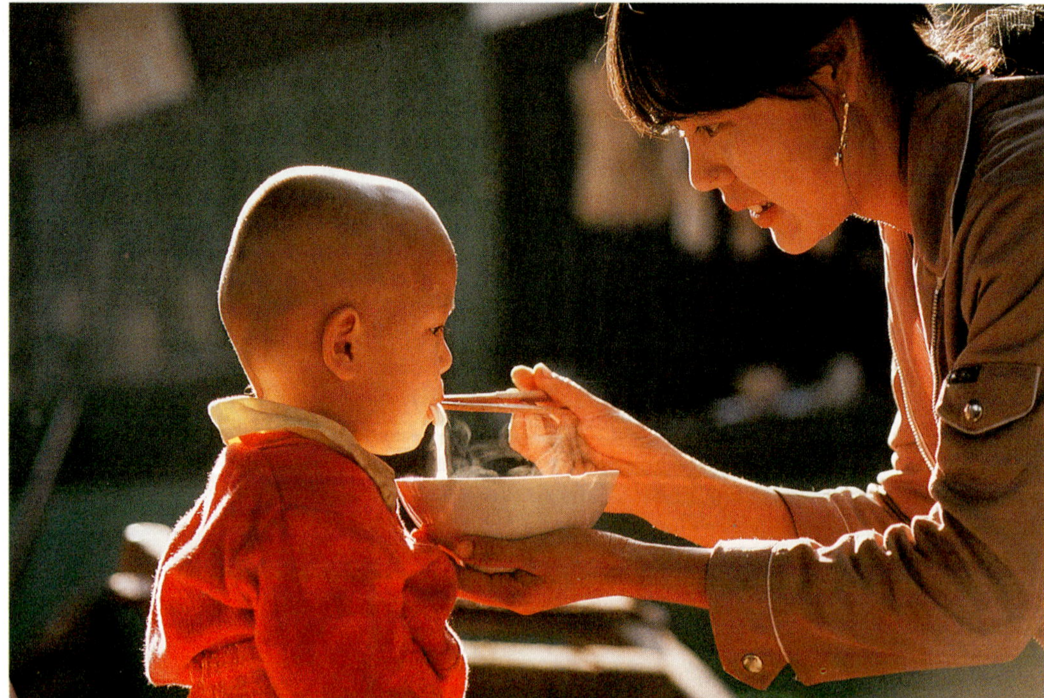

We try to be sensitive to the way light falls on a subject. This mother feeding her baby was strongly backlit in a market in southern China. The quality of the light made the picture unforgettable. After Ann had grabbed a few shots, she ran through the market to find Carl. "I have a gift for you!" We both returned to get many rewarding photos of this scene.

*Chapter 3*

# SHOOTING FOR STOCK

## BASIC EQUIPMENT

A stock photographer must decide which camera system to use. We have already indicated that the most widely used and most acceptable format is 35mm and we urge you to choose this format to maximize your sales and minimize your logistical problems. There are always some instances when a client will specifically request a larger format such as 4-by-5 inches or 2¼-by-2¼ inches, but these are exceptions to the rule. Most clients are willing to accept an image in a larger format, but usually they are accustomed to looking at and working with 35mm slides. From the point of view of a photographer or a picture agency, 35mm slides are always easier to catalog, file and ship.

The most important advantage of the 35mm format, however, is the difference in photographic style made possible with a smaller, more compact camera. Today's publications often prefer the spontaneous, candid image that was made popular on the pages of *Life* magazine in its heyday and which it continues to publish so ably. This style has even had a profound impact on advertising photography, but a portion of advertising images are still created in the studio with the larger cameras. Modern, high-resolution film enables the 35mm camera to adequately record a studio style subject, but no photographer can use a view camera with the speed and convenience possible with a 35mm SLR. Add the advantage of the multiple high-speed lenses and zooms available with most 35mm camera systems and you have a final, convincing argument for choosing this type of camera for the major portion of your stock shooting.

Once the 35mm format decision has been made, a potential stock photographer must choose from a wide array of brands available on the market. With only a few exceptions, these cameras are manufactured in Japan and Germany.

The Germans were the ones to pioneer the 35mm camera. The best-known brand was the excellent Leica, famous for its high optical quality and mechanical precision. It is still a commendable camera, but many pros feel it has lagged behind the Japanese in its internal design and operational features. As a result, the major Japanese brands such as Nikon, Minolta, Canon, Olympus and Pentax have pushed the Germans to second place in the worldwide sales of 35mm cameras.

Quite honestly, it is difficult to pick the clear winner among these leading brands, but if you are shopping for a 35mm camera for the first time, there are certain features that, as a stock photographer, you should be sure to get. The automatic exposure and autofocus features are indispensable, but these features can always be disabled or deactivated at will, allowing you to revert to manual operation. The ability to disable the automatic functions of a camera is a requirement for a professional. The following are features we recommend:

1. **Matrix averaging automatic exposure.** Some cameras offer this option. A computer chip inside the camera can read an incredible number of light situations and automatically determine what speed is needed to make your subject sharp and perfectly exposed, taking into account the amount of light, or lack of light, around the subject.
2. **Autofocus.** This is an option we strongly recommend, even for those photographers who have excellent eyesight. Most modern cameras can focus almost as fast as the eye and, in some cases, faster. As you grow older, the automatic focus of the camera can often be more accurate than your eye.
3. **Multimode exposure options including program, aperture priority, shutter priority and manual.** The program option will be your main workhorse and will be the one you use the most. In some cases, you will want to set the aperture or the shutter speed specifically. Manual will put you totally in control.
4. **Dedicated flash with TTL metering.**. It is more accurate if your flash will take all its readings directly from the camera and read the light through the lens.
5. **A flash synch speed of at least 1/125th.** 1/125th of a second is fast enough for hand-held shooting without problems of ghost images.
6. **Plus and minus exposure compensation control.**. Even if your camera reads the film ISO automatically, you can overexpose and underexpose your film as you choose. We underexpose all our film at least ½ stop, or minus 0.5, to get a richer color saturation. We would overexpose, however, in a snow scene to get all the details of our subject while keeping the snow white.
7. **Compact size and lightweight.** A camera might not seem heavy in the shop, but after eight hours of walking, the smallest difference in weight and size will be important.

When purchasing a new 35mm camera, make sure it has all of the above features. The next step is to choose the lenses for your camera. This will be determined, at least to some extent, by your budget, but let's pretend you can buy all the lenses you want.

For those of you who have never thought about it, remember that on a lens the smaller the millimeter number the wider the angle. Thus a full-frame fisheye lens of 16mm can take a photo of nearly 180 degrees; a 24mm is perfect for the interior of a room, showing wall to wall; and a 90mm lens is ideal for a head shot or portrait. A 300mm lens will catch a full-frame cheetah at 100 yards and a 300mm with a doubler will do a loving portrait of the cheetah's eye and nose.

Zooms are ideal. Using one lens, you are able to go from a wide angle to a long shot. The disadvantage of a zoom lens is loss of speed, especially in poor light, but the newer (and more expensive) zooms are faster. With the newest high-speed lenses, you can hand-hold your camera in relatively poor light and get excellent, sharp, well-focused shots.

Here is what we recommend in the order of preference:

1. 28mm to 85mm zoom
2. 100mm to 300mm zoom or a 70mm to 210mm zoom
3. 20mm or 24mm wide angle
4. 50mm high-speed lens
5. 35mm high-speed lens
6. 16mm full-frame fisheye lens
7. 300mm high-speed lens with doubler
8. 28mm lens with movable elements for linear corrections

This is a good lens to use for architectural shots. If you are taking a photo of an entire building by tilting your camera up, there will be a linear distortion, making the building look as if it were leaning away from you. The movable elements for linear correction allow you to take a photo looking upward while the camera remains parallel to the ground. The result is that you have a photo of the entire building without the linear distortion.

All of the above will cost you a bundle and give a boost to the Japanese economy. If you can't buy these all at once, you can shoot 80 percent of all your stock shots with items one and two. After the checks start coming in from your stock sales, hopefully you can afford to buy the rest, one by one.

While not absolutely necessary, it is highly desirable to have at least two identical camera bodies. It is very helpful to have an extra camera body in case your first body malfunctions. Many pros like the convenience of shooting with two bodies fitted with different lenses. In addition you will need an electronic flash with coil cord, tripod and cable release for time exposures, and some type of lightweight, expandable camera bag. In addition to your cameras and lenses, your bag should also contain extra batteries, your favorite filters, model releases and items for cleaning your camera gear. So equipped, any photographer is ready to shoot for stock.

## TRAVEL EQUIPMENT

As travel writer/photographers, we have honed the art of traveling with cameras to a sharp edge. As a stock photographer, you are adding anywhere from twenty to fifty pounds to whatever you normally carry in your suitcase. Ideally, you should be able to carry all of your luggage and your cameras yourself if you have to. This can often be achieved by wisely purchasing luggage with built-in wheels and handles and using a collapsible wire frame on wheels for your camera bag or bags. With the help of these optional wheels, a photographer can navigate in airports or train stations without a porter. We have actually hauled as many as two suitcases and one camera bag each through a crowded airport when porters were not available.

Our favorite carry-on luggage is hard-sided with built-in wheels. The one we use is called the Piggyback by Samsonite and is large enough for our camera bag, several books and even our laptop computer. It was designed to fit under the seat of most airplanes, but locks if you need to check it during flights on smaller aircraft.

We recommend hard-sided suitcases with combination locks and straps for maximum security. Such luggage can also serve as locked compartments for your cameras when it is necessary or desirable to leave them in your hotel room. Soft-

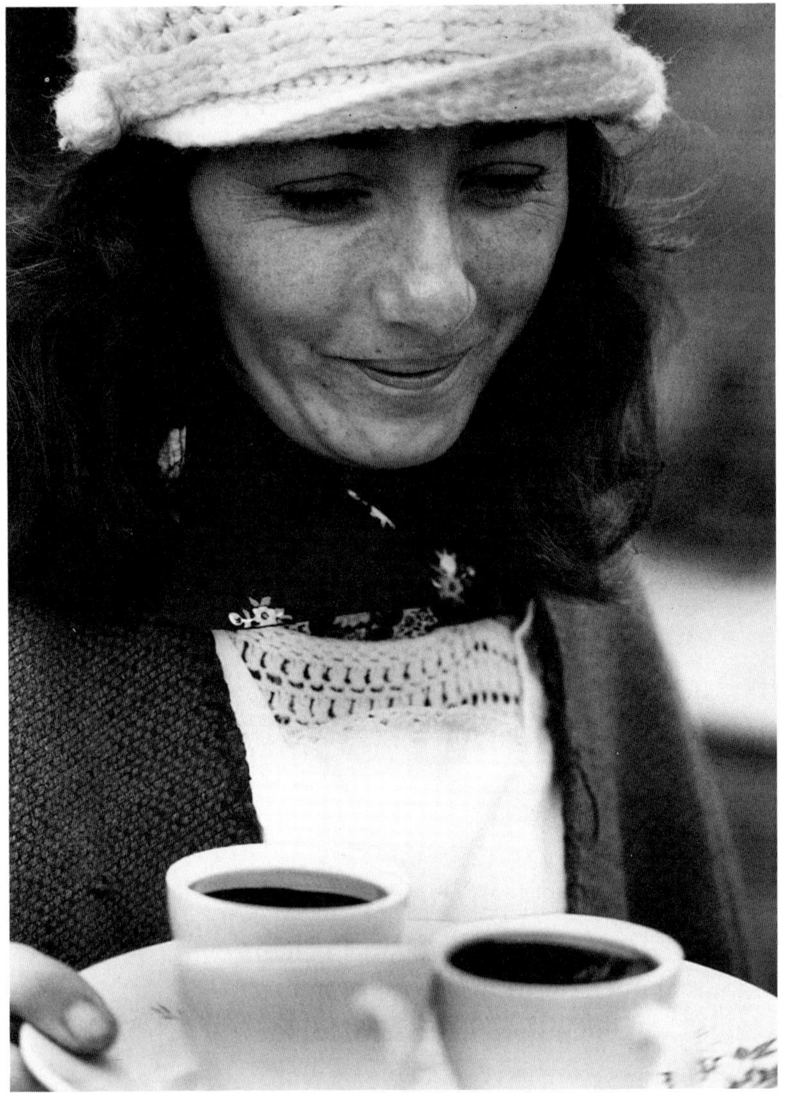

Colombia is known for its fine coffee. This lady near Bogota may not be Juan Valdez, but she made a fine stock picture as she served her rich brew to visitors. Remember that people are the place. Try to catch sights that would be familiar if you were a native. These will most often be the sights that identify a country.

sided luggage is usually lighter, but it can be easily cut open, making the contents accessible to thieves. Current airline regulations control the number of pieces of luggage a traveler may check for a flight, but do not place serious restrictions on weight. Flights originating in some foreign countries insist on a fairly restrictive weight limitation, so check with the airlines when planning your trip.

Some photographers like hard-side aluminum cases with foam, cut-out inserts for carrying their cameras, but we prefer soft canvas bags with adjustable compartments. The aluminum cases are attractive targets for thieves and tend to be much heavier than canvas. Our choice of camera bag is the Domke Pro bag, designed by a working press photographer. It utilizes Velcro-type flaps and metal clips for closure of most compartments, and a nylon zipper for others.

When you buy a tripod, be sure that it will fit in your suitcase, yet still be sturdy enough to be stable. As there are two of us shooting, we travel with two professional tripods. We use a Bogen tripod and a Slik tripod, each of which will accept a detachable Slik pistol grip panhead. The panhead makes recomposition of the photo, sometimes awkward with a camera on a tripod, an easy flick of the wrist.

It is always our policy to carry our cameras with us and pack our film in our suitcases on the way to a destination and to carry both our film and cameras on the way back. If we must make a choice, cameras can be packed on the way back. We knew a young photographer who flew to Hawaii on his first assignment for *National Geographic*. He shot for three weeks and flew home. Unfortunately, he packed his film in his suitcase, which was checked through. He never saw that suitcase or his exposed film again. The moral of that little story is very clear. You can almost always purchase fresh film if your luggage is lost on your way to an assignment and cameras can be replaced at a price if they go astray on your way back. The loss of a prizewinning stock picture, and you should get many on a productive trip, cannot be assigned a price tag. Over the years that photo may well earn you many thousands of dollars. In the hotel room, we normally put exposed film in a dresser drawer to avoid the possibility that a chambermaid might not recognize what it is and throw it out with the trash. When actually traveling, we prefer to keep exposed film with us inside lead shield containers in a shoulder bag.

## Protecting Your Film From X Rays

Professional and amateur photographers have understandably been concerned about possible damage from X rays to their film when they travel. There has been much conflicting information given out about the potential danger or lack of danger of X-ray machines at security checkpoints in airports. These are the facts:

1. Airport X-ray machines *can* fog film.
2. The low-dosage machines used in the U.S. will not normally fog film with an ISO rating of less than 1000 if the film only passes through a security checkpoint once during a trip. Nevertheless, if you are planning to come back home, your film is already guaranteed a minimum of two dosages.
3. Repeated exposure to X-ray machines will almost certainly result in some fog level on both exposed and unexposed film.
4. X rays will have no detrimental effect on developed film.
5. FAA regulations require that airline security personnel in the United States hand-inspect a bag containing film if the passenger requests a hand-inspection.
6. Many foreign countries can, and often do, require passengers to put all carry-on bags through the X-ray machine. Foreign-made machines are not always the same low output as the U.S. machines.

Even knowing these facts, it is hard for a passenger to know the best way to protect his film on an extended trip. From experience, we have come up with what has proven to be an effective procedure.

All of our film is taken out of the cardboard boxes and put into clear plastic ziptop bags. Then we place the ziptop bags in lead foil bags and put these inside our hand luggage or camera bags. We run these bags through the X-ray security machine. Often the security guards, seeing a solid black block on the machine, will ask us to open our bag and they then hand-inspect the film. In foreign countries we never argue with a guard at the front of the X-ray machine to keep him from putting our film through. Not once has a guard insisted that we take the film back to the front of the machine and put it through without protection.

There are two types of lead foil bags. The SIMA lead bag, available in many camera stores, is relatively inexpensive and comes in regular and heavy-duty weights. These do eventually wear out. The other type is constructed of lead-saturated fabric, similar to the aprons you wear when your dentist x-rays your teeth. These are a bit more expensive, but ours have lasted for years. These can be purchased from Photak, P.O. Box 415, Menasha, WI 54952. Call (800) 723-9876 or (414) 722-6960 for prices and a free catalog.

Security checks and X-ray machines may seem like a pain-in-the-neck, but we should always remember that these efforts are for our own safety.

## Portable Studio Lighting

While we are on the subject of Photak, there are some other indispensable pieces of equipment we order from them:

our slave flashes. The Morris Mini and Morris Midi are tiny flash units that would fit in your palm. They can be hidden in flowerpots or behind marble columns and take their orders from any flash being fired in the room. With four of them, you could light an entire (middle-sized) room. They are not very expensive, a little over $25, but they are the most exciting innovation since potato chips. The Morris Midi is about two-and-a-half times as strong as the Morris Mini and can be very useful in photo situations requiring a brighter light. The only drawback that we could find to the Morris flashes is that they will fire every time any photographer in the room uses his flash. Carry extra batteries so that you'll have all the flashes you need for your trip. The Morris Mini uses two AAA batteries, and the Morris Midi, two AA batteries.

## PLANNING A TRIP

The key to a successful stock trip is careful planning. The Boy Scout motto of "Be Prepared" could well be applied to stock photographers. If you are visiting a foreign country, by all means call the tourist office of that country for brochures and literature that might be helpful on your shoot. Find out what the weather is likely to be during your visit. Most photographers would want to avoid the rainy season in the Caribbean, Africa or South America. If the weather will be cold, you'll need warm clothes. If it will be hot and humid, you'll want light cotton clothing.

Find out if you'll need special permissions to do professional photography in a particular country. We spent over a year obtaining permission to shoot an assignment in Gabon in Africa, but it does not normally take so long. In many places, there is an advantage in appearing to be a tourist. Almost all countries welcome a tourist with a camera and in many instances you'll be taking the same pictures. The only difference is that yours will be better.

From time to time there will be some countries where you could face possible danger. In planning a trip to shoot stock, it is wise to check with the State Department in Washington, D.C. to see if there are any travel advisories on that country. The telephone number is (202) 647-5225. They will provide a recorded report on the countries on your itinerary.

What makes good stock on a foreign destination? The first thing you want is an "establishing shot," one or more pictures that can be a symbol of that country or city. It might be the Eiffel Tower in Paris, the Clock Tower of Parliament housing Big Ben in London, or the Vatican or Colosseum in Rome. It is always a good idea to take the skylines of major cities, but at the same time realize that skylines change from year to year and they can become dated. Photo coverage of any city requires that you take an establishing shot. That could be the skyline we already talked about, an aerial view from an aircraft or high building, or just a wide-angle street scene of the downtown area. An establishing shot is one of the first things a picture editor asks for.

## THE IMPORTANCE OF PEOPLE

Another important subject is people and, for some photographers, the most difficult thing they can do is ask a stranger to pose for their camera. If you really want to succeed in stock photography, you'll

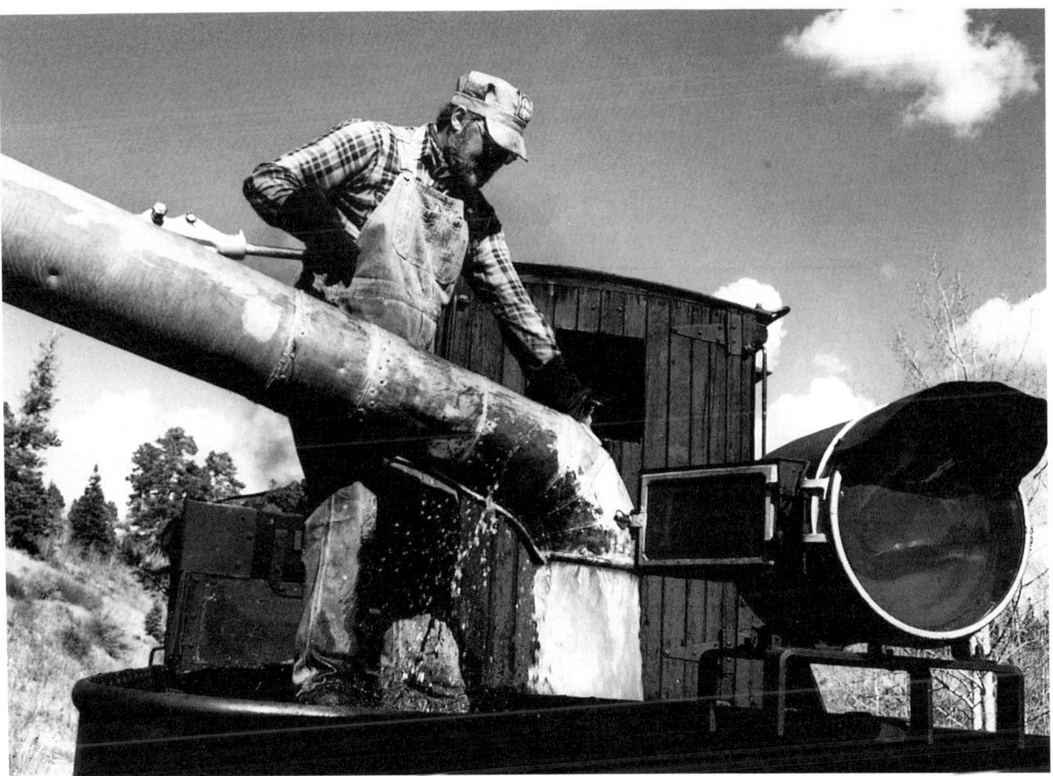

A railroad engineer puts water into the steam engine of a train in Colorado. Because of his timeless clothing and the natural background, this could illustrate a steam locomotive today or long ago.

need to overcome the people barrier. *People are the place* and photo coverage of any destination is incomplete without pictures of people. Our policy is to get people to pose and think they're having fun doing it. In fact, you're paying a person a compliment when you ask to take her picture. Obviously you think she is interesting or attractive enough to spend your time and your film on her. Explain to your intended subject why you believe she would make a good picture. It might be the way the sun plays in her hair or the color of her jacket or sweater. If you can interest her and get her involved in the creative process, you've already won cooperation and your picture will be more lively as a result.

When taking people pictures, we make it very clear that we are professionals. We even wear name tags with the name of our business, Words & Pictures, spelled out. We also carry business cards. People like the idea that their picture might appear in a magazine or newspaper. We ask for a model release. This is very important. It automatically doubles or even triples the potential value of that picture. The release we ask a person to sign is very short and simple. A copy of our model release form is on page 54.

Unless we hire professional models for a shoot, we normally do not pay people to pose. We do, however, offer to send them one or more color prints of the pictures in return for their cooperation and signing the release. This takes time and effort, but it is far less expensive and less demeaning than handing out small amounts of money at the moment. We should mention here that model releases are not usually necessary for pictures of people in Third World countries and are rarely required anywhere for pictures that will be used only for editorial purposes. As a rule of thumb, we always try to get releases for the people in Europe, North America, Japan and major cities in South America.

What kinds of people pictures sell best? If you're in a foreign country, naturally you want people who are typical of that country. You might photograph a Frenchman wearing a beret and sipping a glass of wine. The Chinese farmer may wear a cone-shaped hat to protect himself from the sun while working in the rice fields. The Masai woman in Kenya is adorned with brightly colored beads. In building a stock file of people, you first shoot the typical, but picture agencies also get requests for the atypical shots of people. They may want the Masai woman in Kenya in business dress working at a computer. One of the interesting things about the stock business is the variety and diversity of requests you will receive.

When traveling anywhere, we come back with a variety of people shots. We most often shoot pretty girls, old men, adorable children and attractive couples of all ages. If possible, we show people in different occupations, both living in the city and in the countryside. We shoot close-ups of faces, head and shoulders, full body shots of people in varied activities, and people interacting with each other. One of our pictures from China shows a mother feeding noodles to a child with chopsticks (see page 32). Such an image has a universal appeal and makes a good stock picture.

## SHOOTING IN YOUR OWN BACKYARD

Some photographers assume that the best stock pictures come from exotic destinations such as Tibet or Afghanistan. In fact, the very best stock pictures, ones that will sell again and again, can be taken in your hometown and often in your own backyard. The best-sellers in the American market are American subjects. The ideal subjects might be your own family. Photographer Wayne Miller, once an assistant to Edward Steichen, photographed his own children for several years as they were growing up. The resulting book, *The World Is Young*, is a classic of intimate family pictures, all done in black and white. Eugene Smith's unforgettable picture of his two children walking hand in hand along a shaded garden path has been used again and again as a stock image to depict the innocence and wonder of childhood. Never, for an instant, make the mistake of assuming that a stock picture needs to be a trite cliché. The really good ones tug at your heart and bring a smile to your lips or tears to your eyes.

Let's assume you're going to use your house, your family and your backyard for shooting stock. You'll want a place or a room to create a small studio, preferably a location with good, indirect sunlight. Pick up two telescoping stands from your local camera store to hold a paper roll on a horizontal pole. The best paper color is white, but you should eventually add some earth tones like brown and gray. You will want to add some floodlights and possibly a kicker light, or slave flash, also on portable stands. This simple studio can provide a setting for taking portraits of people and pictures of objects.

You might ask, "What can I possibly photograph at home that will be useful stock?" Our answer is to use your creative imagination. Stock pictures are all around. Photograph the face of your grandfather clock, a bottle of wine with a wedge of cheese, or an old globe of the world with some rare books bound in leather. A stock picture can be almost anything. It is up to you to arrange objects of interest into strong compositions.

We will stress again and again the importance of using people in your pictures. While we often use models for assignments when our client pays the modeling fees, we usually turn to family, friends, neighbors and even strangers for models when our budget will not cover such fees. We would urge you to follow our lead when shooting stock pictures on speculation. While really good professional models can be a joy to work with, there are also distinct advantages to using nonprofessionals to pose for your camera. Perfect beauty pales in comparison to the fresh scrubbed, smiling face of the girl next door. Remember, you are not looking for people who look perfect. Real people often make better models for stock pictures than professional models, and you can be sure they won't charge you as much. In fact, our normal payment for a nonprofessional model is an 8-by-10-inch color print and most people appear glad to get it, especially if the picture makes them look good.

When we are on assignment and must have models, we usually first try the local modeling schools. If they have acceptable models with some experience, getting your models from such a school has its advantages. The model's hourly rate will be less than that of a professional, although the model will often have all the advantages of a professional model. The models almost ready to leave their school to look for jobs are always glad to have good photographs of themselves for their portfolios. Your fee will sometimes be lowered if you will provide portfolio shots to the model.

## POSING YOUR SUBJECT

Many nonprofessionals are, at least initially, ill at ease in front of the camera, but there are a few things you can do to make them more comfortable when posing. Here are various methods:

1. Get your subject involved in some familiar activity, something the person can concentrate on while you're taking pictures.
2. Get two people doing something together such as two men playing chess. In a few minutes they will be thinking about the game and almost forget that you're taking pictures.
3. Ask your subject to stand in favorable light and look off to one side of the camera.
4. Have that person lift their chin slightly and open their eyes to catch the light. It will make your subject look ten years younger and ten pounds lighter.
5. If you ask your subjects to move, walk or turn their heads, let them try it once before you actually take the picture. If you need to correct the action, explain carefully and clearly before they try it again.
6. Whenever possible, photograph several generations together and interacting with each other.

Again, don't forget to get a model release.

Where can you find attractive, photogenic people to pose for your pictures?

While shooting aboard a cruise ship in the Caribbean, we asked the cruise director if some of the young people who appeared in the floor show would volunteer to be our models around the pool and on shore excursions. They were glad to do it and, in fact, enjoyed themselves during the shooting. As usual, we promised to send them all color prints for signing model releases.

When staying at resort hotels, we have approached the management and asked if some members of the staff would pose for us on their time off. They were glad to agree, realizing that our pictures would generate favorable publicity for the hotel.

Obviously, there are many instances when it is not practical to get a model release when taking candid pictures of people. On some occasions we will work as a team. For instance, when covering people at a party or a reception, one of us will shoot pictures while the other person will follow along and request model releases from the subjects. As pointed out earlier, we keep the model release simple and short. The wording should cover editorial, electronic media (TV), advertising and public relations. If someone objects to advertising, we suggest they cross out that word on the release, but in fact that rarely happens. We point out that a magazine cover is used to advertise and promote the magazine. We almost always offer to send a color print to the subject and make sure that we follow through on that promise.

There will be some instances where you need professional models and when you need them, you can't afford not to have them. When shooting pictures for a guidebook on Bermuda, we hired four models through a local model agency for two hours for only $115. We explained to the agency manager that we did not have any budget to hire models and she agreed to provide them at this low rate. We planned the shooting carefully to take advantage of the limited time. We each shot six rolls in the two hours. Many of the images were used in the book and the rest went into our stock file and to our agencies.

## DISCOVERING GREAT STOCK PICTURES

Some outstanding stock pictures require planning and preparation. On a recent trip to South Florida, we saw people feeding a flock of sea gulls on the beach at Fort Lauderdale. It was a great stock subject, but we were on our way to give an illustrated lecture and could not stop. We did, however, go back the following day with a volunteer model in a brightly colored bikini and a loaf of bread. The gulls were delighted to see us and we took about three rolls of our blonde friend tossing bread to the gulls. The results were worth the effort.

On that same trip we covered the art deco hotels of Miami Beach, a subject that is often requested by art directors. These unique hotels have become so fashionable that many fashion shoots are done in South Miami Beach, using the small hotels as backgrounds and settings. We enjoyed taking pictures of the photographers taking pictures.

We also spent some time scouting for a perfect location to shoot the Miami skyline at sunset. Friends had suggested the Bayside restaurant and shopping complex, which is located directly on Biscayne

Bay, but we found it was too close for an ideal picture. Finally we located a spot in the parking lot of the Royal Caribbean Cruise Line offices at the Port of Miami. It offered a view of the major buildings of downtown Miami from across the water. We came back just before sunset and set up our tripod and camera, attaching a cable release. As the sun set behind the buildings, we started taking pictures about every five minutes. Gradually the sunset faded and the lights started to come on in the skyscrapers. Once again, we shot every few minutes, bracketing our exposures to be sure we had at least one right on the mark.

On yet another trip, this time to Lower Manhattan in New York, we were fortunate to be there in late spring during a stretch of beautiful, clear weather. We wanted to be near the base of the Brooklyn Bridge on the Brooklyn side of the river with a clear view of the skyline near the time of sunset. Not being familiar with the area, we hired a car and driver through our hotel and set out to locate this spot. After exploring several streets and making a few inquiries, we located an area almost directly under the bridge. By this time, the sun had set behind the buildings, turning the sky to a rosy pink. We set up our tripods, attached cameras with cable releases, and started taking pictures, one frame every five minutes. The approach was similar to that used in Miami.

Our basic setting was aperture priority at f/8 with Fujichrome 100 film. Each camera automatically set the shutter speed, which started off at about 1⁄10th of a second and, by the time it was really dark, was as slow as about twenty seconds. For some shots, we shifted our position to include the bridge.

The point in describing this photograph is that it took some special effort, a certain expense and planning on our part. The results, which were spectacular, were well worth the effort. The stock pictures we took that night will sell again and again.

Closer to home, our son Peter and his wife Stacey were expecting their first baby. We often receive requests for pictures of pregnant women and mothers with new babies, so we knew this was a golden opportunity. We took pictures of Stacey all during the term of her pregnancy, including some warm shots of Peter and Stacey together. When Stacey was finally taken to the hospital, we visited and recorded our daughter-in-law shortly before she gave birth to an eight pound baby girl. After the mother and child could receive visitors, we took pictures of both mother and father proudly holding their daughter, grandparents with the baby, and even great-grandparents holding the baby. Peter and Stacey will have these precious moments recorded on film and we will have strong images to fill future photo requests.

The point we make is that you should always be aware of potential stock pictures as you travel or go about your daily life. Keep asking yourself, Is this a subject that will sell as stock? We find pictures in both expected and unexpected places. Over a period of years we have collected, with our cameras, some interesting neon signs. One of our favorites was in the window of a beauty salon. The name of the shop was "Curl Up and Dye!" Sure enough, we recently received a picture request for amusing signs.

A more common subject is people working with computers. Since computers have become indispensable in our daily lives, art directors and picture editors often request striking pictures of computers in use. We shoot pictures of each other working on our office computers and these have sold many times.

## PERMISSIONS

There are instances when you will need authorization to shoot at certain locations. On a trip to Asheville, North Carolina, we visited the Vanderbilt Mansion. Normally visitors are asked not to take pictures in this magnificent structure, but because we were travel writers planning to write about Asheville, we were granted special permission to shoot. The curators reasoned that good published pictures might encourage more visitors.

Not all permissions are easy to get. As we mentioned previously, we spent almost a year obtaining permission to take pictures for a children's book on the African nation of Gabon. When a positive response was finally received, the government wanted one hundred free copies of the book and the right of approval on the final text. We have not yet done that coverage in Gabon. Negotiations are still going on between the publisher and the government. When and if we do the coverage, we will come away with valuable stock images of an African country that is not frequently covered by photographers.

Department stores such as Bloomingdale's in New York, Harrod's in London and Galleries LaFayette in Paris require that photographers obtain permission before taking pictures in their stores. They don't want competitors taking pictures of their displays and duplicating the arrangements elsewhere. Go to the public relations office for such a store, present your credentials such as an ASMP press card or business card, explain your purpose, and you will often be given the necessary permission. Even better, write ahead for permission. Be sure to use your professional letterhead.

Later in the book we will talk about where to get repro-quality dupes of your best color slides. For now, we will tell you how to save the high cost of duping by taking multiple shots of the same subject. When you find or set up a "gee whiz" stock picture, one you know is a sure winner, take anywhere from eight to ten shots of that same subject. In addition, be sure to bracket ½ stop under and ½ stop over at least once on that subject. (Set your compensation meter at –½ and + ½ or change your ISO meter to be one mark above and one mark below the normal ISO rating you give the film.) If your evaluation of the subject was correct and it is a winner, you already will have made the dupes in the camera and saved yourself time and money. Under these circumstances, we keep three or four originals for our own file and send the others to our picture agencies throughout the world.

## PHOTOGRAPHIC STYLE

There are two distinctive styles of stock shooting: editorial and advertising. In general, editorial tends to be more documentary and realistic. This is the kind of shot you will see in textbooks, illustration for magazine articles and newspaper articles. Advertising tends to be more posed and idealistic. You've seen this style every time you look at an ad or watch a TV commercial. Each style can be very effective for stock and we do both. The advertising style is more often done on advertising assignments. Public relations (or PR) firms often need pictures that appear editorial in style, but that could be called "soft advertising." They understandably avoid pictures that make their product or destination look anything less than perfect or ideal. Public relations pictures should appear unposed and should look real, avoiding the glossy style of many advertising shots. Public relations firms often provide photographs to the media and no editor wants an advertising picture to illustrate an article in his publication. Public relations photos also are often used for brochures and press releases.

We follow certain self-imposed rules when shooting for stock. Keep in mind, however, that rules are actually guidelines. Ours are:

1. Keep your pictures simple and uncluttered.
2. Use color as a graphic and design tool.
3. Include people in your pictures when possible.
4. Closer is better for most stock pictures.
5. Shoot couples, babies, pretty girls and cute animals in that order.

As you shoot and learn, you'll gain your own insights into what sells as stock photography. Keep a record of the subjects that sell again and again. Be sure that you re-shoot these subjects from time to time. It is satisfying to see your credit line on magazine covers and national advertisements. It is even more satisfying to receive the checks.

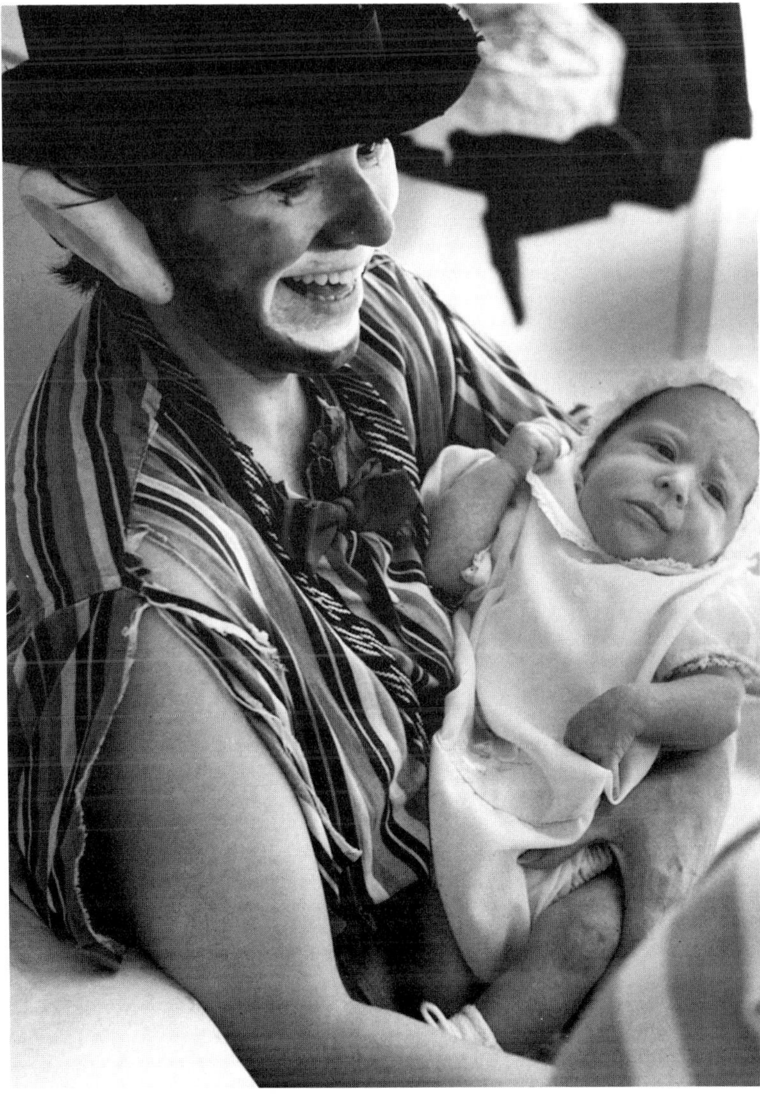

A mother with a baby is always a popular stock picture. When the mother is a clown, it is a more unusual shot.

*Chapter 4*

# THE BUSINESS OF STOCK PHOTOGRAPHY

## ORGANIZE!

You can have thousands of the best photographs in the world and they won't earn you a penny if they are still sitting in little yellow boxes in a jumble in your basement. Most photo requests have a short deadline and must often be mailed the same day the requests come in. We had a friend who admitted ruefully that he had received a call asking for an eagle in flight over mountains. He had exactly the picture the editor had described, but he couldn't remember in which little yellow box it was. The deadline passed and he missed the sale. It is important for you to get organized if you want your photo stock to make money for you.

### Pre-editing Your Stock

Pre-edit your slides carefully with a hand viewer that has a good magnifying window, such as an Agfascop200 viewer. Any slide that is not technically good should be thrown away, even if you feel that the subject is extraordinary. Try to remember what it was like to squirm silently with embarrassment for your host when you were being shown a poor home slide show. Even while you are looking at a harp seal giving birth, if the picture is out of focus, it is a poor photo. If it is overexposed, it should be tossed. That gorgeous landscape shot will have to end up in the trash can if the horizon isn't level. Remember that these slides will have your name on them and you do not want to have a reputation for anything but excellence.

After we have turned all the slides so that they are top side up, we hold the slides together like a pack of cards and draw a black marker line across the top middle edge of the mounts. Thus every slide has a small black mark at the top middle edge of its mount. This small step will save you endless hours if a drawer of slides should ever spill or if you are preparing a slide show. Without looking at the slide, you can now tell which side is up.

When a slide is a real winner, better than most of the others in its category, we mark the upper left corner of the slide mount with a blue marker. Now we can travel or be away from the office with a feeling of true ease, knowing that even if the editor of *National Geographic* should call for slides in our absence, anyone, even a totally untutored person, can do a superlative pull for the most demanding client as long as he or she pulls slides with blue marked corners.

## Filing Your Slides

Until now, you have been interested only in the quality of the slides you shot. Now you must determine category breakdowns so that the slides can be filed by subject. Before the slides can be permanently filed, they must be copyrighted and captioned. For this step, we use the plastic containers for silverware drawers sold in grocery stores, as they have long narrow channels in which slides can stand upright. For category headers we use pieces of stiff cardboard that we have cut to the width of a slide but a bit taller. We often use old business cards, flipping them over so that we can write category headers on the blank side.

Our slides are filed alphabetically, first by continent, then by country, then by city and then by subject. We also have "Miscellaneous" files, in which we keep generic subjects, also filed alphabetically. (An example of this is "Clouds." Although you will caption the slides as "Cumulus clouds in Kenya" or "Nimbus clouds in Miami," the slides will be filed under "Clouds" in "Miscellaneous." Then, when you are asked for cloud slides, you won't have to remember where you shot good pictures of clouds.)

Our miscellaneous files are massive and it is important that we keep these files in order. We also keep a list of the subjects on the wall, so if we forget that "Skating" will be found under "Sports," or that "Asian children" will be found under "People," we can easily look it up. The miscellaneous files also help us know where we can find more slides of any kind. Remember that we have 650,000 slides from 94 countries. If, for example, we are asked for "Asian children" we will often go first to "Miscellaneous." Under "Asian children" we can check the captions on the slides and know exactly in which country files we will be able to find other pictures. As a backup, we also have a cross-reference card file that lists subjects and all the countries in which the subjects will be found.

## Captioning and Copyrighting

Now you have all your slides filed by subject in plastic silverware trays. Each slide must be copyrighted and captioned at this point. The copyright should include a "c" surrounded by a circle, followed by your name and the year. This copyright, for example, © Ann F. Purcell '92, must go on one small side of the slide mount. Before our current method, we used a stamp that we ordered from a stationery or office supply store.

The caption goes on one large side of the slide mount. Remember that any slide going to a stock agency must have one small side and one large side of the slide mount left clear for the agency's use. Thus you have the task of entering as much information as possible on one side of the mount. It should include the loca-

Never write on more than two sides of a slide mount. If the slide is ever to go to a stock photo agency, the agency will need one fat side and one thin side of a mount for their own use. Do try to get as much information in your caption as you can. Editors like captions to be complete. On a least one occasion, we were given an assignment on the basis of a caption that intrigued the editor. If your photo is model released, it is very important to write MR in the upper right-hand corner of the slide mount.

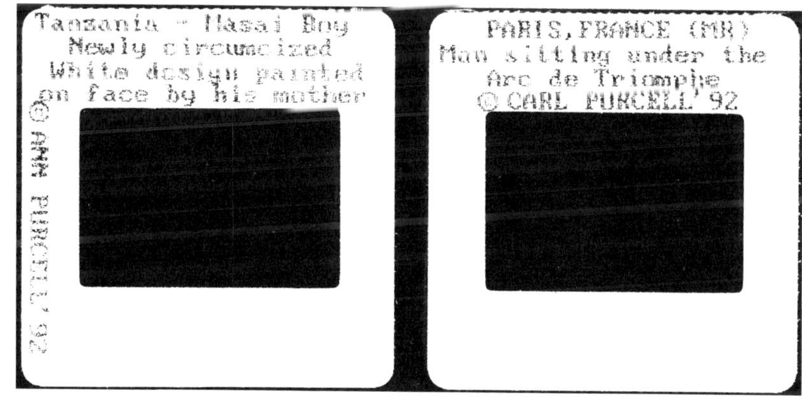

tion and something about the subject. If the slide is of a person, it should have "MR" in the upper right-hand corner to show that the slide is "Model Released."

When we were getting started, we used the 1¼-by-1¼-inch Avery labels, which are precisely the size of the fat side of a slide mount, and hand-typed each caption.

Later, as we became more sophisticated and acquired a computer, we used file folder labels (3½-by-7/16 inches), which can be bought in bulk (10,000 per box) at any office supply store. Two captions will go on each of these labels and, when cut in half, each piece will fit exactly on the large side of a slide mount. We programmed our computer to give us extra small type. We also bought a small metal device that fits over the roller of our printer and has sprockets to hold the labels taut as they feed through the printer. With a little experimentation, we were able to set the margins exactly to fit the labels and the tabs so that there would be a space right in the middle between the two labels.

Using a computer for captioning slides saves us a great deal of time. Rarely do you take only one or two pictures of any one subject. When we come back from a trip, for example, we might have 254 slides of the flower market, 32 slides of the cathedral, 188 slides of downtown street scenes, 46 slides of bicycles and so on. If you type a caption such as "Flower Market, Beijing, China" on your computer, you can have the computer repeat the label again and again so that you can have the necessary 254 labels without retyping.

Eventually you may go still another step in making your job of slide captioning easier. Typing captions and putting pressure sensitive labels on slides can be extremely time-consuming. TRAC Industries in Doylestown, Pennsylvania, (215) 345-9311, puts out several versions of Slidetypers, which have greatly increased our efficiency in captioning. Slide captioning machines traditionally had been attached to the slide mounting machines in the photo laboratory, and the captioning machines cost up to $20,000. Now, with the advent of the smaller machines, it is possible for each photographer to have one.

We shoot approximately 6,000 slides a month and the TRAC Slidetypers can caption all of these slides within a few hours. Over the years, we have tried several TRAC Slidetypers. Some are less expensive (Model CM/4 runs about $850) but only one slide can be captioned at a time and only two lines can be typed on each fat side of a slide mount.

The one we currently use is another model—the most sophisticated of five small models available, the TRAC A/10 Slidetyper, which looks like a small box with a loading stack attached to a small computer keyboard. You load a stack of slides (our machine accepts round cornered, square cornered or plastic mounts), type in your caption on the computer keyboard (the A/10 will let you put up to five lines of twenty-two characters each on each fat side of a slide mount) and push a button. The machine sends each slide between padded rollers, prints the caption using a silent ink jet printer—the first of its kind for any slide captioning machine—and then deposits the slide in the second loading stack. Us-

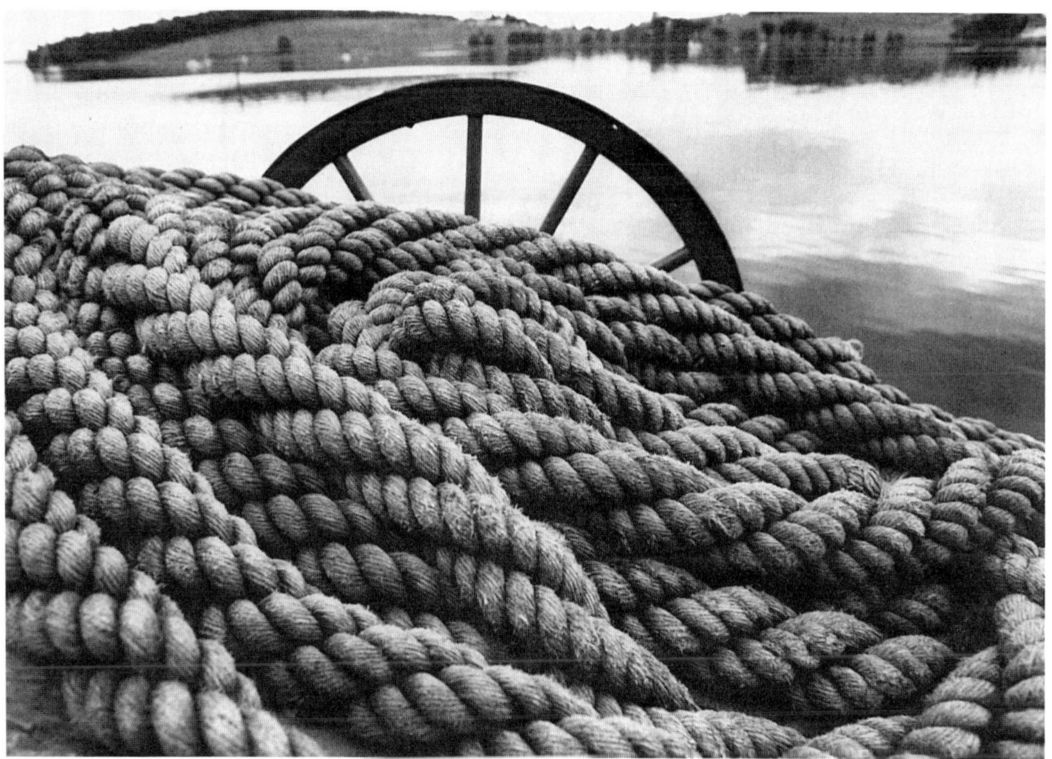

This pile of heavy rope in Lunenburg, Nova Scotia, reflects the maritime heritage of that community. Such an image could also be used to convey strength. This is the kind of detail that a normal tourist might ignore, but is a shot that a stock photographer could not resist.

ing our example from the preceding page, your "Tulips in Flower Market, Early morning in Beijing, China," captions, consecutive numbers and copyrights can be neatly typed by ink jet directly onto the 254 slide mounts in less than three minutes.

TRAC Slidetypers are expensive—they can cost up to $4,500 new—but you may be able to obtain one secondhand for less, or you could even lease one. TRAC also puts out a software for IBM-compatible and Macintosh computers so that you can run the slide caption printer directly off your computer. We chose to have the extra NEC computer that comes with the SlideTyper because we didn't want either of our computers tied up for hours while slides were being captioned. Certainly, considering the time you save, buying such a machine will more than repay the money it cost if you are dealing with a large slide file.

## Options for Filing Your Pictures

If your good slides number less than 4,000, then perhaps you'll want to file them in archival plastic sleeves. These sleeves hold twenty slides each and each sleeve has one stiff wide edge with perforations, so the sleeve can be stored in a standard three-ring binder. Over the years, we have probably tried just about every design of plastic sleeve made. Our preference is the top-loading plastic sleeves; we feel that the slides are easier to get in and out.

If you decide to file your slides in plastic sleeves, be sure that you buy archival sleeves that over the years won't chemically react with the slides. Most sleeves sold today are archival. At first you may be able to keep the sleeves in large binders on shelves. (Don't forget to treat all cracks, creases and corners of the shelves against bugs before you put the binders on them!) Later, as you expand your files, you may need to buy standard metal filing cabinets to keep your slide sleeves organized; hang the slide sleeves from filing cabinet bar racks, which are available at most office supply stores and are easily inserted into the file drawers.

If your slide collection numbers greater than 4,000, you may want to consider our form of filing, that is, in NEUMADE slide cabinet files. (Some camera stores will be able to supply these, but if not, they can be ordered from NEUMADE Products, 200 Connecticut Ave., Norwalk, CT 06856, (203) 866-7600.) These are five-drawer metal cabinets with six channels in each drawer. We have found that we can file as many as 5,000 slides in each cabinet.

Unfortunately, as in most modern products, these cabinets are not inexpensive—approximately $300 each. However, the advantage of the metal slide file cabinets over the old handmade wooden cabinets we did use is that bugs will not choose to live in the corners of the metal drawers.

Whether you decide to keep your slides in drawers or sleeves, your main insect enemies are silverfish and cockroaches, both of which like to eat film emulsion. You will know that you have a problem if there are tiny pinprick holes of light on the transparency around the edges of the slide mount. If that happens, you may need to debug your files, an undertaking that is somewhat more complicated than it sounds. Ideally, each slide will be removed from the file, individually cleaned with film cleaner and canned air, and stored separately from the uncleaned slides until the files have been cleared and fumigated. If the slides are kept in plastic sleeves, the notebooks and sleeves will also have to be cleaned and aired. Bright sunshine is a good way to get the bugs to leave. The slides, however, should not be exposed to bright light for long as it causes fading.

Pest control companies like to spray, fog and powder homes against insects. You have to warn the people who service your home that none of the products they use must touch or fog any of the slides. Before you set up your slide cabinets, you may want to saturate the floor and walls with some sort of insecticide. We keep our slide cabinets about one foot off the floor so that we can treat the floor periodically, being careful not to let any of the solution near the slides and keeping it far enough back so that children and pets cannot accidentally come into contact with it.

Fortunately, our only problem so far has been with a few slides that were out for a long time with clients who obviously had bug problems.

## Categorizing Your Files

When you are captioning your slides, you may decide to allocate a number to each slide. The TRAC Slidetyper we use for captioning can be programmed to number the slides as they are being captioned. Each slide will be given one number higher than the previous slide. We have found that there are advantages and disadvantages to numbering slides.

The advantage of numbering your slides is that each then assumes a unique identity. Occasionally, a client will call to ask questions about one of the slides that you sent. One of your stock agencies may call to tell you that they have had a big advertising sale of one of your slides but that their agreement includes exclusive use of that slide for a certain amount of time. You may also have the misfortune to be dealing with a client who did not return all of your slides. You may wish to set up a computer tracking system that can tell you at a glance which of your slides are earners and how much they have earned. In all of these cases, it could have been an advantage to have numbered your slides.

One disadvantage of numbering your slides is that the number will take valuable space on your slide mount and will diminish your caption. Good captions that provide interesting details often prompt sales of the use of slides. Another disadvantage is the confusion of keeping each slide's number unique. You will not stop taking photos after you have numbered all of your existing slides. Suppose you decided to number all of your slides from a Colorado shoot and the last slide was #CO-93-3264, "CO" standing for Colorado and the 93 being the year you took the 3,264 slides. Suppose that late in '93, you were assigned to shoot Colorado again. You will have to know where to pick up the last number for Colorado. Then suppose that you were also assigned to cover Colombia, Cologne and Cordoba in 1993. Obviously, you will have to find a different code than "CO" for these destinations.

If you are a studio photographer, numbering your slides may become even more complicated. Babies, Backgrounds, Balls, Badminton, Bachelor Degree ceremonies and Bar mitzvahs will compete for "BA" as well as the necessity to keep your clients' names separate by code.

The easiest way to resolve this confusion is to have a series of identifiers on each slide. The first few sets of numbers could pinpoint the location. The second set of numbers could identify the type of image and could also help with cross-referencing. The third series of numbers could simply be a signature of the specific slide.

For example, suppose that we decided that Europe is 6, while England is 12, London is 5, People is 4, Child is 17. We usually divide our files into continents and then into countries, except for countries such as the United States, where each state could have the rank of a country, or Canada and China, where provinces assume the rank of a country. For example, assuming that AFRICA = 1, AMERICA = 2, ASIA = 3, CANADA = 4, CHINA = 5, EUROPE = 6, etc., then a country breakdown could look like:

Example: (6 - EUROPE)
6 - 11 — Denmark
6 - 12 — England
6 - 13 — Finland
6 - 14 — France

Then the photo of a child in London might have an identification number of. 2-12-5-4-17-869 and the next photo of a child in London would have the identification number 2-12-5-4-17-870. With the help of a simple catalog compiled by you, anyone could know what slide the client is holding by being told the identification number. What's more, if you keep separate drawers or notebooks in the order of the numbers, you would be able to locate slides immediately. To that end, your catalog should be carefully alphabetized according to the numbers. The numbers can be as simple or complex as you want them, so you should think out your system carefully before you start marking your slides. Do you want to add the year? You should have a "country code" for your miscellaneous file of generic shots and subcategories in your generic file can be put in the number space where city numbers usually go. If you go strictly by the alphabet, giving "AA" #1, "AB" #2 and "AC" #3, and so forth, the numbering will become fairly straightforward.

The best and most simple way to identify your slides individually is with bar coding. There is a new computer program, called the Photographer Image and Client Tracking System (PICTS), on the market that produces bar-code labels, a submission memo listing all of the images you are submitting, a photographer receipt listing all the kept images, a return receipt listing all the returned images as well as all of the images a client still has, a receivable report, an invoice and late payment notices. Best of all, it produces a client history report, address labels and an image use report. PICTS is put out by Douglass Systems Corporation in Washington, D.C. (Telephone: (202) 723-2647) and can be used with a Macintosh computer with a minimum of 2MB of RAM, System 7 or system software 6.0.5 or later and a hard disk. The software costs around $900, and the bar code wand around $600.

PICTS has one more sterling capability. We used to scan hundreds of our client records each month to learn which clients had held slides longer than they were supposed to. Then we'd write a note asking the client when we could hope to see the slides returned. Sometimes, when we were traveling or struggling with deadlines, the job of tracking late slides would be delayed for as much as a month or two. PICTS, however, can generate, on demand, an instant image receivable report, telling who has which slides, how many they have, and how long they have had them. With a few keystrokes, you also can generate late image notices for any slides that have been out longer than thirty days, sixty days or ninety days.

Do not despair if your slide files are already very large when you switch to bar coding. Simply bar code each slide sent out of your office.

## Computer Assistance

Some people enter all their slides on their computers so that they can check, by doing a computer search, if they have the picture that is being requested. Others use the traditional library system, putting all their slides of a category at a certain place in alphabetical order. If you are just setting up your system, it is good to use both computer and library system. If you are asked for a woman on a water buffalo, there is an advantage in knowing that you have this picture in Nepal and Thailand (computer check) and being then able to put your hands on those slides immediately by going to the Near East and South East Asia files.

There is one important point about using computers in your business that must not be forgotten. Any computer or computer program is only as accurate or thorough as the information entered by its user. Unless you are prepared to be consistent about entering all new information in a timely fashion, you cannot expect the computer to give you accurate feedback. Clients quickly lose their patience when accused of holding slides they have al-

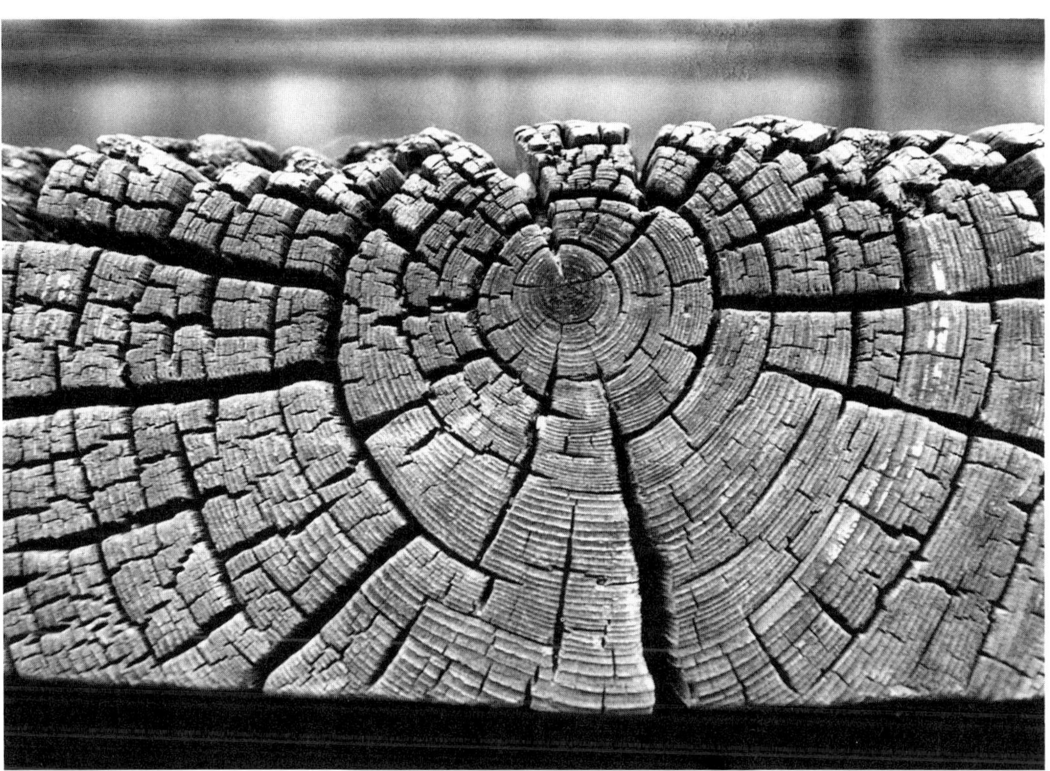

We are constantly on the lookout for strong patterns in nature that can be added to our stock file. Start taking note of magazine advertisements. You'll be surprised how many ads are a combination of two photographs—a middle-page insert on a graphic or scenic background.

ready returned, or when asked to pay a bill that was already paid. Conversely, when you are submitting two to four hundred slides each day, it is nearly impossible for any human brain—even yours!—to keep track of who is holding what slides and which clients have not yet paid you for their use of the slides.

## BUSINESS INSURANCE

There are possibly some monsters lurking around unexpected corners in your stock photography business. The worst is fire. Another disaster could be caused by someone suing you for slander because your slide was used inappropriately. Your photo researcher could suffer bodily damage while on your property. Your camera equipment could be lost or stolen on your next trip. If a hurricane blew down your office wall, water damage could wipe out your slide collection.

Insurance cannot go back to a foreign country, line up the identical model with that special light situation, and retake the photo for you. It can, however, help you with house payments while you accrue a new stock file. It also can replace lost or stolen equipment. If you work out of your home, you should be aware that most home owners insurance does not cover business and property liability. If someone is hurt on your property while involved in your business, you will need a business liability policy. Even camera insurance floater policies, which protect your cameras while you travel, will not be honored if you are using the equipment as a business tool. Talk with your insurance company about a Business Owners Package policy and the various floater policies they offer for business equipment. Although we have never found an insurance company that would insure our color slides (how could you accurately predict the future earnings of each and

Our standard model release.

MODEL RELEASE

I hereby give photographers Carl and Ann Purcell, their legal representatives and assigns, the right and permission to publish, without charge, photographs of me, ______________________

taken at ______________. These pictures may be used in publications, audio-visual presentations, promotional literature, advertising, calendars or in any other manner. I hereby warrant that I (or undersigned Parent/Guardian) am over eighteen (18) years of age, and am competent to contract in my own name in so far as the above is concerned.

MODEL ______________________ __/__/__
Signature of Model or Parent/Guardian Date

ADDRESS ______________________ PHONE ______________

CITY ______________ STATE ________ ZIP ________

WITNESSED BY ______________________ __/__/__
Signature of Witness Date

every slide?), we do make sure that the structure around the slides (our house) has a very high pay-off in case of fire or water damage.

Fireproof safes may protect your slide mounts from getting charred, but the heat still will have melted the film. Water damage can be ruinous, particularly if mold is allowed to grow on the slide. Storing a duplicate set of your best slides in a different location can keep you from being wiped out in case of fire or water damage. Storing a computer disk with all your client records (updated every few months) in a safety deposit box will help you make a new start after a total disaster.

A legal suit can be almost as devastating, even if you are not in the wrong. Assuming that it was a publication who used one of your photos in a demeaning or inappropriate way without your knowledge, you could nevertheless spend $10,000 to $50,000 just responding to the accusation. You can buy a "Commercial Umbrella Policy" for protection against this, but you should check with an independent agent who works with many companies to find out where you will get the best rate.

## STANDARD BUSINESS FORMS

We spoke about one of the standard business forms for a stock photographer—the model release—in the last chapter. The wording is simple and fairly standard and we have it printed on a 3-by-5-inch card. We try to make it a practice always to have some of the standard model release forms with us anytime we are carrying a camera.

In addition to model releases, you will need other standard business forms for your stock photography business. These include business cards, stationery with your distinctive business logo, your printed slide catalog, client record sheets, submission forms, slide request forms, invoice forms and mailing labels. Other optional forms, as your business progresses, might include return postcards with your name preprinted in the mailing address space, checks with your business logo, fax cover sheets with your logo, photo assignment proposal forms and photo assignment invoices.

## Establishing Your Business Logo

The design of your business card and your business logo is important. Many of your clients will never see your face. They will, however, learn to know and recognize your business logo as if it had a personality of its own. It should be distinctive and tasteful. You may want to have your logo designed by a commercial artist. Once you have a business logo, it is a good idea to keep it consistent on all your business forms. When you decide on the color and paper quality of your business card, letterhead and envelopes, you should keep it the same, every time you have a new supply made, so that it can be easily recognized by the clients who have seen it before.

## Color Slide Index

Your color slide index, or catalog, will be sent to potential clients to let them know what you have in your stock files. It also will go out with stock that you have pulled by telephone or fax requests for new researchers or art directors. Whether your slides for the immediate submission are returned used or unused, your catalog will sometimes prompt the art director to request another subject from you. The slide index, like your other correspondence tools, also should be distinctively yours, and perhaps follow the design and color of your letterhead and business card.

The slide catalog should be comprehensive and easy to read. You want your clients to locate their current needs quickly if you have them. Alphabetize your listed categories and briefly give details about the depth of your coverage in that category.

Most computers are able to do desktop publishing and the slide catalog is a good chance to use this capability. Clip art can enhance your catalog so that it is not just a dry list. A laser printer will give you the most professional-looking catalog. If you do not have a laser printer, you can save the catalog on disk and then take the disk to a print shop to do your final printout. A fast service copy store or print shop can make and even collate several hundred copies of your catalog in a few days. You'll be doing updates every year, perhaps even every six months if you are doing a great deal of shooting. Limit the number of copies to those you'll use before it is time to do an update.

## Client Records

Paper client records can be designed for your personal needs on accountant ledger sheets. Use correction fluid to mark out unnecessary lines, and draw in others where you want them. When you are happy with the design, you can mass-copy the sheet, punch holes and clip the sheets in large three-ring binders. The client records need to give you the following information at one glance:

- Name of client (business name)
- Name of contact
- Address of client
- Telephone number of client
- Fax number of client, if available
- Federal Express or Airborne number of client, if available
- Date the slides were sent

- How many slides were sent
- Subject of the slides
- Date slides were returned after pre-edit
- How many slides were returned after pre-edit
- How many slides were held after pre-edit
- Date slides were returned after final edit
- How many slides were returned after final edit
- How many slides were held after final edit
- How many slides were used
- How much money the client paid for use
- Date the last slides were returned
- How many slides were returned

The client record sheets also should have space to give information about the client, particular likes, dislikes, company policies, slide return reliability and payment reliability. You will also want space for information about the rates you give these clients or their standard rates (often provided by the clients themselves).

All this information can be kept on computer, but this is emphatically a situation in which your computer will only be as efficient as the information entered into it. Be sure to do backups after every business day so that a computer glitch will not lose more than one business day's worth of information. It is a good idea to use a paper trail on clients until you are sure that you will remember consistently to enter client information on your computer every time you handle your stock file.

It will be a problem to interrupt other computer work to enter slide submission information. If you do not have an extra computer that can be dedicated for this purpose, you may wish to keep a paper file on clients and then once a day, or once a week, enter the information on computer. Again, be sure to make a backup copy at least once a day so that you won't lose all your records if the electricity goes off or if your computer burps.

There is one more paper trail that you should keep religiously. When you have submission forms and invoices printed up at your local print shop, it is a good idea to have three-part forms made. Then you can keep one copy and send two copies to your clients, with the request, printed prominently, that the client returns one with the slides or with the payment. It will also keep you from getting confused when you send slides or an invoice to a specific magazine and the slides or check comes back from a parent publishing company who is not mentioned by name in your books. This is a situation that happens often and can cause great trouble and embarrassment for you if you cannot identify the clients from whom you are receiving your slides or payment.

## Submission Forms

The main purpose of a submission form is to state the terms on which you are lending your slides, your count of how many were sent, and the terms for their return. At the bottom of your submission form will be a line stating that all terms are considered to have been accepted unless you receive notice to the contrary within ten days of receipt. Most clients will accept the terms, as they are normal for the stock photography industry. Some clients, however, will not agree to research fees or holding fees. Other clients will not

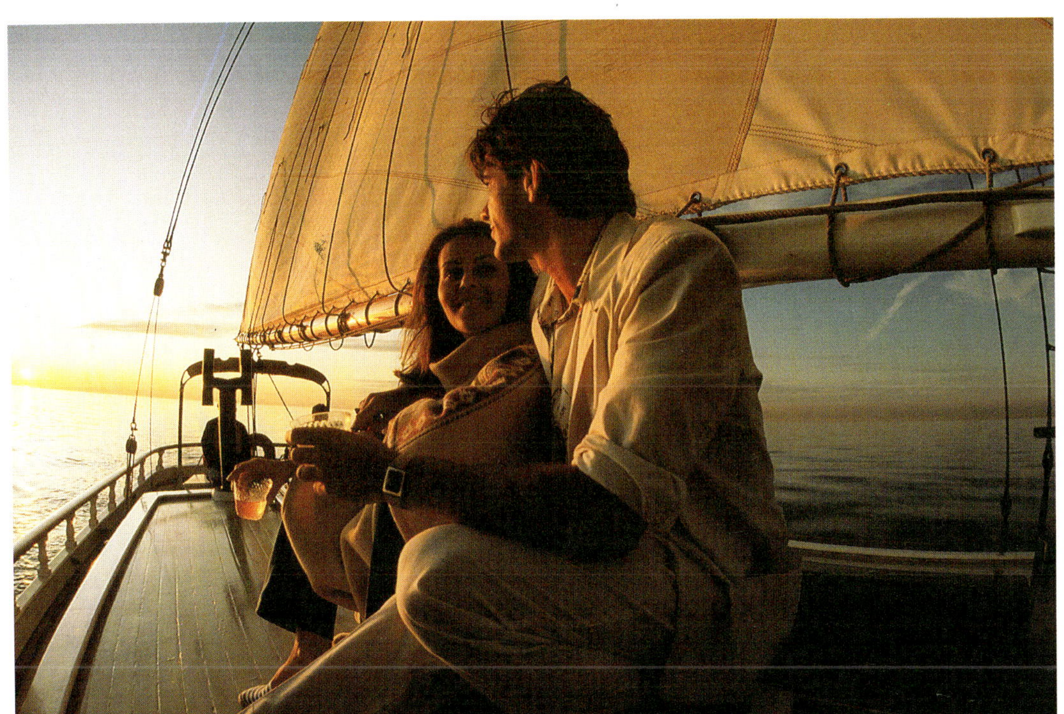

These young people were invited to go sailing with us in California. The only catch was that they were asked to volunteer as models. The day turned out to be quite hazy bright, but an amber filter gave a romantic glow to the picture.

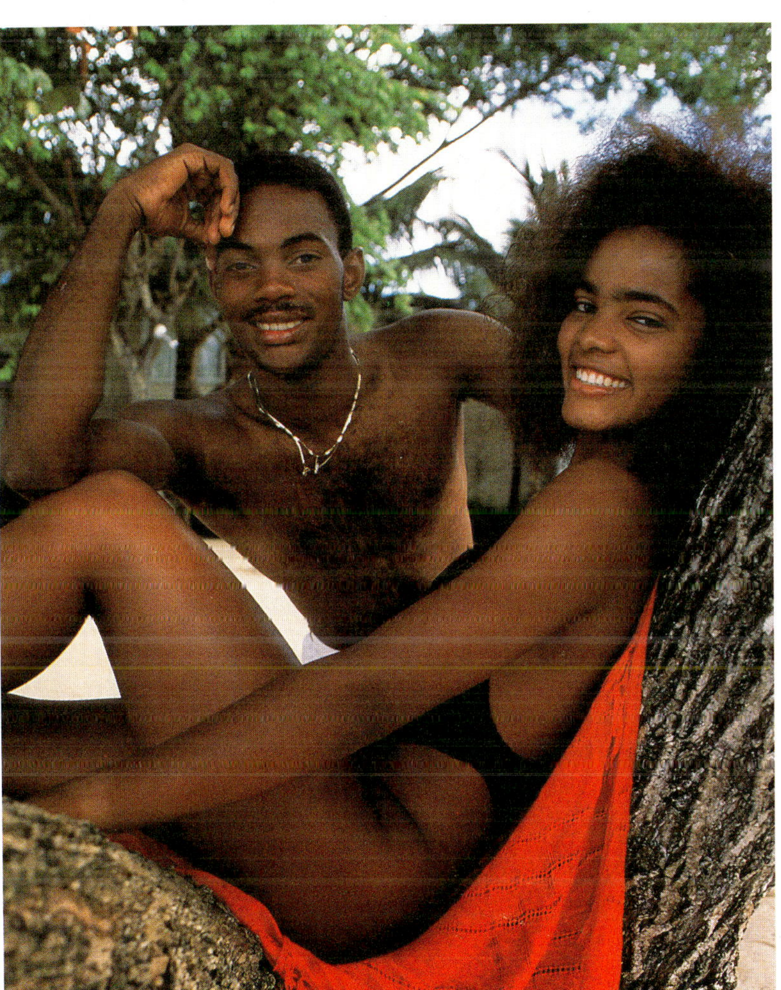

There is a demand for pictures of attractive black couples. We used two staff members of a beach resort in Jamaica to pose for this shot, a useful and good generic image that can be used for vacation, cruise and beach advertisements as well as "happy/ healthy couple" concepts.

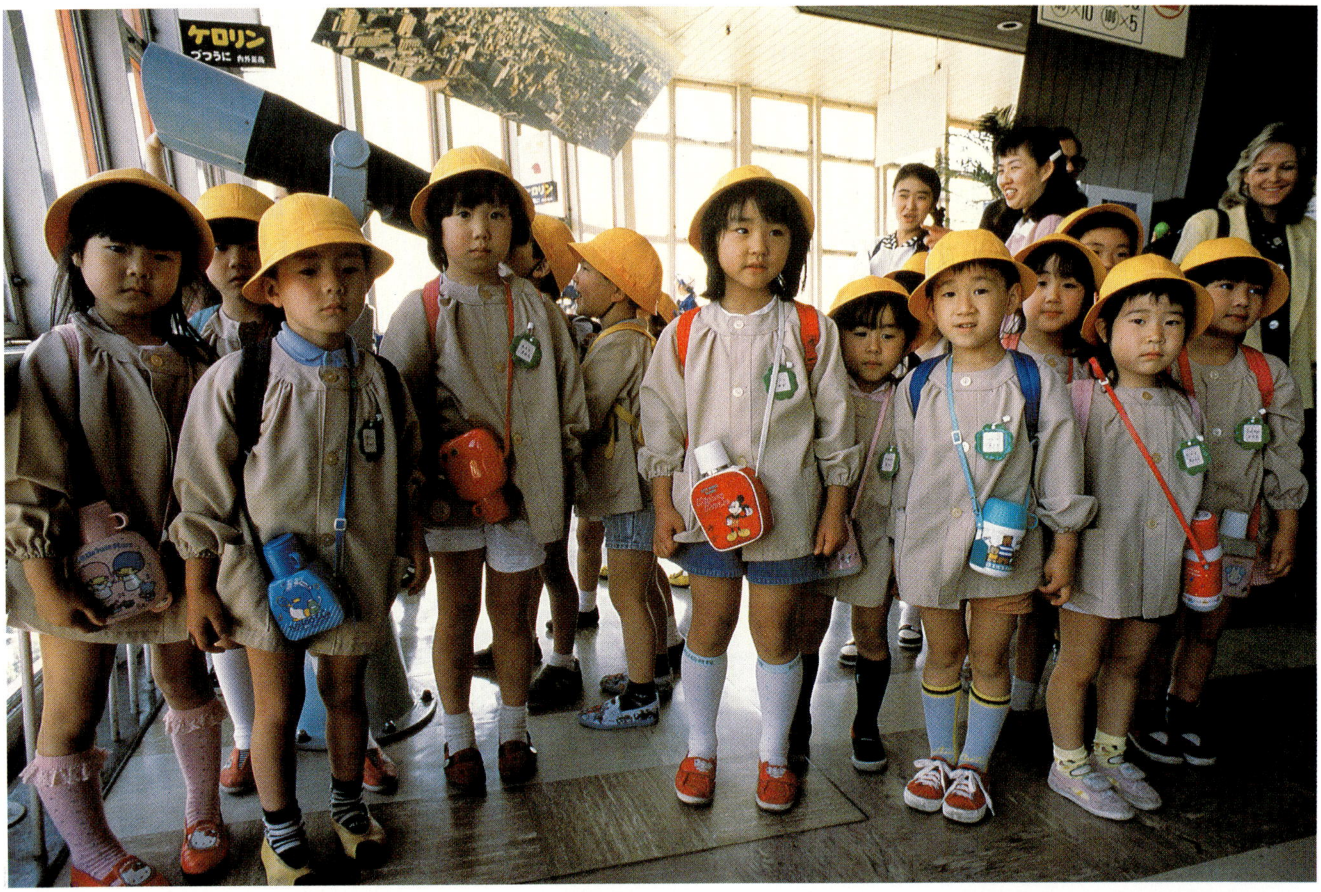

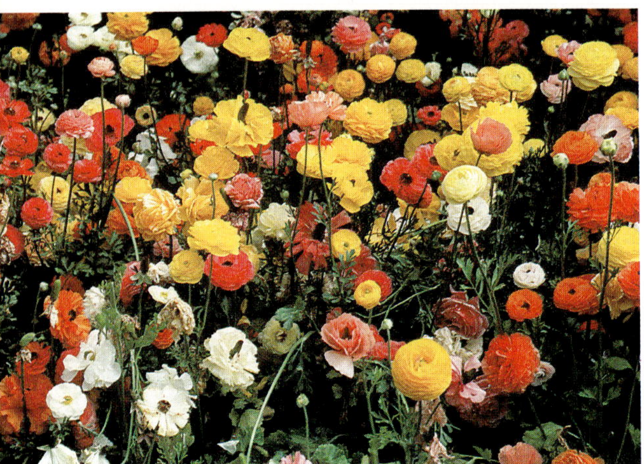

Gardens and fields of flowers can often provide an effective background for an advertisement. These flowers easily could serve as the background for a perfume ad with a perfume bottle insert.

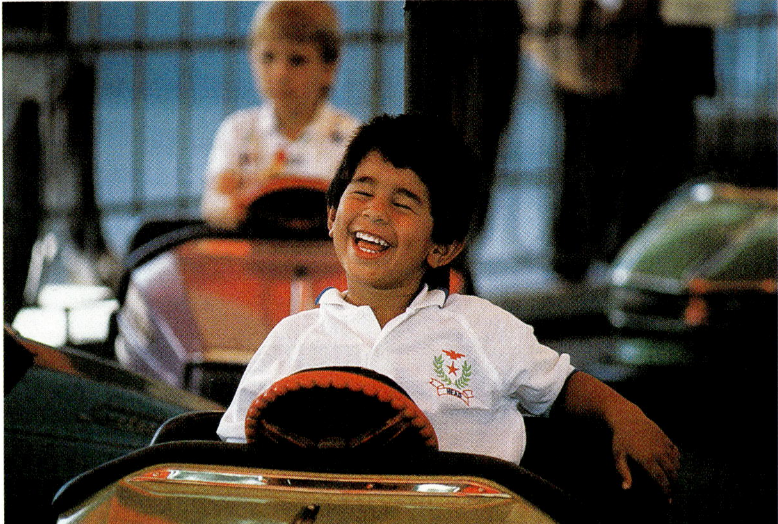

(Top) School children have a universal appeal and are delighted to pose for any photographer. Unfortunately, it was not possible to get a model release for this shot taken in Japan. This then is a good editorial shot, but it will never earn as much money as an advertising shot.

When shooting pictures of children, look for that perfect expression that symbolizes the joy of childhood. After getting the father to sign a model release on the carousel, we managed to meet up with the family during the day at several attractions. Although we got some nice family pictures that included this youngster, this shot turned out to be a real prize—and it was already model released!

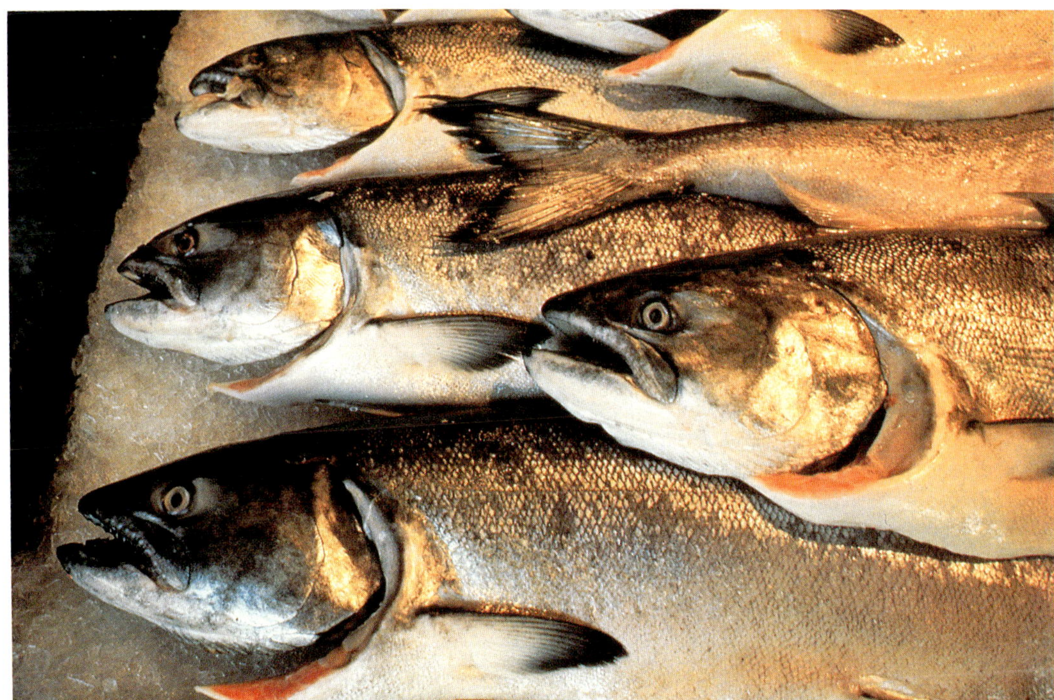

This picture of fish, attractively displayed, was taken at the Pike Street Market in Seattle. Such photographs are often needed to illustrate food articles in travel and homemaking magazines. In an inside market, you'll get the best results near an entrance or large window where the artificial light can be mixed with natural light.

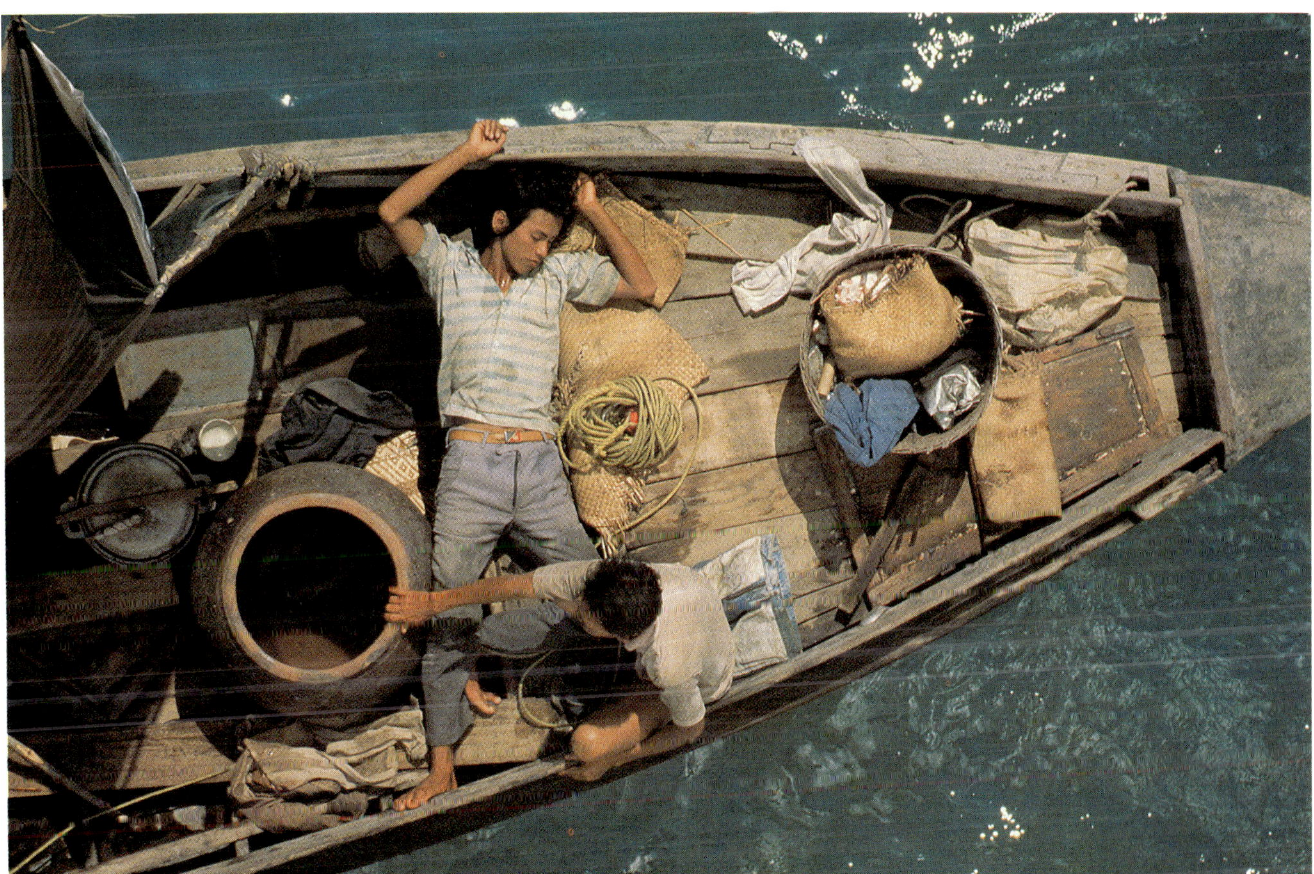

As travel photographers, our paths sometimes cross with the drama of people in need. In this rare case, we had a chance to photograph boat people fleeing Vietnam who were trying to hitch a ride on a cruise ship.

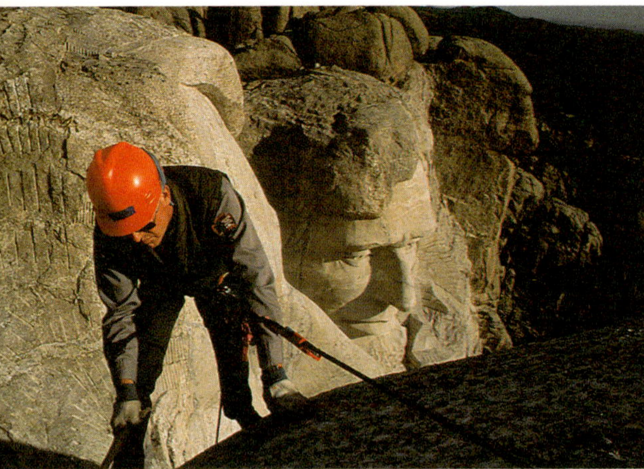

The traditional shot of Mount Rushmore is a great stock picture, but this unusual picture of a worker atop this massive group sculpture also has value for stock. Shoot any famous landmark from as many angles as possible.

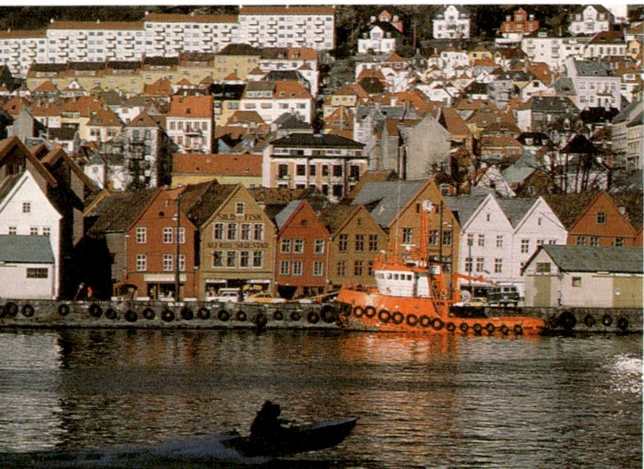

The historic harbor of Bergen, Norway, looks like a picture-perfect postcard. It has already been used as a calendar photo and may someday be a postcard sold through one of our European picture agencies.

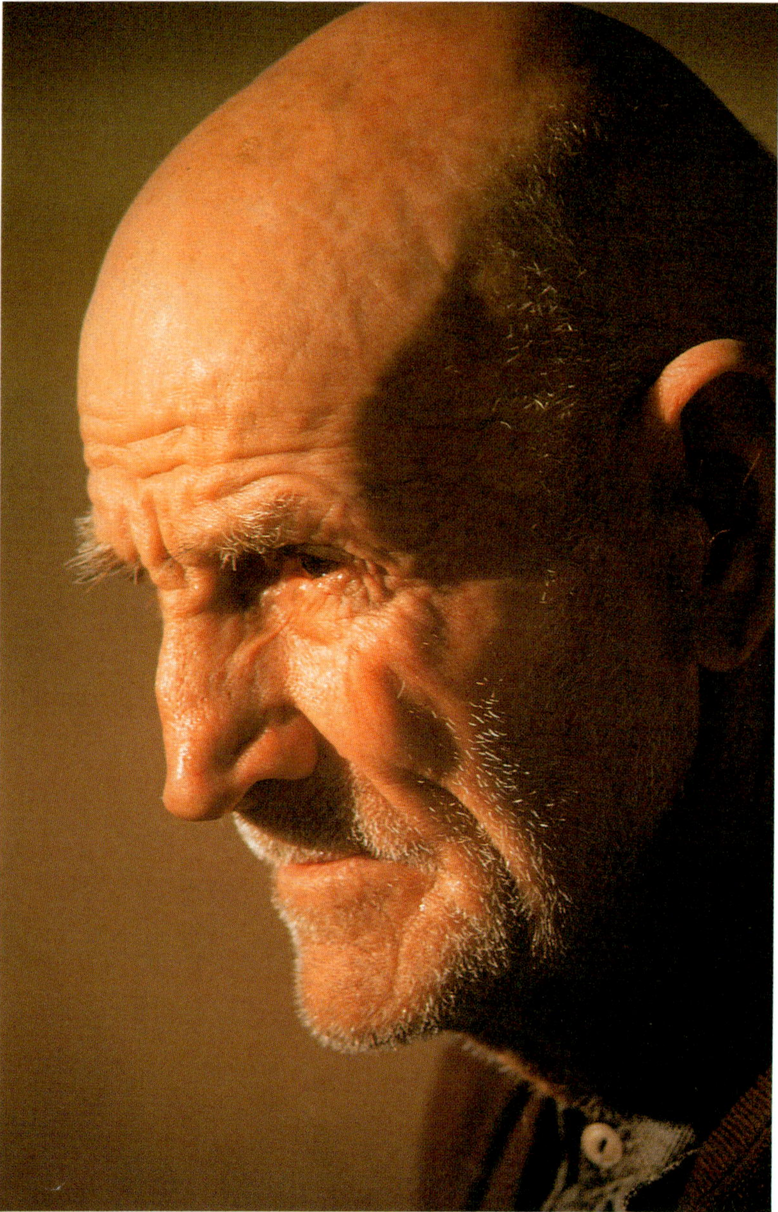

This grizzled opal miner in the outback of Australia has a face that reflects a lifetime of hard work and years of experience. Remember, when you are taking people pictures, closer is better. Being so near to this man's face makes the photo much stronger than it would have been if we hadn't been as close.

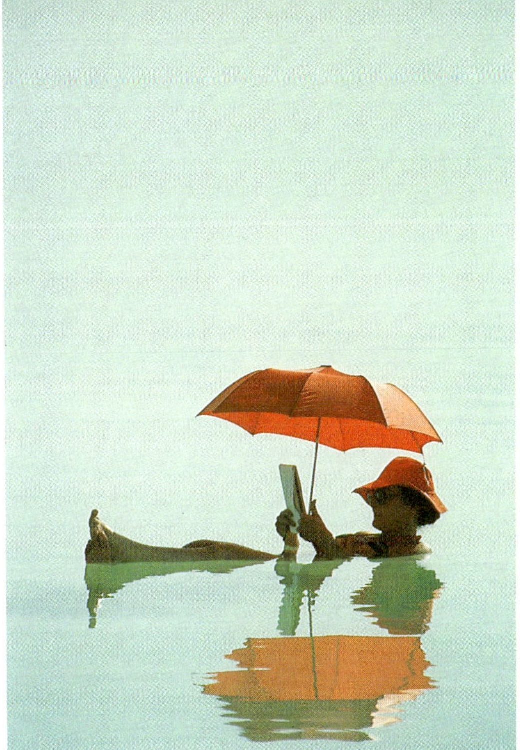

This picture of Ann Purcell floating in Israel's Dead Sea has been used on several magazine covers, one with a subtitle "How to Keep Cool in Summer." It is ideal for a cover because it has ample space at the top for a magazine logo and space on the sides for article subtitles. We gave this shot a great deal of thought and it was carefully set up.

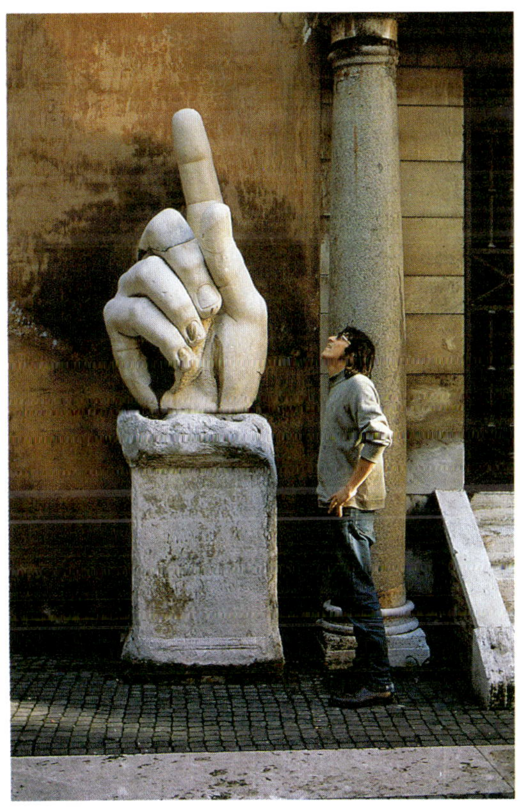

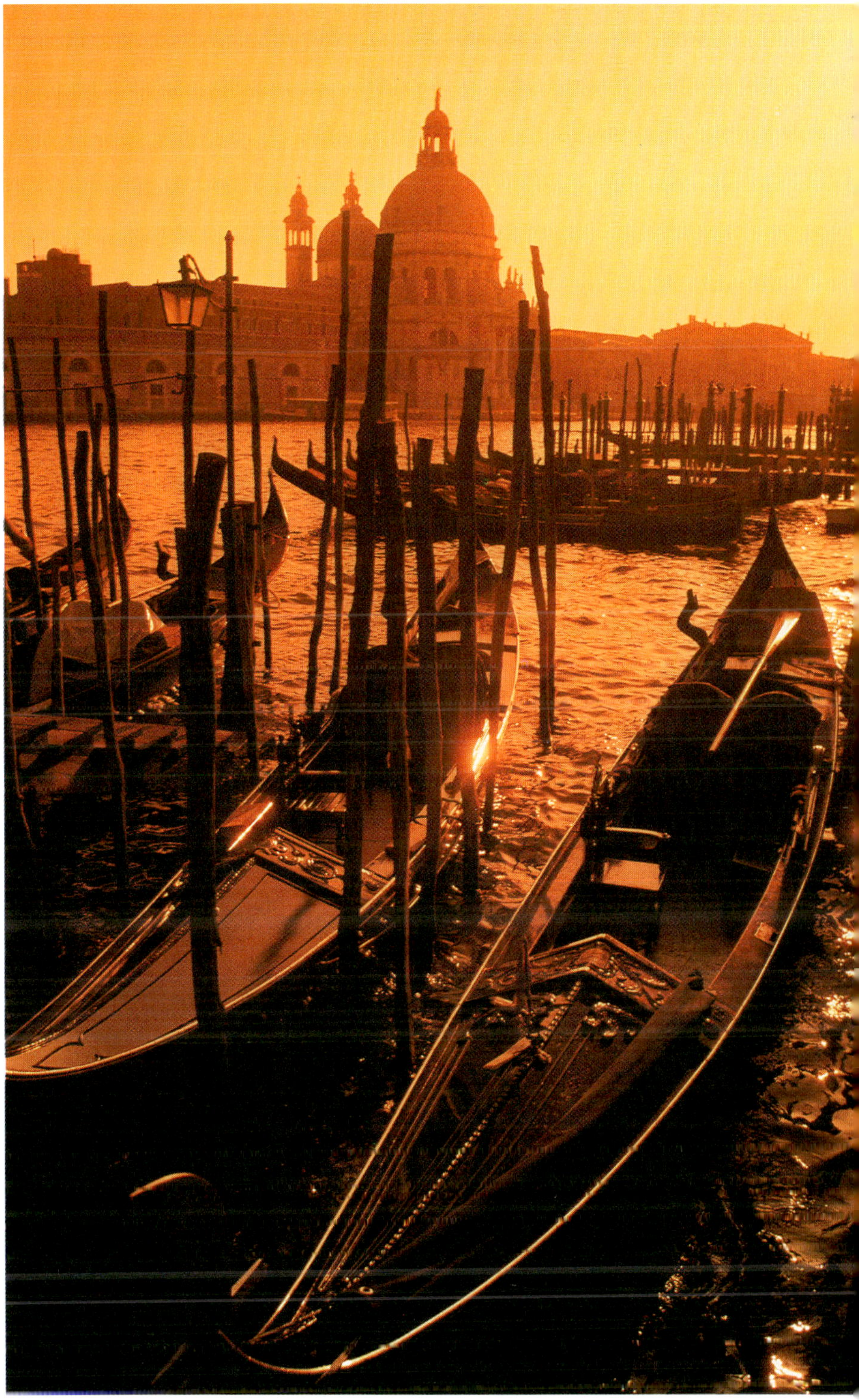

(Above) The gondolas of Venice are symbolic of that historic Italian city. We enhanced this picture with a graduated Cokin sunset filter to give the late afternoon shot the feeling of sunset. A graduated Cokin sunset filter can also be used to enhance a real but nonextraordinary sunset.

(Left) Pictures can represent verbal concepts. For instance, this photograph of a gigantic hand with its finger pointing skyward (found outside the Capitolene Museum in Rome) could pose a question such as "Do you want to go to the top in your profession?" Such a picture is also amusing, even without a caption or headline.

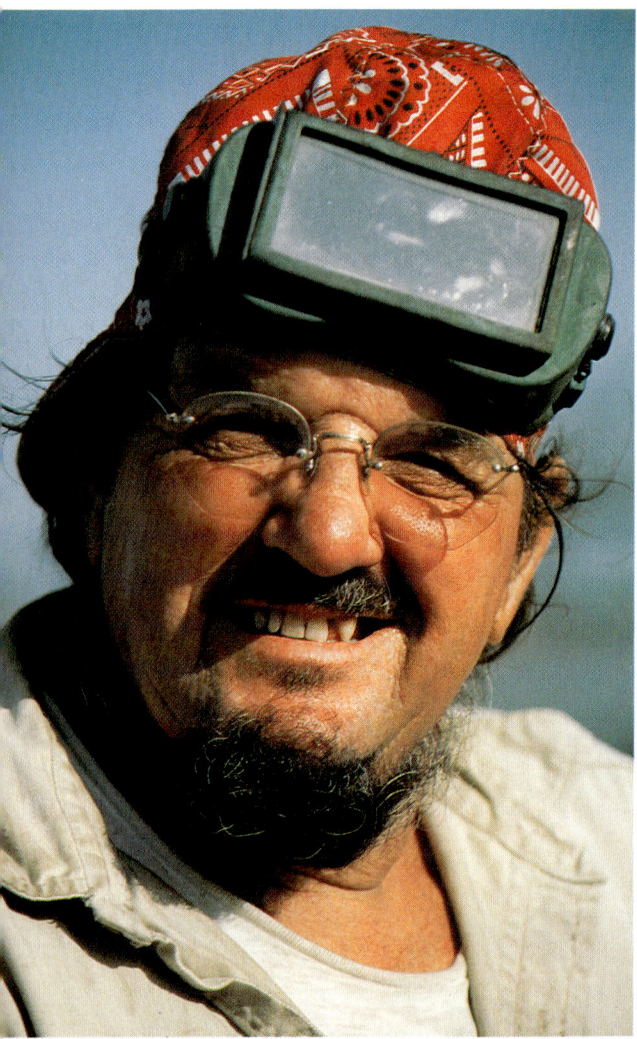

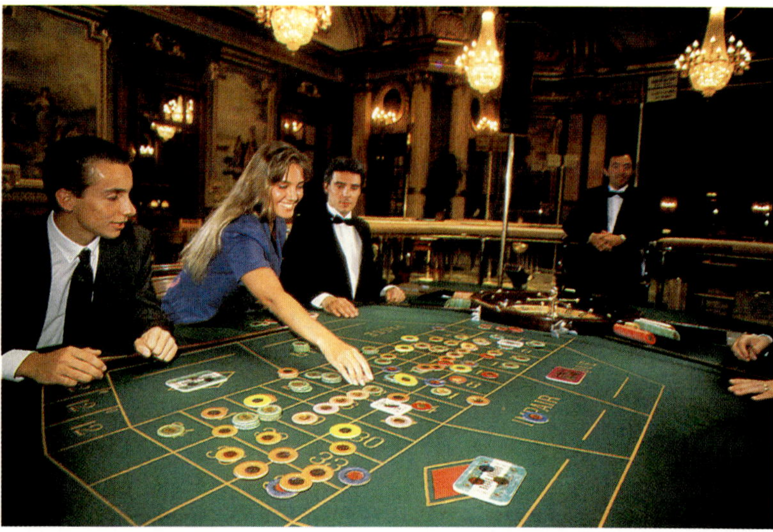

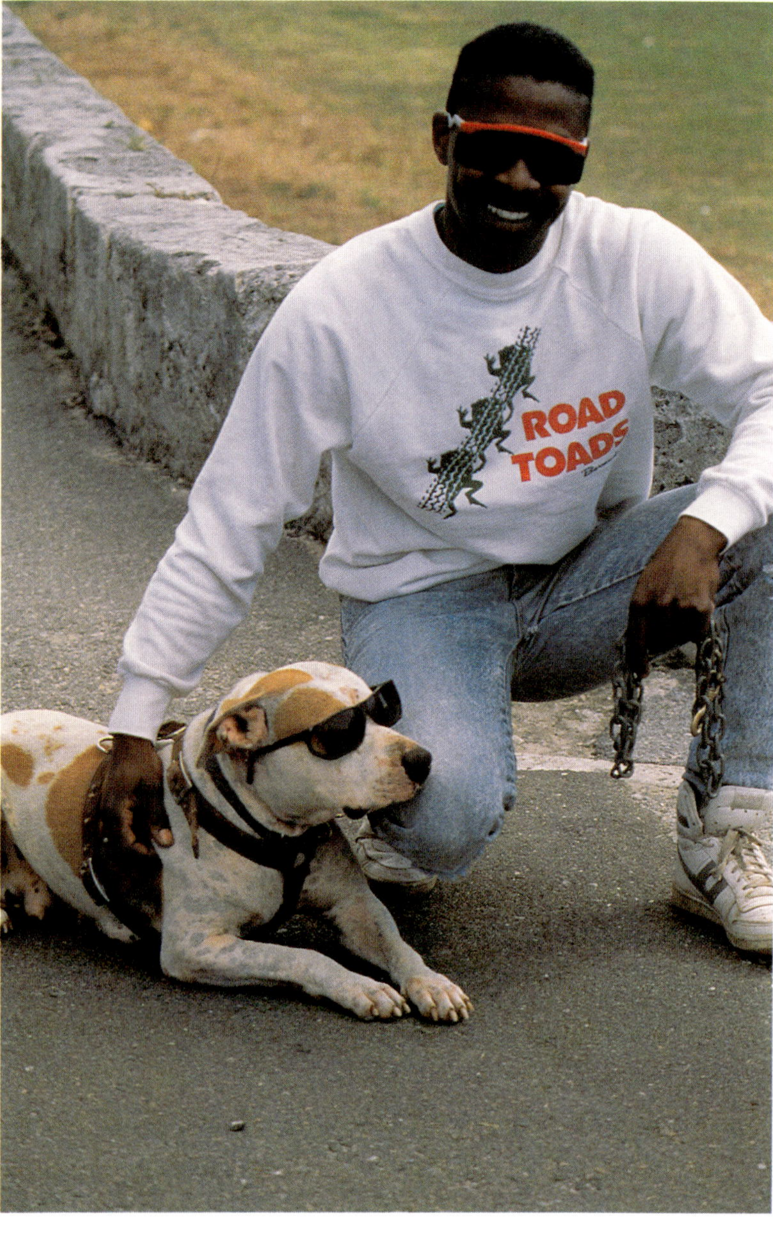


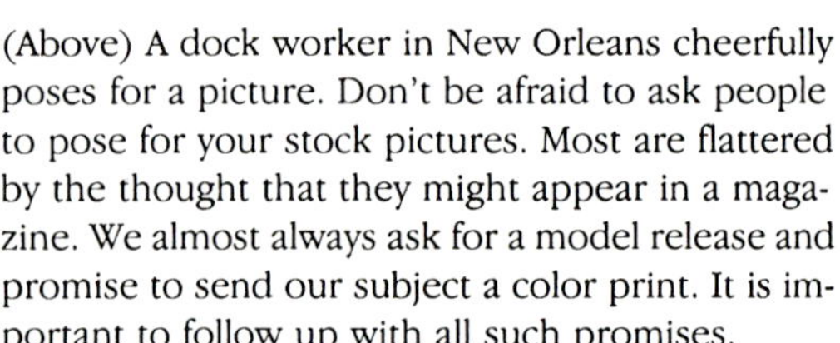

(Above) A dock worker in New Orleans cheerfully poses for a picture. Don't be afraid to ask people to pose for your stock pictures. Most are flattered by the thought that they might appear in a magazine. We almost always ask for a model release and promise to send our subject a color print. It is important to follow up with all such promises.

(Top right) Model released pictures of people gambling in casinos are difficult to find. We set up this shot in the casino at Monte Carlo through the local tourist office. They even provided the models and, of course, we got model releases. The picture has sold many times for travel brochures, magazines and newspapers. We have set up similar pictures in Las Vegas and the Bahamas.

(Right) When you see a good picture, stop whatever you are doing at that moment and take it. We saw this cool man with his dog in Bermuda, jumped off our motorscooters and asked him to pose. He even signed a model release for his equally cool dog.

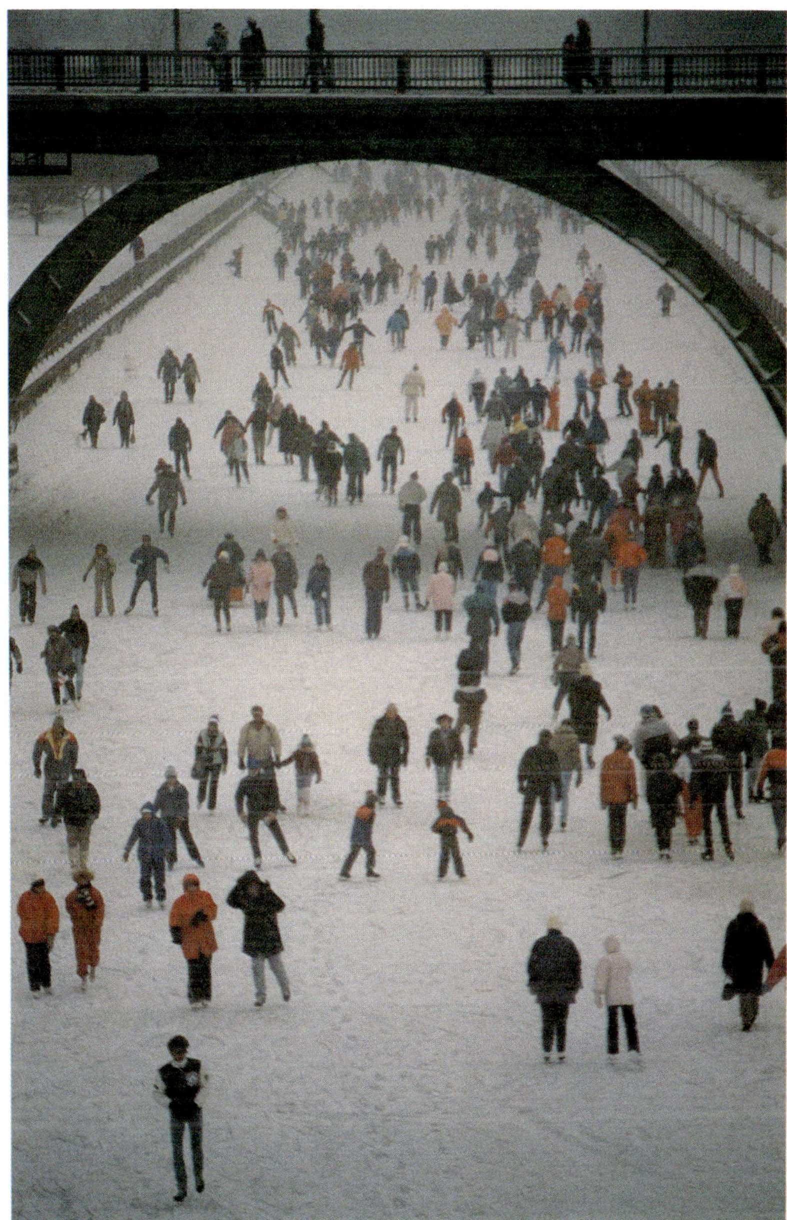

Clouds are often needed for backgrounds. These can be placed, either electronically or superimposed in the traditional manner, behind foreground images by an art director. Such clouds can be used as a background for models, houses, statues, etc. This picture was taken in the Florida Everglades with a wide-angle lens, but it could be placed just over water or desert with virtually any subject in the foreground.

(Above) Winter fun is an eternally popular subject for stock. This Currier & Ives style skating scene from Winterlude in Ottawa has been a good seller. When temperatures drop and the snow falls, pick up your camera and start shooting. Keep your batteries next to your body so that they won't stop working because of the cold.

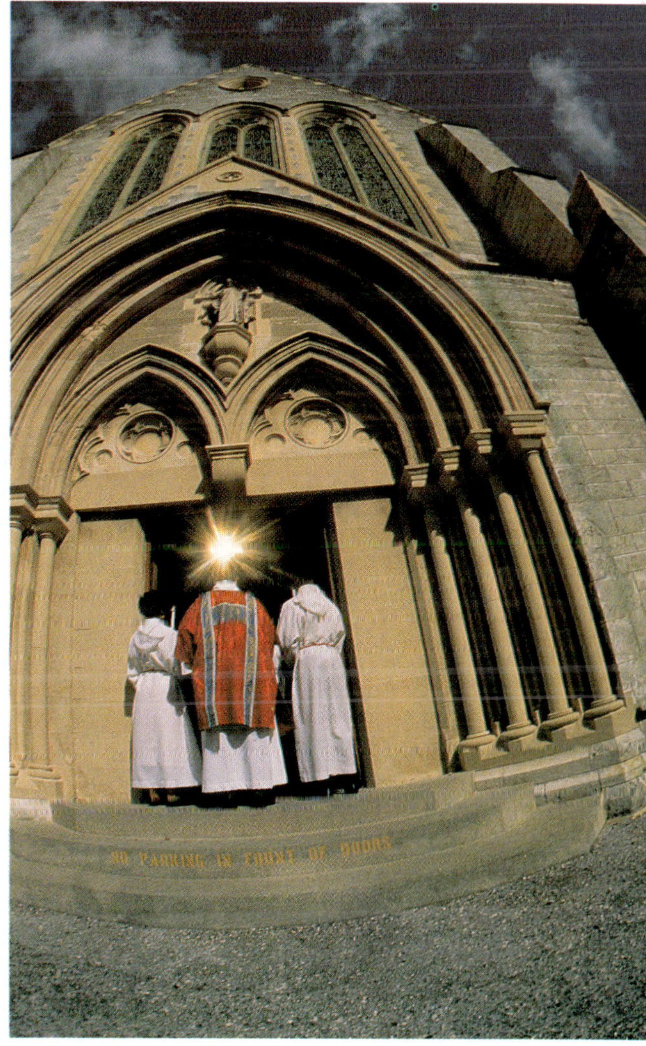


(Right) There is a good market for strong religious images. We were taking photos of the installation of a new Bishop in an Anglican Cathedral in Bermuda. As the Bishop started to enter the back of the church, we noticed that the sun was shining directly on the door. Dropping to our knees, and scooting to the right, we caught the sun's reflection off a golden cross being carried by one of the altar boys. As we were using a 16mm full-frame fisheye lens, the cathedral was distorted, but the entire building was in the frame.

Signs can often tell a story about a place. These lonely signs direct people to the coastal homes and cottages of residents of Prince Edward Island in Canada. Oddly enough, this shot has been chosen often to illustrate editorial articles about Prince Edward Island. To an editor, it is evidently symbolic of PEI's countryside.

Markets always say a lot about a foreign country. This picture of a produce market in Helsinki, Finland, is colorful and interesting. Such a picture works very well to illustrate a travel story for a newspaper or magazine. Always look for the unusual angle. In this case, the carrots become a graphic design and the focal point of the picture.

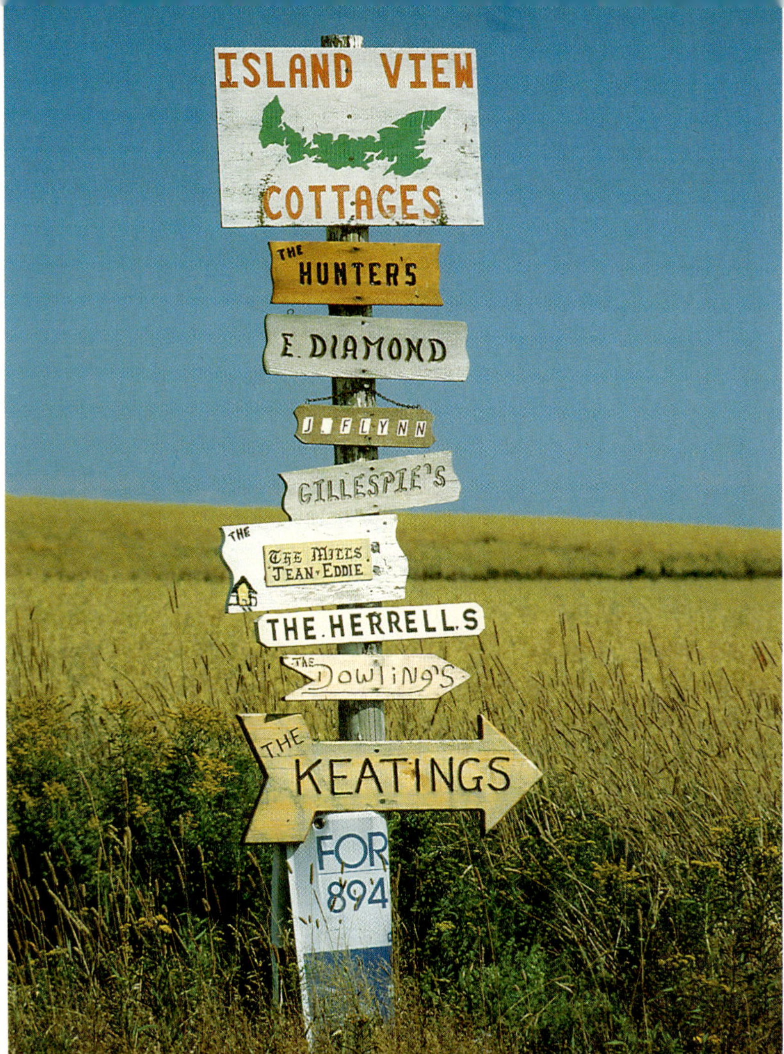

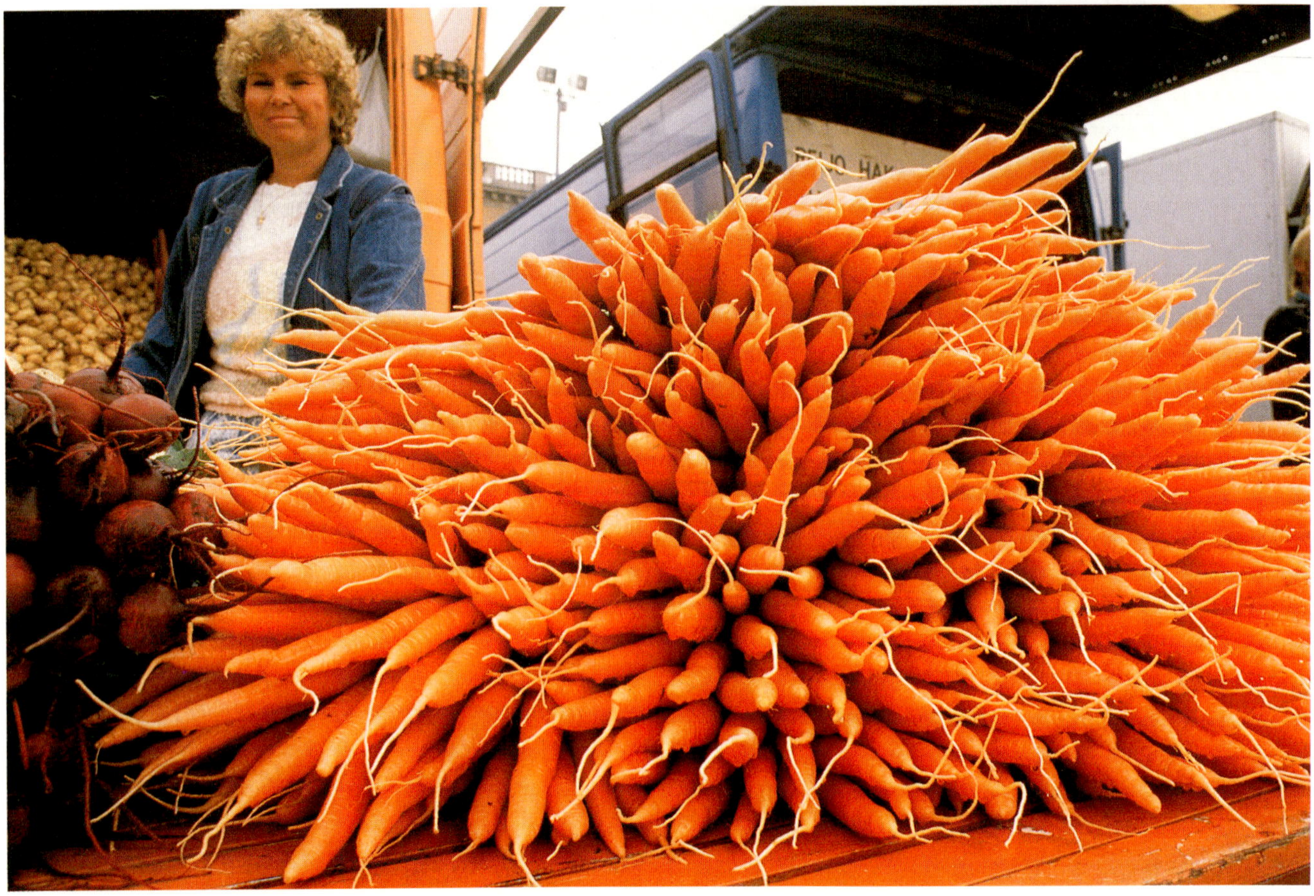

accept responsibility up to $1,500 (again, a stock photo industry norm) for each original slide that is either lost or damaged.

No slide or photo should leave your office without a submission form, but you cannot send a submission form with unsolicited material.

There are several ways of learning who wants which picture. Lots of our clients call us knowing, from experience and from looking at our slide file index, that we have what they want. We also subscribe to several photo request services through which we get picture requests that are being submitted publicly to photographers at large. (In our experience the three most productive photo request services are Telefoto (801) 569-1155, Photosource (715) 248-3800 and Photonet (800) 875-3686. We used to receive the messages from these by computer modem. Now, however, they transmit to our fax machine each night.)

Before any slides leave your office in response to a public picture request through a photo request service, you should call the clients, tell them that you have slides to fill their needs and ask if they would like to see the slides. If the answer is yes, then the slides are solicited and you can send the submission form. If the original slide request was made to you personally, the submission form will automatically go out with your slides.

When talking to the client, don't forget to ask for their Federal Express number. Most clients will give it to you, saving you enormous postage costs.

ASMP (The American Society of Media Photographers) published a booklet called *Stock Photography Handbook* that gives details about optional wording on submission forms. The Society of American Travel Writers has suggested another form with similar wording. A copy of our standard submission form is pictured on page 68.

We staple photocopies of the slides submitted to our copy of the submission form, as well as any Federal Express, Airborne or other delivery forms. In this way, if the slides don't arrive, you have a quick way to find out what the airbill number is when you want to track the slides.

From your nearest office supply store, you can get alphabetical accordion files. These are perfect for storing submission forms until the slides have been returned. In our office, the submission forms are then relegated to another alphabetical accordion file that is placed in dead storage. Often a client will call you and ask for a slide that was submitted a year or two ago. It helps to be able to track precisely which slide is desired.

## Slide Request Forms

Slide request forms will be written and designed by you, photocopied, stapled together and stored next to your phone. They will remind you of all the questions you need to ask so that you don't have to call the client back because you forgot to get an answer. The information you will need includes:

- Client name (business)
- Contact name (the person to whom you are speaking)
- To whose attention are you to send the slides?
- Address
- Telephone number
- Subjects needed

The Purcell Team color slide index.

# *The Purcell Team Color Slide Index*

**1992-93 Update**

*A unique world-wide collection of outstanding color images for magazine, book, and advertising illustration*

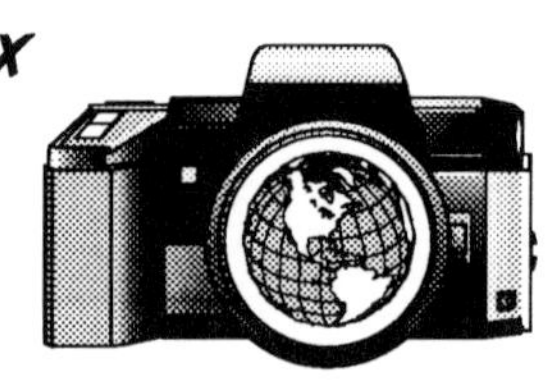

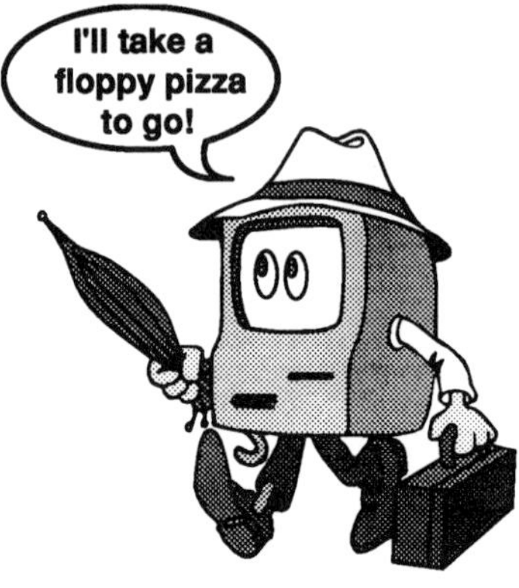


THE PURCELL TEAM (Carl & Ann Purcell) are multi-talented travel writers and photographers who cover the world. They have accumulated an impressive collection of captioned color slides, almost 650,000 from 94 countries, mostly shot on 35mm Kodachrome and Fujichrome. The Purcells' specialty is travel and travel-related topics, but their slides include such varied generic subjects as culture, religion, wildlife, flora, industry, space technology, art, architecture, underwater scenes and marine life. Their file is especially strong on people, with many pictures model-released.

The Purcells have provided images for advertising, public relations, and editorial use throughout the world and in leading publications such as Life, U.S. News & World Report, Travel-Holiday, Conde Nast Traveler, National Geographic, Travel & Leisure, Signature, Popular Photography, Associated Press, Copley News Service, and the New York Times. Their color photographs have appeared on over 200 book and magazine covers. Pictures are provided on a regular basis for audio-visual productions, television, calendars, text books, and encyclopaedias.

The office staff is comprised of full time professional picture researchers who stand ready to fill your picture requests, both by want lists and via telephone requests. The Purcells can also shoot assignments tailored to your needs at any location in the world and can often arrange to be where you need them, when you need them to be there. In many instances they can cover many of their own travel expenses, keeping location assignments within your budget.

This color slide index is broken down both by geographic and subject matter categories. While it does not list each picture, it will serve as a guide to general subjects and geographic locations. The file is constantly growing, with new listings being added every month. Text and story material is available for most destinations.

***We can take any picture and customize it to fit your needs. Image manipulation on the computer makes possible any type of color illustration. Dramatic sunsets, for instance can be combined with palm trees. Lions can walk down Park Avenue. We can also shoot destinations for a PR client and put the images on CD-ROM disk for distribution. See page 18 for details on electronic imagery.***

***Carl & Ann Purcell***
***5913 Skyline Heights Court, Suite 100***
***Alexandria, VA 22311***
***Phone: (703) 845-1104 Fax: (703) 845-1103***

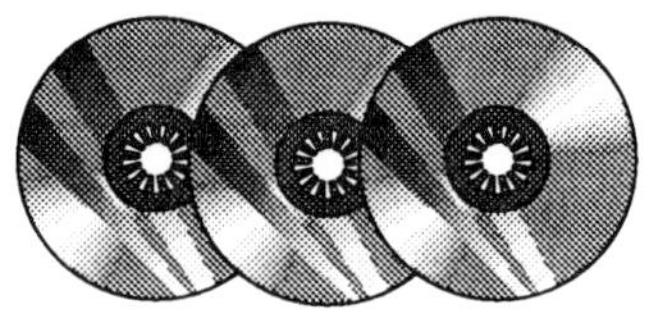

1

- How slides will be used
- Circulation of publication
- Number of copies to be printed (if a textbook)
- Vertical or horizontal format needed
- Date of deadline
- Express mail service used by client and client's account number
- When will slides be returned?
- Does client pay research fees?

Not all clients pay research fees. As photo agencies usually charge research fees, not having to pay research fees is

quake damage.

**Honduras:** Tegucigalpa, rural and coastal areas.

**Mexico:** Good coverage of Yucatan, Mayan ruins and Cozumel. City and market shots of Merida. Beach and underwater reef shots in the area of Cozumel. Cancun, Chichen Itzu, Mexico City and Talum.

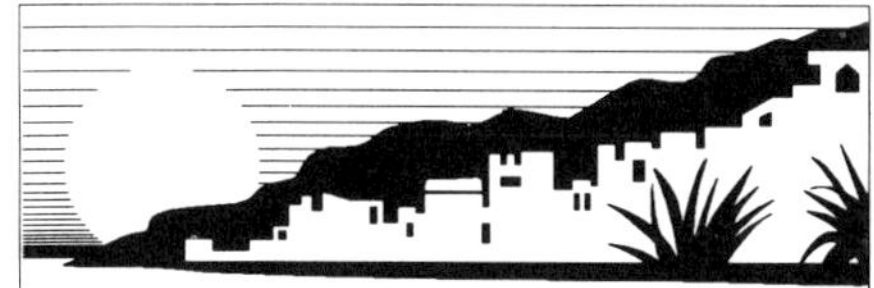

**Nicaragua:** Managua and rural scenes. Farmers and families. Earthquake damage.

**Panama:** Panama City, Canal and Canal Zone with locks and ships. Fish farming and rural scenes. Kuna Indians with colorful molas on San Blas Islands.

**Peru:** Extensive coverage of Lima. Scenes of urban migration on fringes of Lima. Mountain passes. Huancayo and Arequipa. Rural scenes. Cuzco, steam train and Machu Picchu.

**South Pacific Islands:** See Islands.

**Venezuela**: Orinoco River, Ciudad Bolivar, Angel Falls and Canaima National Park.

**NORTH AMERICA**

**Canada**: Alberta, Vancouver, Yukon, British Columbia, Nova Scotia, New Brunswich , Northwest Territories and Prince Edward Island.
Coverage of Dawson City (Yukon gold mining town) and the Yukon. Victoria, Butchart Gardens, Vancouver, Bannf, and Lake Louise. Scenes of the Canadian Rockies. Golfing pictures at Bannf Springs Hotel. Snowcoach with giant tires on Athabasca Glacier.
Extensive coverage on all aspects of Montreal including downtown, skyscrapers, architecture, people, restaurants, hotels, St. Lawrence River, historical areas, parks, street markets, Olympic site, etc.
Maritime Provinces of Eastern Canada including Fredericton, NB, St. John, NB, Bay of Fundy, Yarmouth, NS, Shelburne, NS, Lunenburg, NS, and Halifax, NS. Folk art, churches, fishing villages, people, etc. Good coverage of Prince Edward Island.
Excellent coverage of harp seals on the ice floes near Magdallen Islands in the Bay of St. Lawrence to illustrate an article for Black Star Syndicate. Winter festival in Ottowa. Dog sledding in Frobisher Bay.

**Mexico:** See Central and South America.

**United States**

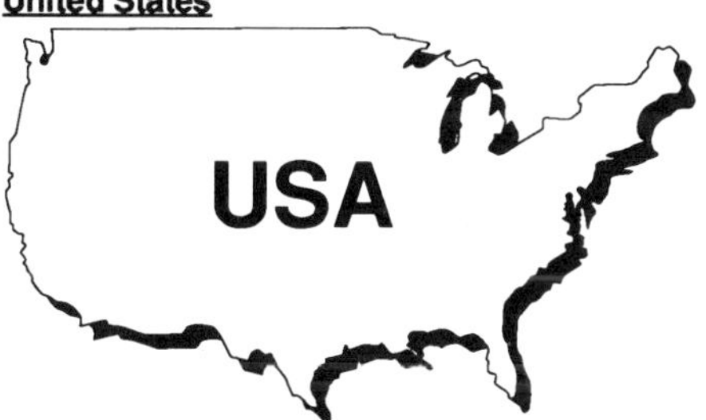


**Alabama**: 1965 Civil rights march with Martin Luther King (in black and white).

**Alaska**: Extensive coverage of Alaska, including: Juneau, Fairbanks, the South East passage, Sitka, Skagway, Petersburg, Tracy Arm Fjord and Wrangell. Dramatic shots of Chilkat Indians, icebergs and these glaciers: LeConte, Margerie, Mendenhall and Sawyer. Nice scenics and also some game shots. Seaplanes with pontoons. Shipboard coverage on Niew Amsterdam. Coverage of Denali National Park and shots of Mount McKinley. Wildlife includes eagles, Dall sheep, and wolves. Super-stretch double bus and observation dome passenger train.

**Arizona:** Spectacular sunrise and daytime shots of the famous Monument Valley. Coverage also includes: cactus, irrigation, lightning, film crew, Tucson. University of Arizona at Tucson. dramatic train tracks at sunset and Canyon de Chelly. Aerial views of the Grand Canyon.

**8**

sometimes the reason the client will come to you, the photographer, rather than go to an agency.

Research takes time and time is money. We have found that to pull slides from the files, do the paperwork, pay the postage and refile the slides in the appropriate files when they come back is costly, up to $75 per submission. Research fees help to repay some of the loss when a client asks for a submission but does not use the slides. If this is a client who pays research fees, we usually charge $25 for fifty slides or less, $35 for fifty to one hun-

Our standard color slide submission form.

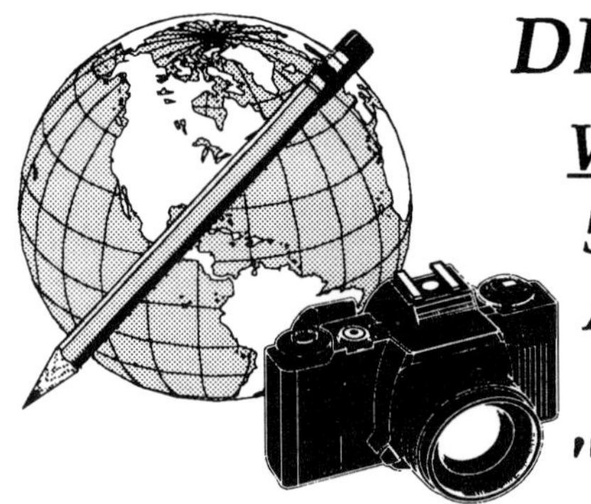

# DELIVERY MEMO

*Words & Pictures*
*5913 Skyline Hgts. Ct.*
*Alexandria, VA 22311*
*Phone: (703) 845-1104*
*"We Cover the World"*

**CLIENT** **PHONE** ____________

**ORDER FILLED BY** ______________ **DATE** __________
**TOTAL SLIDES SENT**_____ **ORIGINALS** ___ **DUPES**___
**SHIPPED VIA: UPS**___ **FED. EXP** ___ **OTHER**_________

The enclosed slides have been submitted at your request. These slides are copyrighted and fully owned by the photographers of THE PURCELL TEAM. Reproducing, duplicating, printing, or copying is prohibited without prior consent.
Please pre-edit and return any slides which you cannot use as soon as possible. With each return shipment include a copy of this submission form with a notation of the number returned and the number still being held. **Do not make any returns without clearly indicating whether or not any images have been used.**
These transparencies may **NOT** be projected.
Each original slide is submitted with the understanding that it has a value of **$1500** in case of loss or damage. If you choose to return the slides via Federal Express, your responsibility for the slides ends when they are picked up by the courier. With any other form of delivery, including regular mail, your responsibility for the slides continues until they are received by this office.
It is understood that this submission has a holding period of 30 days without charge. After that time has elapsed, there is a holding fee of $1.00 per slide per day unless prior arrangements have been made with this office.
The client will indemnify and defend the photographers against all claims, liability, damages, costs and expenses, including reasonable legal fees and expenses arising out of any use of any photographs for which no release was available. Model released pictures are marked on the mount with R or MR.
Any dispute regarding this agreement shall be arbitrated in Fairfax County, Virginia under the rules of the American Arbitration Association and the laws of Virginia.
If we do not receive written objections to the conditions of this delivery memo within one week of its receipt, it is assumed that the client accepts the terms stated above.

**PLEASE CHECK SLIDE COUNT**

*Carl and Ann Purcell, 5913 Skyline Heights Ct.*
*Alexandria, VA 22311 FAX: (703) 845-1103*

dred slides, and $50 for more than one hundred slides. We have not, however, turned down clients if they do not pay research fees, unless they have a very poor record of acceptance. We also charge a small fee when we scan a slide and fax the image at the client's request.

## Invoices

Your invoice is not just a bill for the use of your photo. It also states what rights you are conveying and it should reflect the exact use that you have agreed to give for this price. For instance, when giving permission for use of one of our slides in a magazine or newspaper, we usually write "One time North American rights" on the invoice. If the clients want to re-use the picture, or use it overseas, there will be an additional charge. The invoice should also give the name of the publication in which the photo will be used, the size (one-fourth page, full page, cover, etc.), the name to which the check should be made out, your social security number or the federal identification number of your business, and the time span within which you expect payment. Our invoices also state that if we have to re-bill, there will be a bookkeeping charge of $35.

## BASIC PAPER FLOW

Now that you have all your forms, you need to set up your system of slide submissions. When the person first calls, you'll want to fill in all the information about the desired photos on your slide request forms, which should be stored next to the telephone.

After you pull the necessary slides, you'll fill out your three-part submission form. Your office copy will be stapled to the slide request form and photocopy of the slides you are mailing out. If the client has asked you to send the slides by Federal Express, the copy of the Federal Express form will also be stapled to your office copy of the submission form. File everything alphabetically in accordion files. Clients often call with questions and it is a blessing to be able to put your hand on their paperwork without fumbling.

The other two copies of the submission form will go to the client with the slides, one for their files and one to be returned with the slides.

Register the submission in your client records. When the slides are returned, you'll need to be able to verify how many have been held for use. Because you have photocopies of the slides you submitted, you will also be able to circle the slide images that are still being held. You can use another color to circle the slides that have been chosen for use. When you invoice your client, clip the invoice to the submission packet and file it in another alphabetical accordion file. After all slides are returned and you have been paid, mark this packet "PAID" and file it alphabetically under "old submissions," the third and last of the accordion files you'll need. It is important to keep these old submission packets for several years. Often a client will call you and say that he wants the same slide again for another use. You will be delighted to have the photocopy of the slide so that you can do the research without having the client try to describe one specific slide out of the many you took on that subject.

### Mailing Labels

When it comes to looking professional, attractive and well-designed labels are very important. Self-adhesive labels are needed for multiple purposes in the stock photography business. We use them for shipping slides, labeling computer disks, creating return address labels and, in some instances, for creating small copyright labels with our name and address. Even at their best, handwritten labels do not convey the impression of efficiency and they can be, at their worst, unreadable.

For years we used the widely available Avery labels and typed on the information with a typewriter. Recently, we acquired a new software program called MacLabel-Pro, which was designed specifically for use with the Macintosh. (A version called LabelPro is available for IBM and IBM-compatible computers using Windows.) This unique software contains templates for every type of Avery label and allows you to design your own labels with clip art and a variety of fonts. It even includes postal bar code capability. You will get your best results with a laser printer, but a good quality dot matrix printer can be used for printing labels.

The Avery line includes templates for mailing labels, clear address labels, audio and videotape labels, file folder labels, rotary card products, postcards, index cards, name tags with holders, name badge labels and overhead transparencies. The programs can be easily merged with mailing lists on databases.

You can order MacLabelPro by product number 5117 (useable with both laser and dot matrix printer) or LabelPro by product number 5100 (for laser printers) or number 5116 (for dot matrix printers) from your local computer or office supply dealer. Information and brochures are available by calling (800) 462-8379.

## OFFICE EQUIPMENT

### Light Table

If you have the space in your office, you can have a large light table handcrafted or make one yourself. The table should be a good working height for someone sitting in a chair. The table will be made like a giant shallow box and it can have a glass top placed over a white translucent plastic cover used to diffuse the light. The table should be wired so that one switch will turn on the two, if not three, long fluorescent tubes set into the recessed area. You want the fluorescent tubes, which are balanced to match daylight, so the color of your slides will not be altered when you view them. A few telephone calls will locate the electricity supply store from which you can obtain these tubes. A slide-viewing loupe will let you check the sharpness of the slides.

Recent findings reported by *Photo District News* suggest that the ballasts for the light bulbs should be put on the end of a six-foot cable to reduce exposure to the magnetic field produced by fluorescents.

Most camera stores sell small light boxes, which are very useful if you do not have the space or need for a large light table. The slide-viewing loupe, however, is indispensable.

### Word Processor

The word processor or computer will be your best friend in your stock photography business, and the first piece of equipment that you will need to buy after you own your own camera. If you do not already have an electric typewriter, it is a good idea to buy a computer printer that converts to a standard typewriter. (It will have an extra typewriter keyboard and a switch that makes it into a normal typewriter.)

### Typewriter

A typewriter is helpful for all the small work that your computer won't do, such as labeling one envelope, one mailing label, filling out submission forms, typing the odd slide caption label for re-mounted slides, filling out airbill labels, etc.

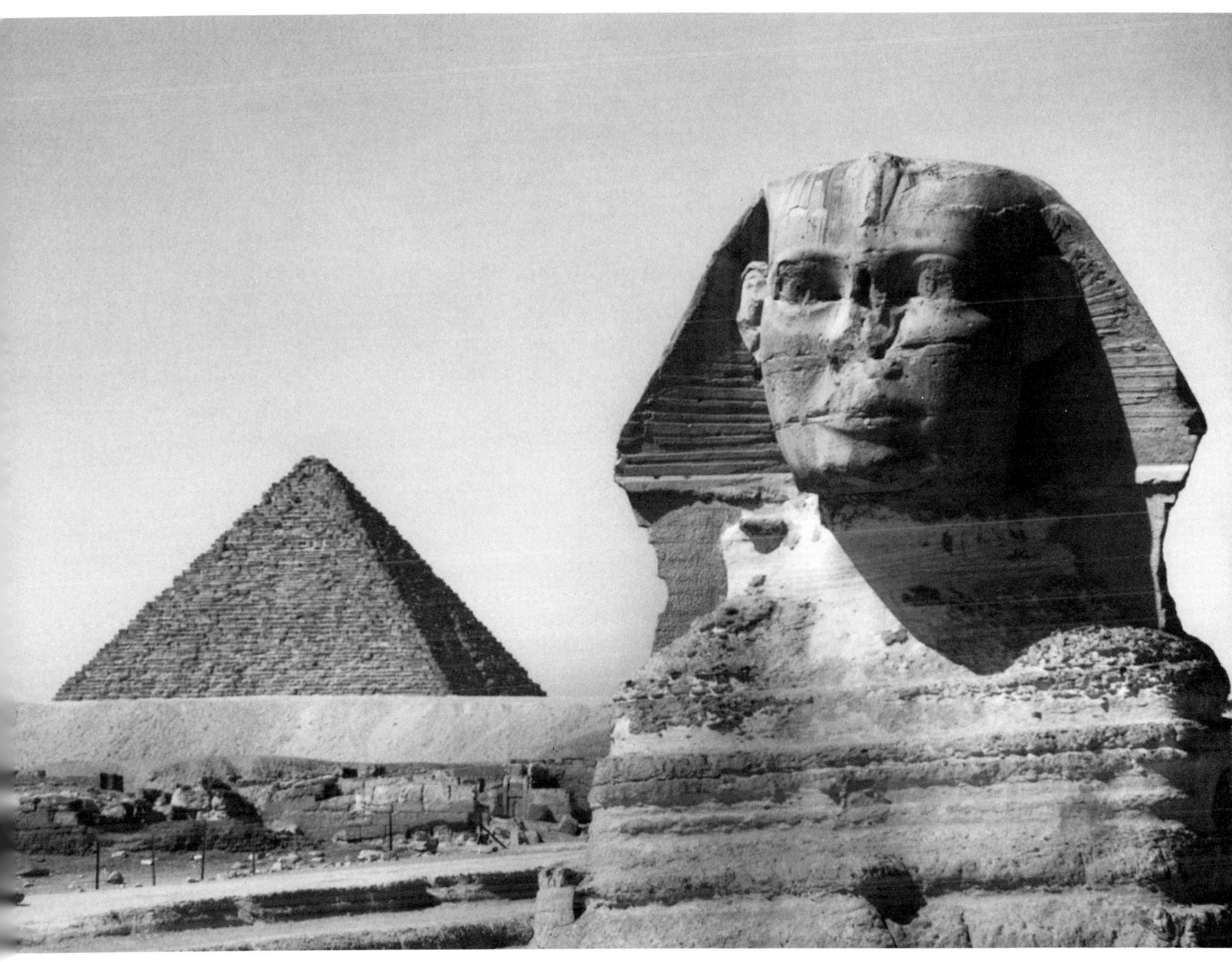

We sold a picture of the Sphinx in Egypt, which has a broken nose, for a cosmetic surgery advertisement. The art director had the concept and $1,450. We had the picture.

## Copier

The next piece of office equipment that you should buy is a photocopier. We have a small Sharp copier that will make 8,000 copies between maintenance calls, and a service contract insures that we have immediate service at no cost if any problem comes up in the meantime. We have also jerry-rigged a device that will let us copy slides to show both subject matter and captions. We built a shelf a couple of feet above the copy machine, just high enough that our copier cover, when open, will clear underneath the two 350 watt photo flood bulbs that we installed on the bottom side of the shelf. (Two 500 watt bulbs also will work if you cannot obtain the 350 watt.) The two bulbs are rigged so that they are side by side precisely over the viewing slit of the copier. A single switch turns on both bulbs simultaneously. The slides, arranged in a plastic slide sheet, are placed facedown so that the copier can read the captions. We leave the copier cover open and press the start button. As the copier passes the slide sheets over the viewing slit, we turn on the spot bulbs briefly, just until the slide sheet has passed the slit. The result is a legible copy of both the captions and the slides. Don't leave the lights on too long or the heat will cause the plastic parts of the copier to warp.

No slide leaves our office without being photocopied. It is necessary to know precisely which slides are being held by which clients. You will not be able to claim compensation for an unreturned slide unless you have a record of which slide did not come back. You also often receive telephone calls from clients asking questions about a particular slide they want to use. By referring to your photocopies, which have been stapled to the submission form, you can determine exactly which slide they are talking about and give the requested information.

## Fax Machine

Another piece of office equipment that you will eventually want to purchase is a fax machine. We delayed buying a fax machine for a long time, but eventually realized that it would more than pay for itself.

It seems odd to us that people will often contract for the written word several months in advance, but will wait to obtain photos until the last possible moment. Sometimes writers will submit photos with their manuscripts at the deadline date and the pictures are not technically acceptable. Some editors will then frantically call or fax their picture request and ask that you get out the slides on the same day.

As we said earlier, we subscribe to several photo-request services who fax us lists of photo requests each night while we sleep. In the morning, we review the lists looking for photos that we have, call the client to confirm that the photos are still needed and pull the slides. We formerly got these photo request lists by computer or by mail several times a week. Often we would have exactly what was needed, but by the time we received the requests and called the client, other slides already had been chosen. Having the fax machine means that we get the lists on a daily basis as soon as the requests come in and it gives us a chance to submit slides before the clients have received a great number of submissions on the same subject from other photographers. A client will usually choose the slide he'll use from the first 150 slides he sees.

Some clients also will ask if you can fax them a photograph so that they can see if they can use the slide before you send it to them. This can be done either by scanning the slide or by using an instant slide printer.

## Instant Slide Printer

Most stock photographers do not have prints of the color slides in their files available. Unless you have a slide scanner, obtaining a fast color print from a slide to fax to a client can be done in several ways, but often it requires a trip to a copy shop or photo lab. These are the other choices:

1. Have a photo print made on a fast printing machine at a photo lab. (Approximate cost is $5 to $10 each.)
2. Have a color laser print made at a copy shop. (Approximate cost is $2.50 to $5.00 each.)
3. Make a Polaroid print on an instant slide printer such as the Vivitar. (Approxi-

mate cost: $1.30 each.) You can buy the Vivitar Slide Printer at your camera store for $139.95. It uses Polaroid film 669, which runs about $20.00 for a 16-shot pack. You slip in the slide and within a minute, you have a Polaroid print (about 3-by-4 inches) of the slide.

4. If you have a high-end computer, a scanner and a laser printer, you can scan your slide into the computer and make a laser print of the image for faxing. Assuming you have the necessary equipment, this is the fastest and most efficient method of getting the rough image to the art director or picture editor.

## WORKING OUT OF YOUR HOME

To claim any business tax deductions for your stock photography business, you will need a county business license. Assuming that you live in a residential district, you are still allowed to conduct business in your house as long as you do not have clients frequently coming to your house for your services. As a stock photographer, you will conduct most of your business by mail. If you have an assignment, you will most often go to the client, or on location, to shoot the assignment.

Some of our friends, also professional photographers, say that they would never choose to work out of their homes. At the end of the day, they like to lock the doors of their studio/offices, commute home and leave the work behind. We choose to work out of our home and have never regretted it. If there is a snowstorm or a horrendous bottleneck on the freeway, our commute to the office is greatly simplified by simply walking upstairs. If one of us has trouble sleeping at night, we will spend an hour or two in the office finishing up some small tasks until we are ready for bed.

Working out of your home also can be an advantage financially because a percentage of your home expenses can be deducted from your income taxes. To calculate what percentage of your home you use for your business, you will probably need to look up the house plans that you were given when you bought your home. Mark each square foot that you have committed to your stock photography business. This will include your slide viewing space, your studio corner or room, your slide storage space and your business office. Compute what percentage this is of your total living space. When you are filing your income taxes, that percentage of house payment/rent, utilities and maintenance is accruable to the business as a business expense. If you have a tax consultant, he or she can help you with this.

## DIRECT MAIL OF YOUR SLIDES AND PRINTS

As most of your business will be conducted by mail, you will need to set up various accounts with delivery services. We made our choices based on cost and tracking ability. We use either United Parcel Service or, at the request of our clients and usually using their charge numbers, Federal Express. Both make a daily run to our house for pickups. These services are able to efficiently track a package if it is lost. As some of our submissions contain several hundred slides, each possibly worth up to $1,500, this tracking ability is essential. Both services allow us to add on insurance for extra large slide shipments.

We pack our slides carefully. We put stiff cardboard protection on both sides of the slide sleeves and we use heavy manila envelopes or padded mailing envelopes, which will not tear easily. All corners and the mailing label are reinforced with heavy clear tape. We have a postage scale, which will measure up to five pounds, that we use to determine the weight of our package. For larger packages, we use our bathroom scales, purchased especially because of an electronic readout that will give us an accurate weight measurement to the half pound.

## TRAVEL EQUIPMENT

As travel photographers, it is not sufficient for us merely to have studio equipment; we also need equipment that will serve us on the road. Everyone who wants to be a traveling stock photographer should check chapter three again before closing the last suitcase. Make sure that your passport and immunization shots are always up to date. Keep all your unpaid bills together in a specific place so that you, or anyone helping you, can have easy access to them as the checks come in. Leave a "To Do List" posted near your desk. After a trip, it is always hard to remember all the details of the busy life you left behind several weeks ago.

## GET ORGANIZED NOW!

We hope that this chapter convinced you to get your slides and your office organized as soon as possible. As we said, you are mining gold with your camera, but you won't enjoy the benefits until you take the necessary steps to move from "stock photography hobby" to "stock photography business."

*Chapter 5*

# PRICING YOUR PICTURES

Negotiation is an art. You don't want to price your photos too low. On the other hand, you don't want to price yourself right out of a sale. Sometimes a client who cannot afford to pay high rates will come back so often that, over time, you make enough money to compensate for a low price on each single sale.

It is important that you figure out how much a submission costs you and weigh that amount against how much the client can actually afford to pay. There are some clients you may have to drop because you are actually spending money to make submissions to them. Remember that postage or shipping costs may be the least of your expenses. Time is spent pulling slides for any submission. Even more time is spent re-filing the slides when they are returned. The massive paperwork involved with checking out slides and checking them back in will take still more time. Obviously, your time is worth money. You could just as easily be spending the same time servicing a client who pays decent rates. There are lots of amateur photographers who are so eager to have their pictures published that they sell themselves, and their pictures, short. Do not put yourself in their league!

When you are determining the price you will charge for use of your slides, there are several important factors to consider. Primarily there are three kinds of photo use: advertising, commercial and editorial.

Advertising pays the best. For advertising, you must determine the size of use, where it will be used in the publication, how many times and the circulation. If it is a spot use on an interior page, it will not pay as well as an inside front or back cover use. A local newspaper advertisement will not pay as well as a national magazine use. There are other ways to use a photo for advertising, such as on packaging, billboards, brochures and advertising posters.

The next highest paying form for the use of your photos is commercial. This is a form of advertising but it is part of the end product. Examples of commercial use are slides used in children's video toys, calendar pictures, postcards and commercial video or slide shows.

The lowest paying, but your greatest source of steady income, is editorial use. Editorial use can include textbooks, newspaper photos, magazine illustrations and encyclopedias.

There are other unusual uses for which people will come to you. Museums sometimes use photographs to illustrate the people or country in which their artifacts can be found. Some exhibitions will have repeating slide shows or use prints. Schools will sometimes use slide shows for geography classes. Ethnic restaurants may want photo prints to set the mood of their decor. Large organizations or companies often use photographs on the workbook folders that they use for their yearly conventions. Office decorations and even wall-sized murals can be made from 35mm slides. Upscale department stores will sometimes run a slide show simultaneously with a fashion show. We once made several thousand dollars from a department store that wanted a running slide show of Spain as the background for their models. Companies who are trying to make an impressive proposal may use photographs in their presentation. The variety of uses of pictures is only limited by human imagination. We are constantly surprised at the new uses people keep dreaming up for our slides.

There are two excellent references to use for seriously studying pricing. One is the ASMP (American Society of Media Photographers) *Stock Photography Handbook*. ASMP headquarters are in New York City (Telephone: (212) 889-9144). Another reference, one of the most helpful books ever written about setting fair prices and giving valuable tips about negotiation, is *Sellers Guide: Negotiating Stock Photo Prices 1992* by Jim Pickerell (available from Taking Stock, 110 Frederick Ave., Suite A, Rockville, MD 20850). We also have found invaluable business hints about negotiating and setting prices from a book written by a master of marketing, Rohn Engh's *Sell and Re-Sell Your Photos* (available from Writer's Digest Books, 1507 Dana Ave., Cincinnati, OH 45207).

We cannot state exactly what any one client will or should pay. Over the years, we have asked for and taken lots of advice in setting basic prices that we feel are fair to the client and fair to us.

When a client calls and asks a price, it is helpful to have some sort of list by the telephone so that you have an approximate idea of where to start negotiations, even if you haven't made such a sale before. There are factors that will come into your negotiations. If the photo is highly unusual, unrepeatable or it was hard to get, you might want to bring the price of using it up. On the other hand, if the client is going to use you exclusively for the project, if this is someone with whom you work frequently, or if the number of slides used is going to be large, the price will normally be negotiated downward.

In the following pages we will give you our own personal pricing guides that we have drawn up to use as a starting point for any price negotiations. After you have gained some experience, you may wish to draw up your own pricing guide to keep near your telephone. Each year, you will probably want to revise the pricing guide slightly to adjust for current economic conditions in the markets where your slides are being used.

PURCELL TEAM PRICING GUIDE

## Editorial Use—Magazines, House Organs & Newsletters

We use the numbers below when we start to negotiate for *editorial use in consumer magazines* and *internal house organs* (a term used for magazines published within an organization, company or corporation for internal distribution to the employees or membership).

- We charge 50 percent (multiply the numbers below by 0.5) when negotiating for *internal house newsletters* that will be used for internal distribution only.
- We charge 75 percent (multiply the numbers below by 0.75) when negotiating for editorial use in *consumer newsletters* that will be distributed or sold to the public at large.
- We charge 170 percent (multiply the numbers below by 1.7) when negotiating for *editorial use in external house organs* (a term used for magazines published within an organization, company or corporation for both internal and external distribution to its membership).
- If the client is using the photograph as an interior shot plus a spot insertion on the Page of Contents, we charge the space fee plus 25 percent (multiply the space fee by 1.25). If the spot insertion is on the cover, we charge the space fee plus 50 percent (multiply by 1.5).

### Magazines, House Organs & Newsletters—Editorial Use

| Circulation | ¼ page | ½ page | ¾ page | full page | double page | cover |
|---|---|---|---|---|---|---|
| Over 3M | $425 | $495 | $565 | $700 | $1,150 | $1,235 |
| 1-3M | 385 | 445 | 510 | 635 | 1,050 | 1,115 |
| 500,000-1M | 345 | 400 | 460 | 575 | 945 | 1,000 |
| 250,000-500,000 | 265 | 310 | 350 | 445 | 735 | 775 |
| 100,000-250,000 | 240 | 280 | 320 | 400 | 675 | 710 |
| 50,000-100,000 | 220 | 250 | 290 | 365 | 600 | 640 |
| 20,000-50,000 | 200 | 235 | 275 | 350 | 550 | 625 |

## Advertising in Magazines, House Organs or Newsletters

Advertising in magazines can be local, regional, national or specialized editions. Most of our invoices specify that we are granting the rights for one year. We charge an additional fee for longer use or repeated use and we base it on a percentage of the original billing.

- In the chart below are the prices we charge for *advertisements in consumer magazines national exposure*.
- We charge 80 percent (multiply by 0.8) of the fees below for *regional exposure*.
- We charge 60 percent (multiply by 0.6) of the fees listed below for *local exposure*.
- We charge the same fee for *advertisements in trade magazines* as we charge for *regional advertisements in consumer magazines*.
- We charge 75 percent (multiply the numbers below by 0.75) when negotiating for *advertisements in newsletters* that will be distributed or sold to the public.

ADDITIONAL FEES:

| | |
|---|---|
| Rights: | One Year Exclusive: Subtotal plus 100 percent<br>Five Year Exclusive: Subtotal plus 200 percent<br>Unlimited use—1 year—Subtotal plus 250 percent |
| Insertions: | 2-4: Space fee plus 25 percent<br>5-10: Space fee plus 50 percent |
| Inside Cover: | We usually start negotiations halfway between the full page price and back cover price. |

**Advertising in Magazines—National Exposure**

| Circulation | ¼ page | ½ page | ¾ page | full page | double page | back cover |
|---|---|---|---|---|---|---|
| Over 3M | $1,300 | $1,750 | $2,200 | $2,600 | $4,200 | $3,500 |
| 1-3M | 780 | 1,020 | 1,250 | 1,575 | 2,575 | 2,080 |
| 500,000-1M | 625 | 810 | 990 | 1,250 | 2,050 | 1,675 |
| 250,000-500,000 | 520 | 675 | 835 | 1,050 | 1,720 | 1,400 |
| 100,000-250,000 | 475 | 625 | 775 | 950 | 1,550 | 1,280 |
| 50,000-100,000 | 400 | 525 | 650 | 750 | 1,200 | 1,000 |
| 20,000-50,000 | 375 | 440 | 540 | 675 | 1,125 | 925 |

## Newspapers—Editorial Use

Editorial use in newspapers normally will not pay as well as photos in magazines or even in newsletters. Newspaper editors frequently are unable to be flexible with their prices.

Most newspaper photos are published in black and white although some newspapers have started to use more color than before. We charge 75 percent (multiply by 0.75) of our normal color fees (listed below) for photos used in black and white.

Sunday supplements have a larger budget than daily newspapers and usually have a bigger circulation than the dailies.

**Newspaper—Editorial Use**

| Circulation | ¼ page | ½ page | ¾ page | full page | double page | cover |
|---|---|---|---|---|---|---|
| Over 3M | $375 | $435 | $500 | $650 | $1,050 | $1,175 |
| 1-3M | 310 | 370 | 425 | 535 | 860 | 925 |
| 500,000-1M | 290 | 350 | 395 | 495 | 815 | 865 |
| 250,000-500,000 | 270 | 325 | 365 | 450 | 765 | 800 |
| 100,000-250,000 | 175 | 210 | 245 | 300 | 495 | 525 |
| 50,000-100,000 | 150 | 180 | 210 | 260 | 450 | 485 |
| 20,000-50,000 | 125 | 160 | 180 | 225 | 410 | 440 |

## Newspapers—Advertising Use

Photos sold for *newspaper advertisement* can be used several times in one newspaper, if the ad is repeated, or it can appear in several different newspapers. We count the number of insertions, assuming either multiple uses in one newspaper, or, more likely, use in several newspapers in different marketing areas. The first-time use fee is listed below.

- For up to two additional insertions, or use in different papers, we charge an additional 25 percent (multiply by 0.25) of the first-time use fee.
- For insertion number three to ten, we charge another 15 percent (multiply by 0.15) of the first-time use fee.
- We charge double the first-time use fee if a client wants unlimited use for one year. We strongly discourage clients who want to buy exclusive use (meaning that the photograph cannot be used for any advertisements throughout the agreed period), but in one case, we gave exclusive five-year use for 400 percent of the first-time use fee.

### Newspaper Advertisements

| Circulation | ¼ page | ½ page | ¾ page | full page |
|---|---|---|---|---|
| Over 3M | $675 | $875 | $1,050 | $1,400 |
| 1-3M | 575 | 775 | 950 | 1,300 |
| 500,000-1 M | 475 | 675 | 850 | 1,200 |
| 250,000-500,000 | 375 | 550 | 700 | 875 |
| 100,000-250,000 | 315 | 425 | 550 | 635 |
| 50,000-100,000 | 280 | 360 | 410 | 525 |
| under 50,000 | 250 | 300 | 375 | 400 |

## Advertorials — Magazine and Newspaper

Advertorials look like an editorial, but their space is paid by advertisers. A country might have several pages of copy talking about various aspects of its culture. A generic advertorial could be, for example, about travel photography, with the advertisers being Nikon, Minolta and Canon.

Advertorials appear in both newspapers and magazines. You should charge less for photos used in advertorials than you do for advertising use but more than you charge for editorial use.

- The prices listed below are for *national exposure*. We charge 80 percent (multiply by 0.8) of the fees below for *regional exposure*.
- We charge 60 percent (multiply by 0.6) of the fees listed below for *local exposure*.

### Magazine Advertorials — National Exposure

| Circulation | ¼ page | ½ page | ¾ page | full page | double page | back cover |
|---|---|---|---|---|---|---|
| Over 3M | $1,200 | $1,650 | $2,100 | $2,500 | $4,100 | $3,200 |
| 1-3M | 1,750 | 1,000 | 1,200 | 1,525 | 2,550 | 2,050 |
| 500,000-1M | 600 | 795 | 965 | 1,225 | 2,025 | 1,650 |
| 250,000-500,000 | 495 | 650 | 810 | 1,025 | 1,695 | 1,375 |
| 100,000-250,000 | 450 | 600 | 750 | 900 | 1,500 | 1,255 |
| 50,000-100,000 | 375 | 500 | 625 | 725 | 1,175 | 975 |
| 20,000-50,000 | 350 | 415 | 510 | 650 | 1,100 | 900 |

ADDITIONAL FEES:

Rights: One Year Exclusive: Subtotal plus 100 percent
Five Year Exclusive: Subtotal plus 200 percent
Unlimited use — 1 year — Subtotal plus 250 percent

Insertions: 2-4: Space fee plus 25 percent
5-10: Space fee plus 50 percent

Inside Cover: We usually start negotiations halfway between the full page price and back cover price.

### Newspaper Advertorials

| Circulation | ¼ page | ½ page | ¾ page | full page |
|---|---|---|---|---|
| Over 3M | $660 | $850 | $1,025 | $1,300 |
| 1-3M | 550 | 750 | 925 | 1,200 |
| 500,000-1M | 450 | 650 | 825 | 1,100 |
| 250,000-500,000 | 350 | 500 | 675 | 850 |
| 100,000-250,000 | 290 | 400 | 525 | 610 |
| 50,000-100,000 | 255 | 335 | 385 | 500 |
| 20,000-50,000 | 225 | 275 | 350 | 375 |

ADDITIONAL FEES:

| | |
|---|---|
| Rights: | One Year Exclusive: Subtotal plus 100 percent<br>Five Year Exclusive: Subtotal plus 200 percent<br>Unlimited use – 1 year – Subtotal plus 250 percent |
| Insertions: | 2-4: Space fee plus 25 percent<br>5-10: Space fee plus 50 percent |

## Books – Textbooks, Encyclopedias, Trade Books & Paperbacks

Photo use in books is usually considered strictly editorial unless the book is a single destination promotional piece. For textbooks, guidebooks and encyclopedias, we offer a special rate if multiple sales are made.

The normal run for a book is around 10,000 copies. Rarely are books published in runs over 40,000, unless they are paperbacks. We have divided out the pricing for books, therefore, into two categories: under 40,000 and over 40,000.

If the run is for 5,000 copies, we will usually negotiate a price of approximately 80 percent (multiply by 0.8) of the under 40,000 fee.

| Press Run | ¼ page | ½ page | ¾ page | full page | double page | jacket or cover |
|---|---|---|---|---|---|---|
| TEXTBOOKS | | | | | | |
| Over 40,000 | $185 | $200 | $225 | $270 | $550 | $550-820 |
| Under 40,000 | 145 | 170 | 195 | 225 | 450 | 450-650 |
| ENCYCLOPEDIAS | | | | | | |
| Over 40,000 | 215 | 270 | 300 | 325 | 650 | 825-1,075 |
| Under 40,000 | 190 | 215 | 250 | 275 | 550 | 435-650 |
| TRADE BOOKS | | | | | | |
| Over 40,000 | 185 | 200 | 225 | 270 | 550 | 550-825 |
| Under 40,000 | 145 | 170 | 195 | 225 | 450 | 450-675 |
| PAPERBACKS | | | | | | |
| Over 40,000 | 200 | 220 | 250 | 285 | 565 | 510-780 |
| Under 40,000 | 175 | 200 | 235 | 260 | 525 | 425-650 |

ADDITIONAL FEES:

- Reuse or revisions: We usually charge 50 percent of the original price each time a new edition comes out or the photo is reused in a foreign edition. If world rights are requested during initial negotiations, we charge 150 percent of the price listed above for a book being published in one language. We charge 200 percent for world rights for a book being published in several languages.
- For chapter openers, we usually charge 125 percent (multiply by 1.25) plus the space fee listed above.
- For wraparound covers, we start negotiations at the top listed price for covers.
- We usually charge $350 for an author head shot, plus traveling costs to get it and $15 per roll of film taken.

## Guidebooks

Guidebook publishers prefer to negotiate for photos without discussing size or placement. If the publisher is willing to let us shoot the entire guidebook, consisting of a guaranteed one hundred or more pictures, we will often settle for a straight price of $80 or $90 per picture, regardless of size or placement.

| Press Run | 1/4 page | 1/2 page | 3/4 page | full page | double page | jacket or cover |
|---|---|---|---|---|---|---|
| GUIDEBOOKS—For Photos #1-5 | | | | | | |
| Over 40,000 | $125 | $135 | $160 | $185 | $300 | $550-820 |
| Under 40,000 | 110 | 125 | 140 | 160 | 240 | 450-650 |
| GUIDEBOOKS—For Photos #6-10 | | | | | | |
| Over 40,000 | 115 | 130 | 145 | 165 | 245 | 525-800 |
| Under 40,000 | 100 | 115 | 130 | 150 | 230 | 425-625 |
| GUIDEBOOKS—For Photos #11-25 | | | | | | |
| Over 40,000 | 105 | 120 | 135 | 155 | 235 | 500-775 |
| Under 40,000 | 90 | 105 | 120 | 140 | 220 | 400-600 |
| GUIDEBOOKS—For Photos #26-50 | | | | | | |
| Over 40,000 | 95 | 110 | 125 | 145 | 225 | 450-725 |
| Under 40,000 | 80 | 95 | 110 | 130 | 210 | 350-550 |
| GUIDEBOOKS—For photos #51+ | | | | | | |
| Over 40,000 | 85 | 100 | 115 | 135 | 215 | 400-650 |
| Under 40,000 | 70 | 85 | 100 | 120 | 200 | 300-500 |

ADDITIONAL FEES:

- Reuse or revisions: We usually charge 50 percent of the original price each time a new edition comes out or the photo is reused in a foreign edition.
- If world rights are requested during initial negotiations, we charge 150 percent of the price listed above for a book being published in one language. We'll charge 200 percent for world rights for a book being published in several languages.
- For chapter openers, we charge an extra 25 percent (multiply the space fee listed above by 1.25).
- For wraparound covers, we start negotiations at the top listed price for covers.
- We usually charge $350 for an author head shot, plus traveling costs to get it and $15 per roll of film taken.

## Other Uses Such as: Billboards, Murals, Postcards, Decorative Prints, Exhibit Prints

| | |
|---|---|
| Billboards (one to twelve photos for one year) | $500-1,000 |
| Murals (3-by-5 feet to full wall) | $300-2,500 |
| Postcards and greeting cards (5,000-20,000) | $200-500 |
| Display prints for decoration (small-large) | $250-450 |
| Bank checks (local-national) | $400-750 |
| Place mats | $325 |
| Key chains & charms | $300 |
| Stationery letterheads | $375 |
| Playing cards | $375 |
| Stamps | $400 |
| Plates or coffee mugs | $375 |
| Apparel (actual photo used) | $350 |
| Apparel (facsimile used) | $200 |
| Telephone directory covers | $750 each (Slide #4+: $500 each) |
| Exhibit prints (small-large) | $250-450 for first time showing<br>50 percent more for exhibits #2-#4<br>25 percent more for exhibits #5-#10<br>100 percent more for unlimited exhibits |

## Film, TV, Educational Filmstrips and Slide Shows

We charge one price for the first five slides used, then a different price for slides #6-10, still another for slides #11-25 and a fourth price for slides #26 and up. This is to encourage multiple sales for slide shows and filmstrips.

| | 1-5 slides used | 6-10 slides used | 11-25 slides used | 26+ slides used |
|---|---|---|---|---|
| 1 Showing: | $165 | $130 | $110 | $ 90 |
| 2-5 Showings: | 175 | 140 | 120 | 100 |
| 5-13 Showings: | 190 | 155 | 135 | 115 |
| Over 13 Showings: | 225 | 190 | 170 | 140 |

## Calendars

Calendars can be either promotional or retail. They can have one photo visible for twelve months, use one photo per month, or have several photos per months as in the desktop appointment book style.

- If we are asked to provide the single photo that is visible for twelve months, we usually ask for twice the rate we would get for the first three photos we provide.
- For a calendar cover photo, we can usually add 50 percent (multiply by 1.5) to the rate we get for the first three photos we provide.

Calendars are good promotional portfolios when all the photos used are by one photographer. When we are asked for calendar pictures by a company who has always put out a fairly sophisticated, good-looking product, we offer the alternative that, if the art director chooses to use only our photos, we will give a 50 percent discount on the cost of the photos for an overrun of 250-3000 calendars (depending on the size of the press run). We then mail the calendars to important current clients and potential clients. When the agreed-on overrun is very large, we ask for a certain percentage to be in finished calendars and the remainder to be in loose photo sheets (without the dates).

| Press Run | Photos #1-3 | Photos #4-7 | Photos #8-12 | Photos #13+ |
|---|---|---|---|---|
| over 100,000 | $1,000 | $700 | $500 | $400 |
| 50,000-100,000 | 800 | 650 | 450 | 350 |
| 20,000-50,000 | 600 | 500 | 400 | 300 |
| 10,000-20,000 | 450 | 400 | 350 | 275 |
| 5,000-10,000 | 300 | 250 | 200 | 150 |

## Brochures and Catalogs

Although brochures and catalogs are technically advertising, most press runs are small. These requests will ask for photos for flyers, mailers, proposal folders and convention folders. It is important to know if this photo request is for the cover of the brochure or for the interior. We always ask if the first run is just a test (usually a low number produced) in which case we charge an additional fee for future runs.

| Press Run | ¼ page | ½ page | ¾ page | full page | double page | cover |
|---|---|---|---|---|---|---|
| Over 1M | $480 | $625 | $750 | $950 | $1,550 | $1,890 |
| 500,000-1M | 400 | 550 | 650 | 800 | 1,325 | 1,625 |
| 250,000-500,000 | 350 | 450 | 550 | 675 | 1,150 | 1,350 |
| 100,000-250,000 | 300 | 375 | 475 | 575 | 950 | 1,150 |
| 50,000-100,000 | 250 | 300 | 350 | 450 | 725 | 975 |
| 20,000-50,000 | 215 | 285 | 325 | 425 | 700 | 950 |
| Under 20,000 | 190 | 250 | 285 | 375 | 650 | 750 |

ADDITIONAL FEES:

Back Cover: Halfway between full page price and cover price.

Inside Front Cover: We start negotiations halfway between the full page price and cover price.

Rights: One Year Exclusive: Subtotal plus 100 percent
Five Year Exclusive: Subtotal plus 200 percent
Unlimited use – 1 year – Subtotal plus 250 percent

## Scrap Use – Artist Reference, Art Renderings, Presentations & Layouts

Use of a photo for *artist reference* results in a finished product in which you cannot recognize the original photograph. The artist is just using the photograph as a reference for details of positioning, color or composition. Depending on the nature of the finished product, we usually charge between $75 and $200 for this use.

*Art renderings* are a faithful reproduction of the photograph and we charge 80 percent (multiply by 0.8) of the money we would charge for using the photograph itself in the end product.

*Presentations and layouts* are used to set up examples of the product for approval, without knowing which photograph will be finally approved. The tacit understanding has usually been that the designer can make a print from your photo to paste into the sample product. We have learned from bad experience that you should make specific agreements as to reproduction rights. (One client made 150 prints from our slide to send out instead of the planned brochure.) We charge a fee of $110-250 for slides used in presentations and layouts. When submitting slides for this use, we seal each slide in an individual plastic sleeve which states that a layout fee of $250 will be automatically charged if the seals are broken.

## Record Albums, Cassette Tapes, Atlas Covers

There is no way to know if these will sell just a few or many. Usually you are approached when the test run is still going on. You can charge a small percentage of the gross receipts but this will cause bookkeeping problems for the publisher and they will usually prefer to give you a set fee.

We charge a fee for the test run, with the understanding that if it goes into mass production, we will receive an additional check.

Test run ............................$300-460, depending how many units are made (the low averaging around 1,000 and the high averaging around 5,000)

Cover use ............................(Lows: 2,000 copies, Highs: Mass production)

Front....................................$490-1,350

Back.....................................$350-975

Wrap-around.........................$900-1,550

Spot use on cover ................$250-875
Background of cover............$375-1,000
Inside brochures ..................$215-475

ADDITIONAL FEES:

Rights: One Year Exclusive: Subtotal plus 100 percent
Five Year Exclusive: Subtotal plus 200 percent
Unlimited use—1 year—Subtotal plus 250 percent

## Posters

If only one poster is made to be used once, we treat it like an exhibit print. Most often, however, people want to make posters in bulk, either to promote their company or a travel destination, or as educational posters or posters to release for sale. In that case, we use the prices below.

Posters are good promotional pieces to mail to important current clients and potential clients. When we are asked to provide photos for posters and if we like the photos being used, we often offer to give a 50 percent discount on the cost of the photos for an over-run of 250-3000 posters (depending on the size of the press run).

| Press Run | Small 8″ × 12″ | | Medium 16″ × 20″ | | Large 30″ × 40″ | |
|---|---|---|---|---|---|---|
| RETAIL POSTERS | US | Worldwide | US | Worldwide | US | Worldwide |
| Over 100,000 | $435 | $600 | $550 | $750 | $625 | $865 |
| 50,000-100,000 | 390 | 550 | 485 | 675 | 550 | 770 |
| 10,000-50,000 | 350 | 485 | 425 | 590 | 485 | 675 |
| Under 10,000 | 325 | 460 | 400 | 565 | 460 | 650 |
| EDUCATIONAL POSTERS | | | | | | |
| Over 100,000 | 375 | 550 | 485 | 675 | 565 | 785 |
| 50,000-100,000 | 350 | 485 | 425 | 590 | 485 | 675 |
| 10,000-50,000 | 325 | 460 | 400 | 565 | 460 | 650 |
| Under 10,000 | 300 | 425 | 375 | 525 | 425 | 600 |
| PROMOTIONAL POSTERS | | | | | | |
| Over 100,000 | 700 | 975 | 890 | 1,250 | 1,025 | 1,435 |
| 50,000-100,000 | 600 | 775 | 715 | 900 | 800 | 1,010 |
| 10,000-50,000 | 475 | 650 | 585 | 775 | 665 | 885 |
| Under 10,000 | 375 | 550 | 485 | 675 | 565 | 785 |

## Packaging and In-Product Use

These prices include the use of photos on blister packs, labels or anything on the outside of packages. In-product use includes things like puzzles, photos used in a film inside a toy, etc.

| Distribution | Small Spot Use | Medium Substantial Use | Large Total Package |
|---|---|---|---|
| National | $475 | $710 | $850 |
| Regional | 375 | 575 | 650 |
| Local | 250 | 425 | 500 |
| Test Run | 235 | 400 | 450 |

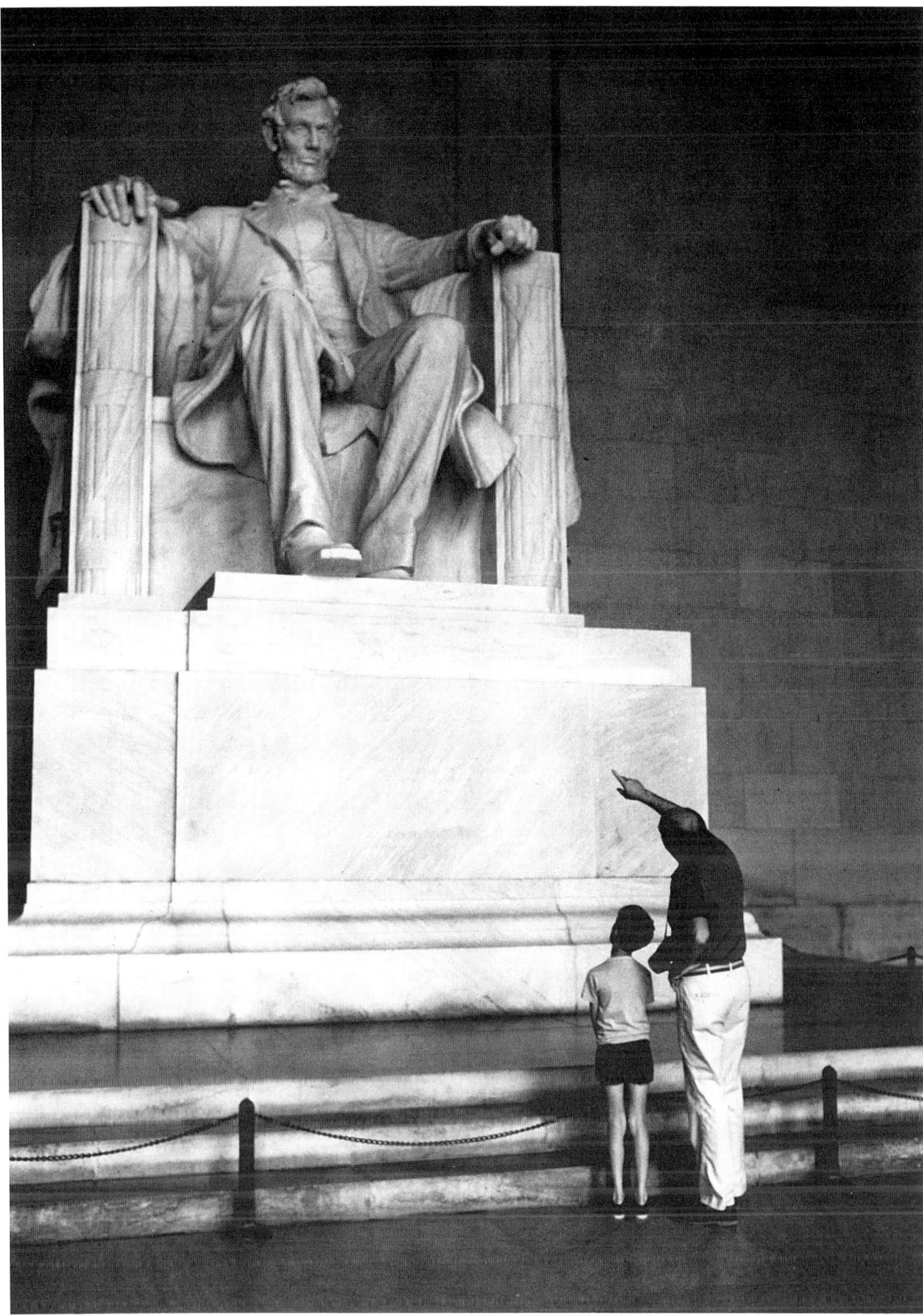

A father and his son stand at the feet of the Great Emancipator in the Lincoln Memorial. When shooting stock pictures, it is helpful to keep in mind the recurrent themes of family values and American traditions. These sell again and again.

## Electronic Rights

These are perhaps the most difficult prices to set because the technology is still so new. If someone wants to put your slides on a high-resolution CD-ROM disk, you may be unable to police the use of the slides. You are usually giving up the right to object to the use of your pictures in any kind of desktop publishing, brochure, etc. If you don't read the fine print, you'll sometimes also be giving up the right to use the photo or similar photos on any other CD-ROM disk. Make sure that all rights, or non-exclusivity, are spelled out in your agreement.

We have so far agreed only once to the commercial electronic rights of our slides on a disk with other people's work (in an encyclopedia) and we set the price of $250 for electronic low-resolution rights. (This was in addition to the original fee charged for use. When they decided to use nine slides on the disk, we came down slightly in price.) The words "low resolution" are very important. High resolution can be used in glossy advertising with almost no loss in quality. If there are only low-resolution photos on a disk, any big advertising agency would come back to you for the original slide if they wanted the image for large or high-quality advertisements.

We also have several disks out that feature our work exclusively, and the price for using these slides is a percentage of the gross sales. About 15 to 20 percent of the gross sales is the normal range for the photographer at the time of this printing.

## ASSIGNMENT PHOTOGRAPHY

Sometimes, after filling a photo request for a client, you will get a call saying that you "almost" had the right picture, but did you take the picture from above? Or, you may get a call from a client who has used you before and likes your work. They will ask you if you have ever taken photos of some view (usually not far from your home base). Perhaps the editor called to find out if you have a face shot of a famous person who lives in your area. In all these cases, if you don't have the shot, you can offer to shoot it on assignment.

An editor for whom you have done work in the past may call and ask you to cover an event or a destination. The destination or the people who are holding the event will sometimes pay all travel and accommodation expenses, while the editor will pay editorial day rates. The most lucrative are the advertising assignments. We frequently get calls asking if we can do a specific shot that the advertising agency has already thought out. The shot is not always difficult to take. We once were asked to take a photo of a telephone in the sand on a beach in the Virgin Islands. The client, an advertising agency for MCI telephone, wanted blue water, sky, telephone, sand and nothing else. We were leaving the next day for Singapore, but we knew of a talented photographer friend of ours who happened to be in the Virgin Islands doing another assignment. We called him and he took the picture. We had already negotiated $3,000 for him for the shot. You've probably seen the photo in a dozen magazine ads.

Your price for assignment photography will change as you become better known. As a beginner, you may get paid only $350 per day, but as a well-seasoned professional, the same day may be worth $1,500, or, in the case of high-gloss advertising, $3,000 or more. You should never accept less for your daily fee than you would get for the photos you are shooting. For example, if you are shooting a cover photograph for a magazine with 50,000-100,000 circulation, the photo, if bought from stock, would cost the client $640. Your fee to shoot that photo specifically for that magazine should certainly not be less than the stock shot would cost. Never forget to add in your expenses: traveling, hotel, food, tips and at least $15 per roll of film for base cost, processing and editing. We usually charge 50 percent, or one-half, of our day rate for travel time and rain days.

It is important that you retain the ownership and copyright of all the slides you shoot. If the client wants a buy-out, try to discourage it. It is better for you to be able to use any "rejects" in your own files and send them to agencies. If the client insists that they do not want anyone to have access to similar shots and, therefore, they demand a buy-out of some particular assignment, you can usually triple your top day rate in exchange for that exclusivity.

Assignment photography is the best of all worlds for you, the stock photographer. Not only are you getting healthy day rates; you are also collecting more images for your stock files and agencies.

## PRICE NEGOTIATION

It is a good idea to ask clients what they have usually paid for a particular use in the past. This is a question people are sometimes reluctant to answer because they've been told to get the lowest possible price, but you can be gently persistent. You may be surprised to learn that they usually pay more than you had hoped to get.

If the client insists that you give the first figure, start high. Too many photographers minimize their own skills and value. The worst mistake you can make is to undersell yourself. We know of some beginners who shot the brochures for a cruise ship and the only payment was the cruise itself. On assignment work, try for at least double what you have decided you really want to earn. You can always go lower if you must. After you have cheerfully but firmly given your price, *be still*. Don't speak until after you have gotten a response. As Rohn Engh reminds you in his book, the person who talks next is the one who is at a disadvantage and you want that to be the client. The client will either agree to your price or he will tell you what his highest budgeted price is. At worst, if his response indicates a budget with a very low figure, then you can reiterate the higher "usual" price, explaining to the client that you would, however, be willing to negotiate. One negotiating factor would be that you have worked with these clients before, or that you enjoy working with them and would look forward to working with them again.

Another negotiating factor would be multiple sales. If this client is doing a slide show, for example, you can give the descending rate: First five slides are $165 each, slides #6-10 are $130 each, slides #11-25 are $110 each, slides #26-50 are $90 each, and so forth. While you wouldn't be happy to give the use of one of your slides for a commercial slide show for $80 each, you certainly could afford to allow it if you were making one hundred such sales in one research pull. Another example would be if a calendar company would agree to use your images for all twelve months. At that point, you might even be willing to let the images go for a very low price plus a certain number of calendars that you could use for promotional purposes.

## COPYRIGHTS, RIGHTS AND PERMISSIONS

The starting point and the first principle you should always keep in mind is to keep the copyright of all the pictures you take. If the issue is raised, you should explain to your clients that, in most cases, it is not really an advantage for them to try to buy your copyright. If someone wants to "buy out all rights," that client is going to have to pay a very high fee, particularly if the client wants to "own" the entire take. (An example of this: You do an assignment taking a fashion shot for a perfume ad, which the perfume company wants to "own" entirely so no one else in the world can use that picture or the similar pictures taken at the same time.) This particular option is called "work for hire" and is often frowned on in the stock photography industry. The exception would be when a particular picture is going to be strongly identified with a specific product. Calvin Klein, for instance, would not want their "Obsession" photo, or any similar ones, being used to advertise any other product. They fully expect and are willing to pay for such exclusivity.

There are alternatives. You can offer to sell exclusive use of a picture, or even a whole "take," for a limited time. (Example: A billboard picture that you will not allow anyone else to use for any purpose for five years.)

The next less expensive level would be to sell exclusive use of a picture for a certain kind of use for a limited time. (Example: A calendar picture that you will not allow anyone else to use in any other calendar for three years. The photo could, however, be used by a textbook publisher as an illustration in their fifth-grade geography book.)

The least expensive option for your client, however, is to purchase non-exclusive one-time use. This is also the most desirable option for you, as it will not limit your use of the photo for future requests.

We would like to stress once again. *Do not undersell yourself!* If you are willing to allow your photographs to be published for nothing, and some photographers are, you have let the client know exactly how much you feel your work is worth. You can feel confident. If the client didn't feel that it was a good picture, you would not be discussing price!

A few days ago we received a call from a friend of ours. He is a brilliant and talented photographer, but stock photography has not been his main business. He had done a striking and unusual wildlife poster. A European photography trade show wanted to use the poster during their show and for extensive advertising in European magazines. Our friend asked if we thought that $500 was a good price for him to quote. We choked. "The price is more like $10,000," we told him. It was his turn to choke, but we are sure that he got it.

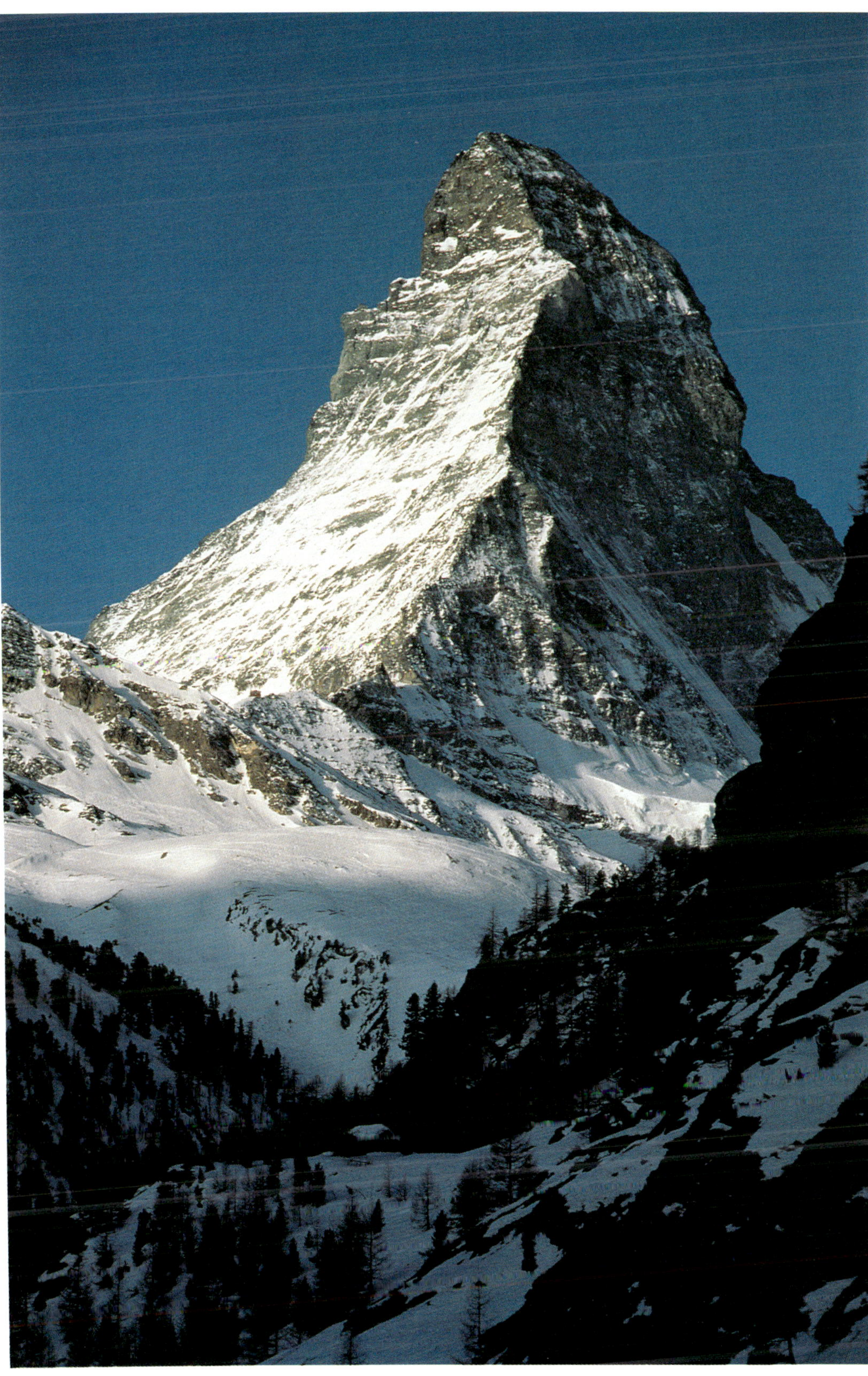

A clear picture of the famous Matterhorn Mountain in Zermatt, Switzerland, has many potential uses for stock. The Matterhorn is probably the best-known mountain in the Swiss Alps and can serve as a symbol of Switzerland to illustrate travel brochures and magazine articles about that country. It can also represent concepts such as "peak experiences" or "reaching the top." Some photographers think every agency in the world will have the Matterhorn in their files and many of them will. Remember, however, that all pictures are different and that the photographer who gets a good shot of the Matterhorn to the picture buyer at the right time is the one who makes the sale.

Nostalgia sells! Whoever grew up in the fifties may have privately lusted after a pink Cadillac with giant tail fins. Such images live in the hearts of Americans and they love to see them in magazines. We found this finned monster at the Art Deco Weekend celebration in Miami Beach. It has been a favorite of art directors.

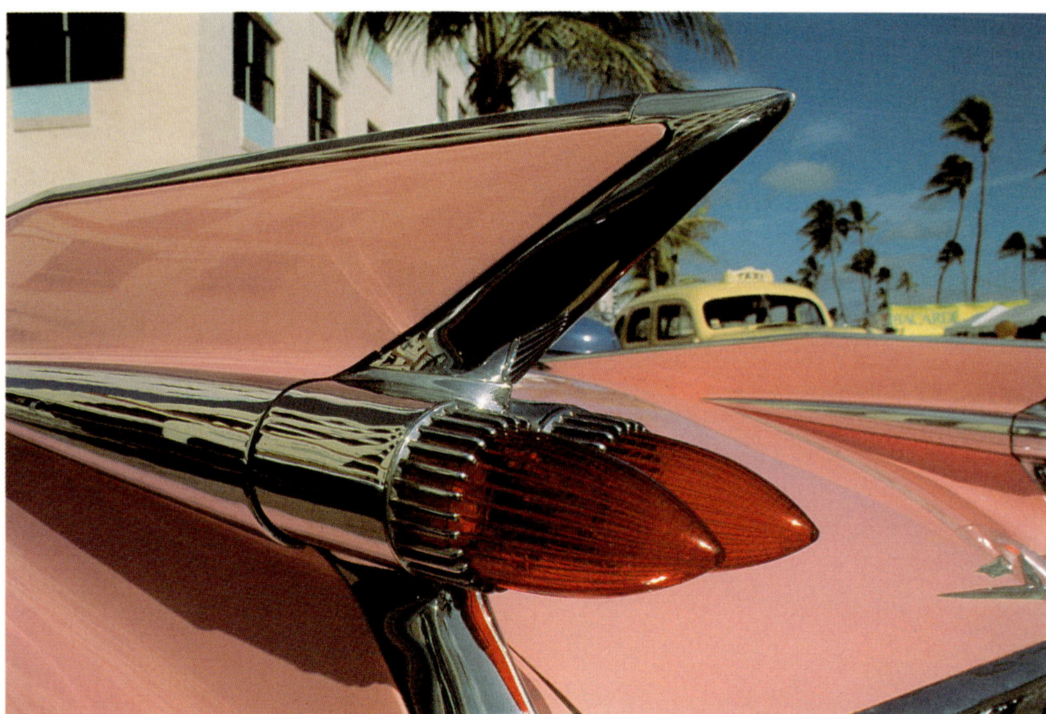

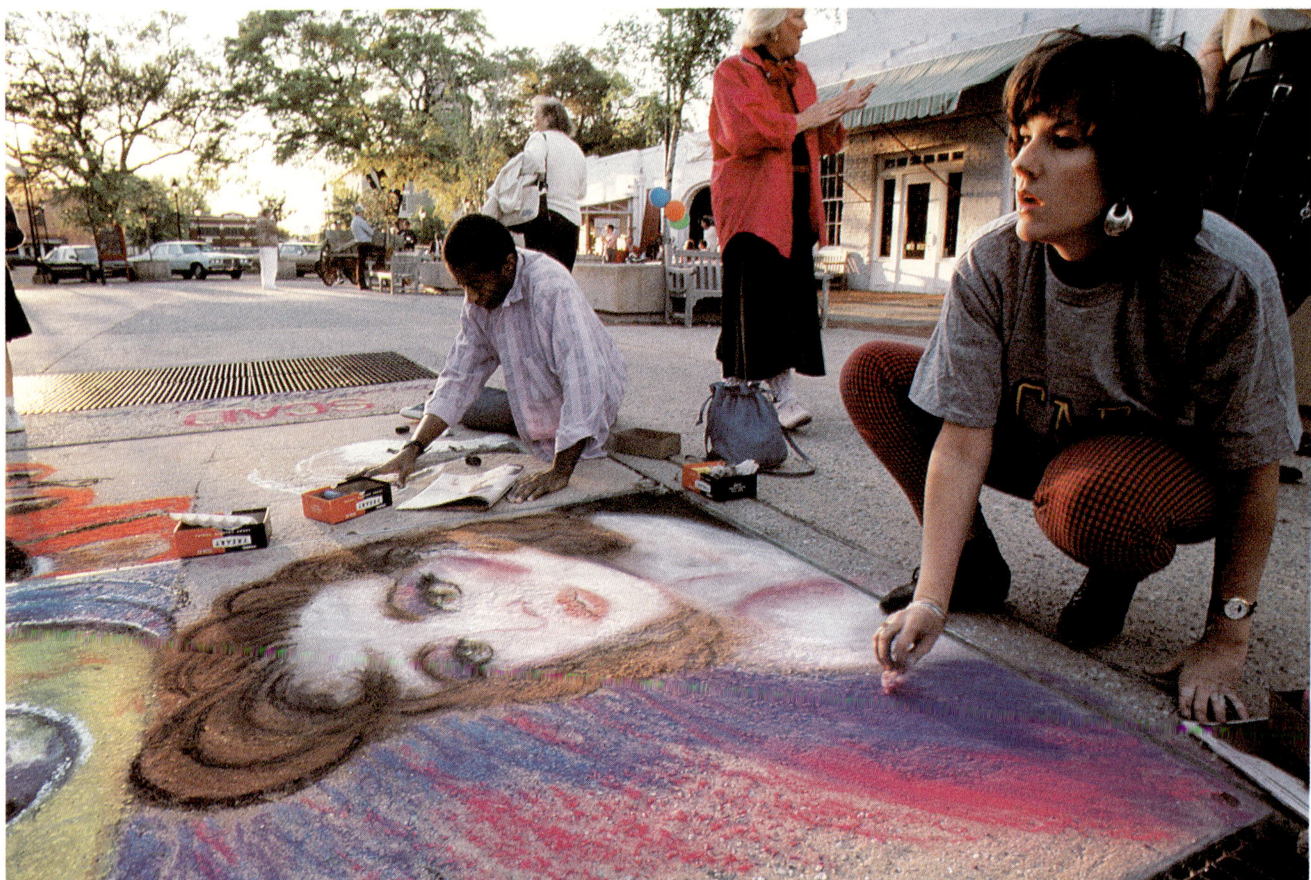

People doing things in a natural way and enjoying themselves frequently make good subjects for stock. We took this picture of sidewalk artists during a visit to Savannah, Georgia.

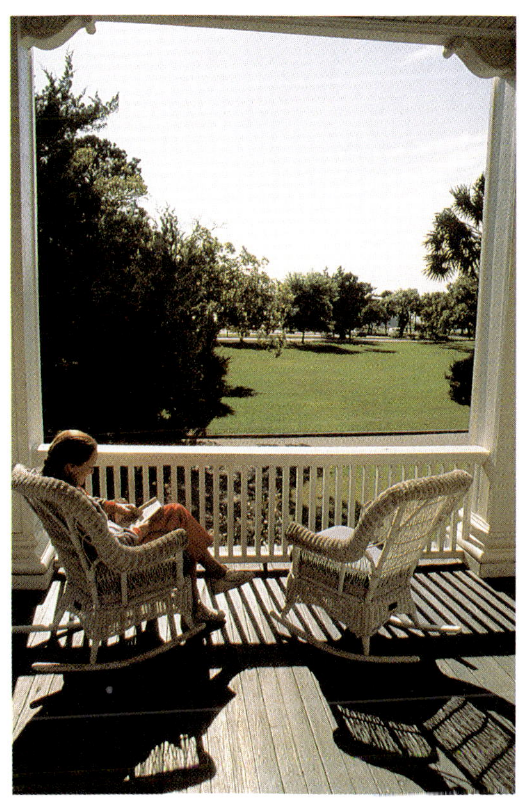

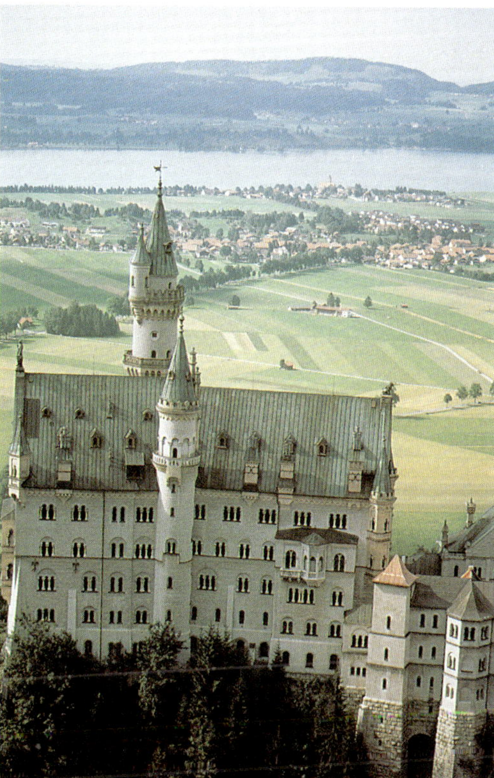

Time and again we are asked for the quintessential fairy tale castle. One of the best, shown here, is Neuschwanstein located in Bavaria. As we travel, we continue to build our file of castles in France, England, Ireland, Spain and Italy. This one, however, is a perennial favorite with the editors.

People travel for many reasons, but the vacationer usually likes to relax. We took this picture of a guest relaxing at the Jekyll Island Club in Georgia. There were several uses for the photo. Using the doorway as a frame, we were able to convey not only the peaceful atmosphere of the hotel, but also could show some of the surrounding countryside.

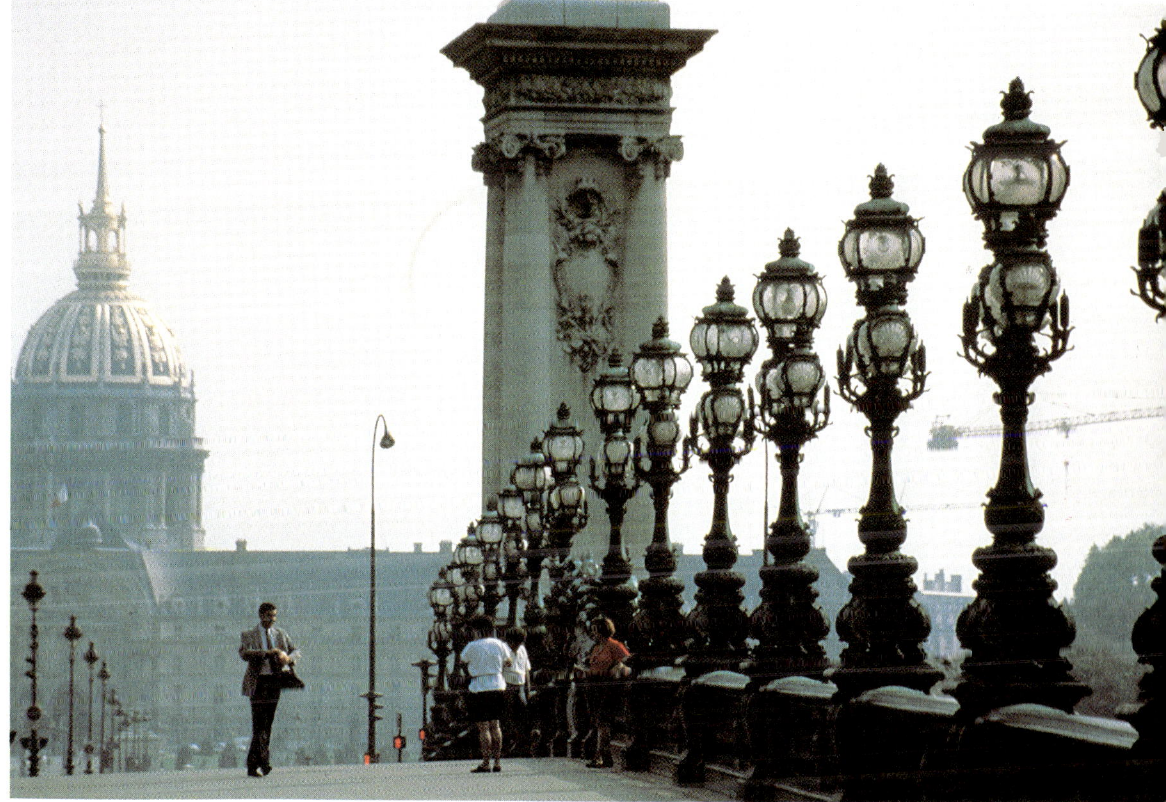

Pont Alexandre is a bridge in Paris, lined with ornate streetlamps, that crosses the Seine. Unlike the Eiffel Tower or the Arc de Triomphe, it is not instantly recognizable but makes a nice illustration for a travel article on Paris. When only using one picture, most editors will select a more recognizable landmark for their illustration. This photo, however, is of the type often used as a secondary illustration, meant to convey the atmosphere of a destination.

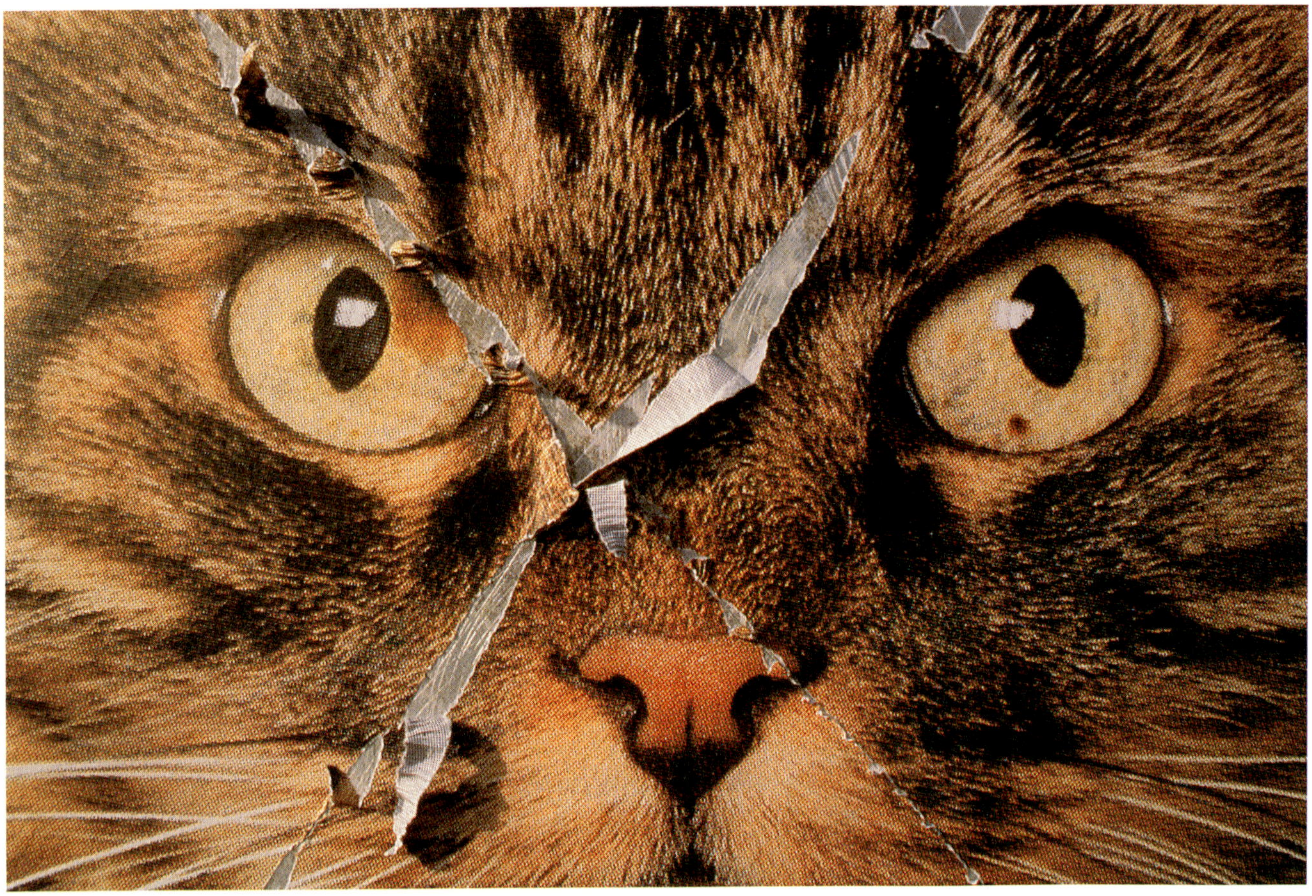

We sometimes take pictures of pictures. This cat's face was on a billboard in Switzerland. Because it catches the eye, it is a good illustration for an article about cats.

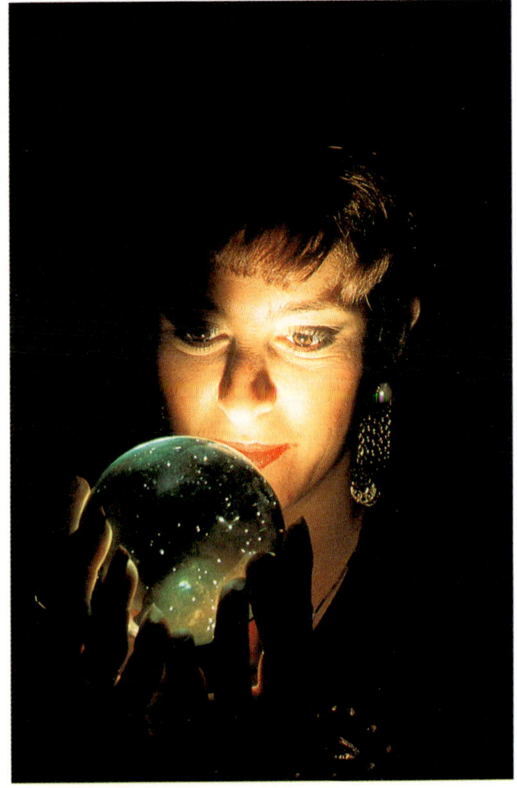

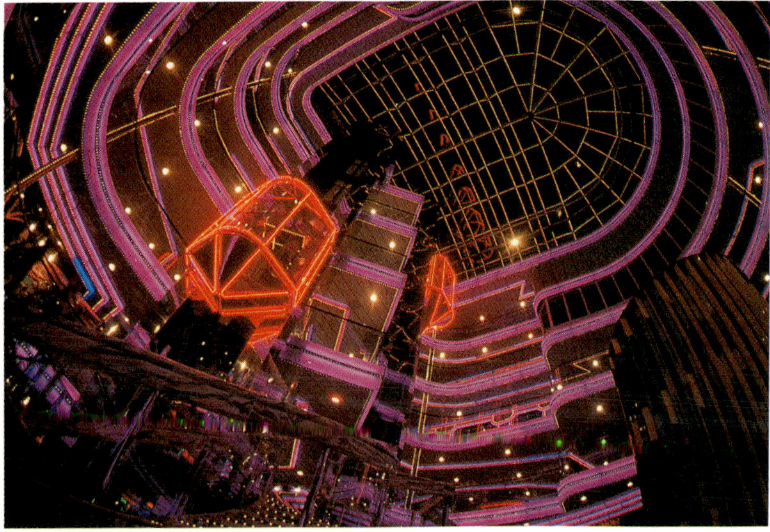

(Above) The Grand Atrium of the Fantasy Cruise Ship is outlined in colored neon. This unique visual feature can be captured effectively using a tripod mounted camera with a very wide-angle lens. The photo has been used with several magazine articles.

(Left) A picture of a woman gazing into a crystal ball can be used as a concept of the common desire of people to predict the future. Such a photograph could be used for an insurance advertisement or a financial investment firm.

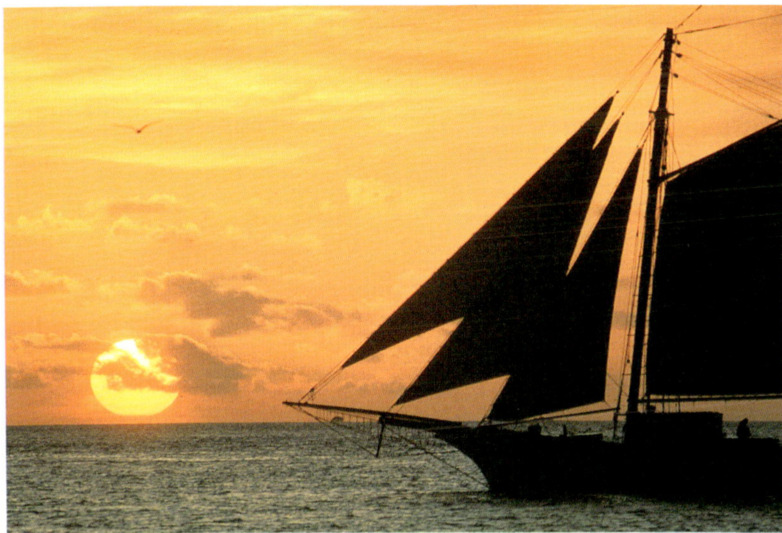

This picture was taken as the sun set in Key West, Florida. Key West is famous for its sunsets. People gather on Mallory Square Pier every night to enjoy nature's display and are rarely disappointed. The two-masted schooner takes passengers for a sunset sail. While our picture happens to be taken in Key West, the sunset and the sailing vessel are generic and could be almost anywhere in the world. This makes it a valuable stock picture. We waited to shoot until the schooner's bow looked as if it were about to pierce the setting sun.

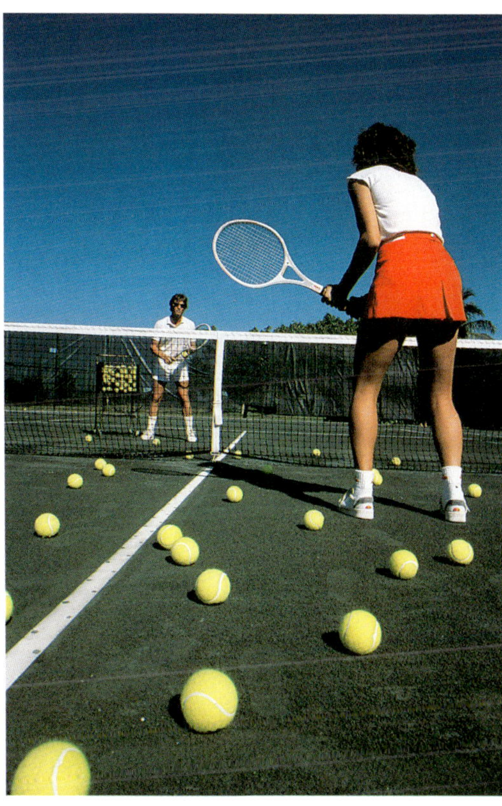

It is difficult to shoot good action shots of tennis for stock. Action pictures invariably show the players in awkward positions or include a busy background. You might get one good shot out of two or three rolls. We carefully posed this tennis picture, positioning the players exactly where we wanted them and placing the brightly colored balls on the green court as if the woman in the foreground was receiving practice serves from the man on the other side of the net. This allowed for a carefully planned composition, taken lying full length on the ground behind the woman.

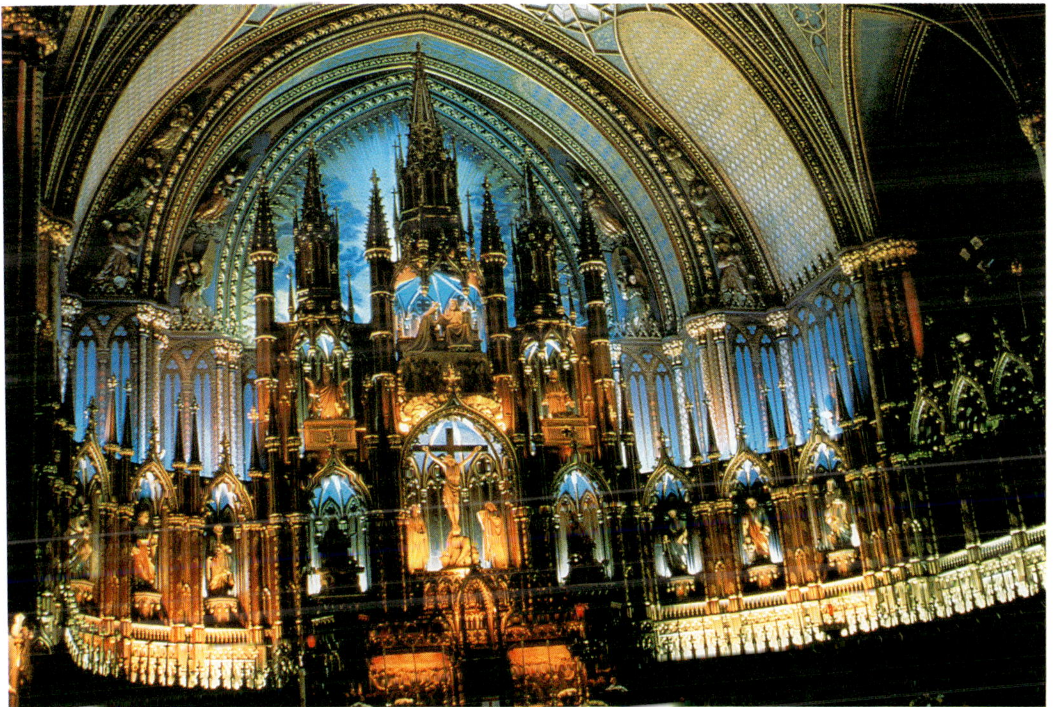

Notre Dame Basilica in Montreal is illuminated with multicolored lights. We mounted our camera on a tripod for a short time exposure to get this picture. It was used in a guidebook on the city. Don't be afraid to attempt interior shots. Ask for permission to use your tripod.

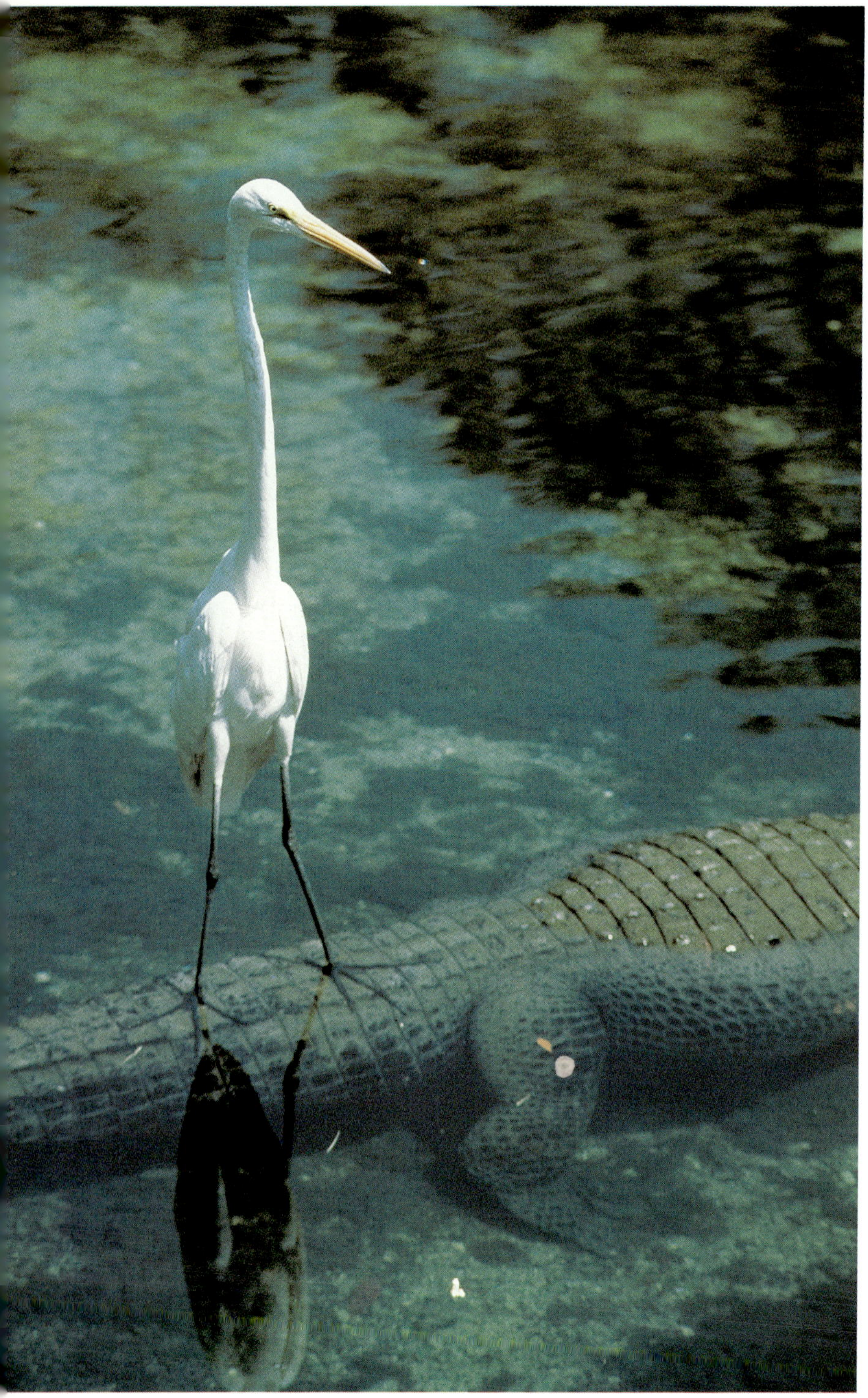

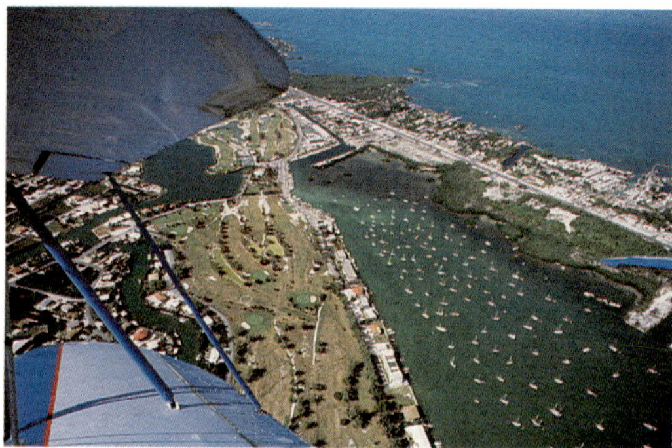

This aerial view of the Florida Keys makes clear the water and land relationship of these small, interconnected islands. It makes a good stock picture for a travel brochure or guidebook. Aerial shots are often used as lead pictures for more specific on-the-ground illustrations.

This amusing picture was taken at Homosassa Springs in Florida. It is a trusting bird who will rest on the back of an alligator. Keep your eye open for life's humorous moments, for the unusual and for strange juxtapositions.

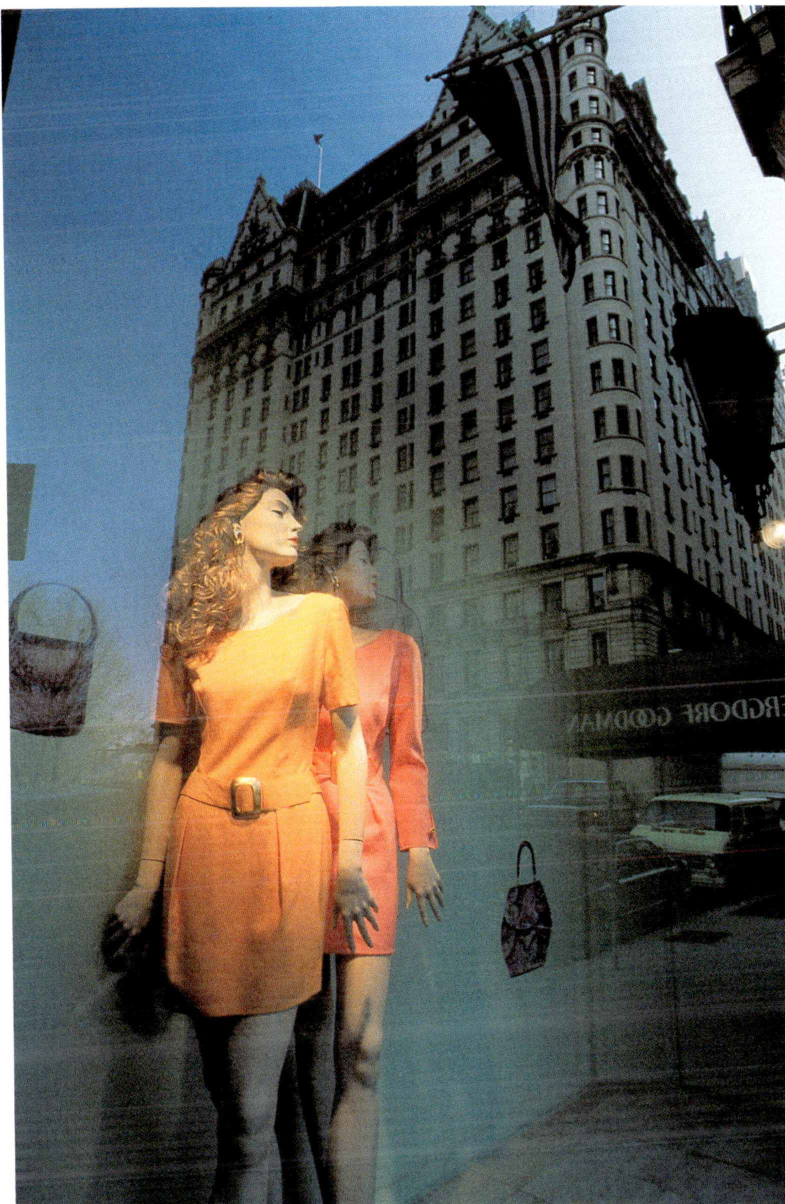

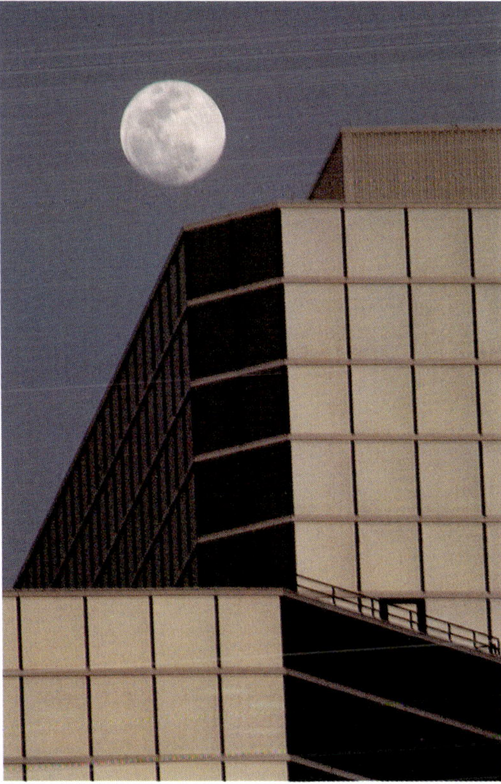

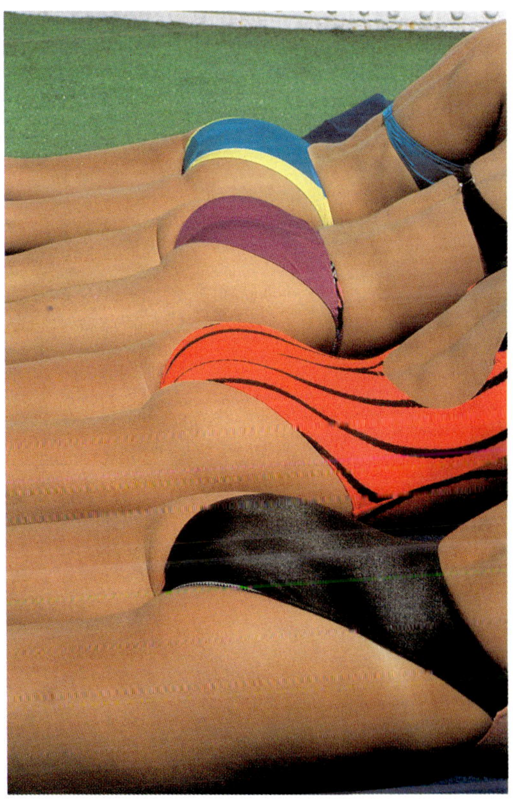

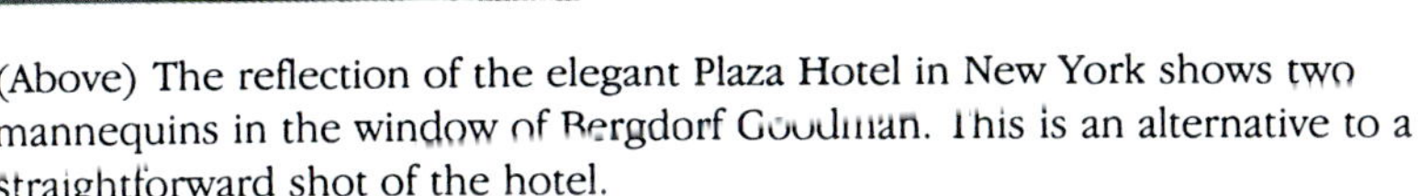

(Above) The reflection of the elegant Plaza Hotel in New York shows two mannequins in the window of Bergdorf Goodman. This is an alternative to a straightforward shot of the hotel.

(Top right) While some photographers put the moon in their pictures via double exposures, sandwiched transparencies, or electronic manipulation, this one happens to be a straight picture of the real thing. We used a 300mm lens for this shot, which magnified the moon and made it appear larger than it did to the eye.

(Right) A perfect line-up of sunbathers aboard a cruise ship rarely happens. We posed these agreeable young women to create an eye-catching and colorful stock picture. Because the name of the cruise ship is not visible, this became a generic shot.

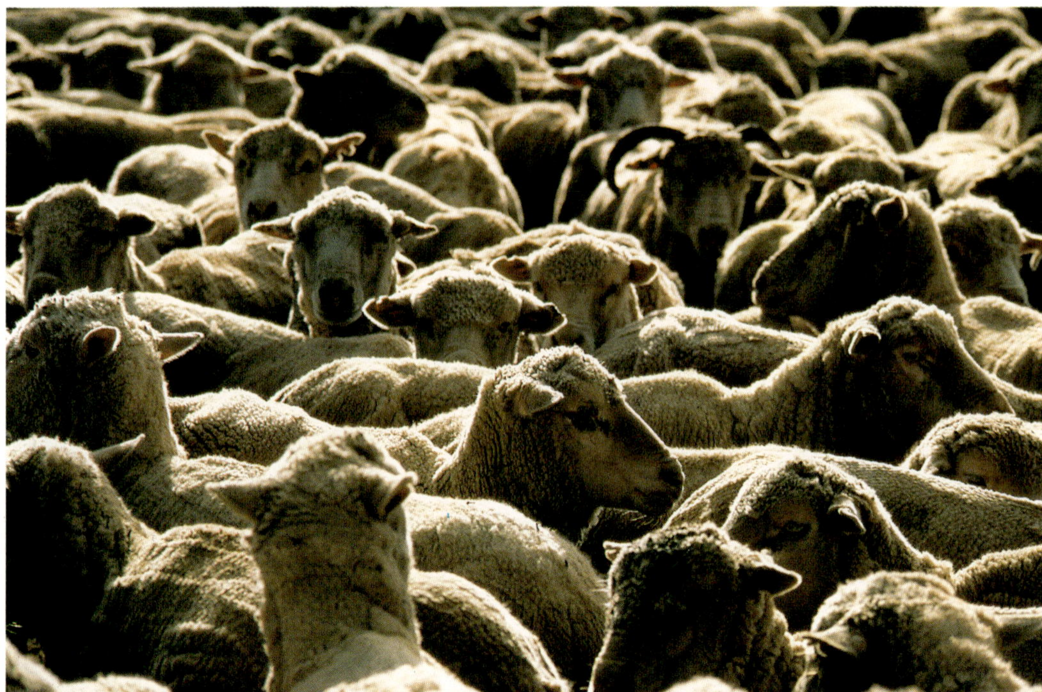

This photograph, if used as an advertisement, might well have the headline "Don't be one of the sheep!" Right or wrong, animals are thought to have human traits such as conformity, bravery, vanity, wisdom or strength. These traits can be illustrated by stock pictures of the appropriate animals.

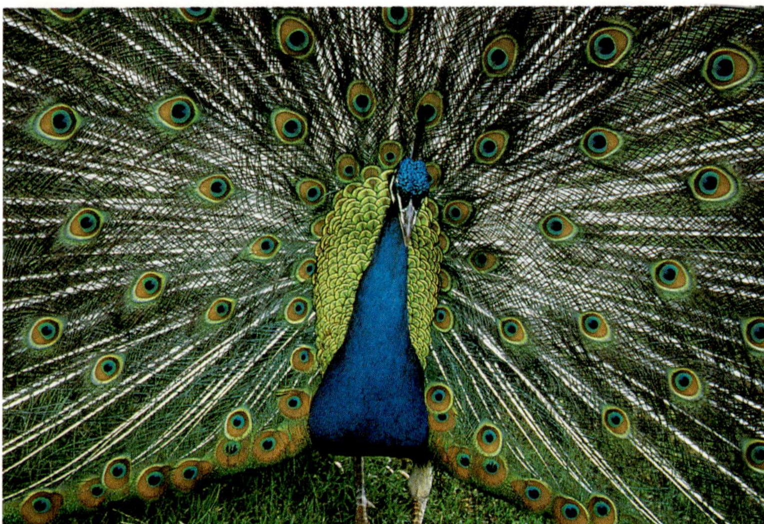

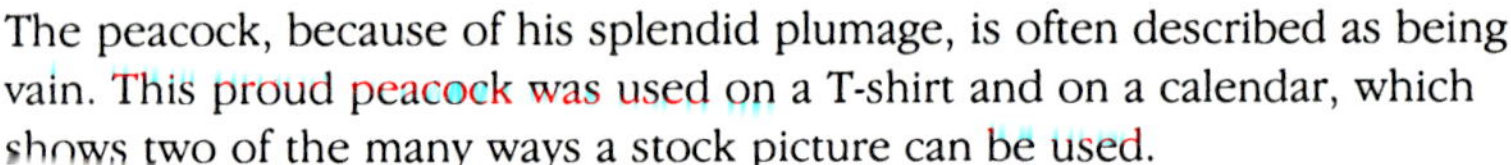

The peacock, because of his splendid plumage, is often described as being vain. This proud peacock was used on a T-shirt and on a calendar, which shows two of the many ways a stock picture can be used.

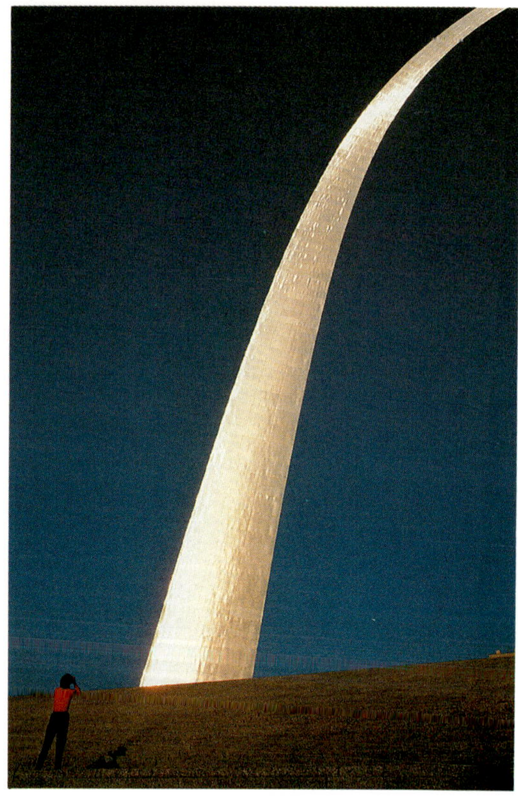

(Right) When photographing famous landmarks, such as the Gateway Arch in St. Louis, we take a traditional, safe shot and then try for an unusual view. This picture shows our unusual angle of the arch as it catches the light of the morning sun. Good photography does not always happen at convenient hours. As first-time tourists in St. Louis, we had to ask several local people for advice about where to be and at what time. We learned that the rising sun caught the base of the arch in the morning about 6:15, in the season when we were there. At 5:45 A.M. we were patiently waiting in place with our equipment.

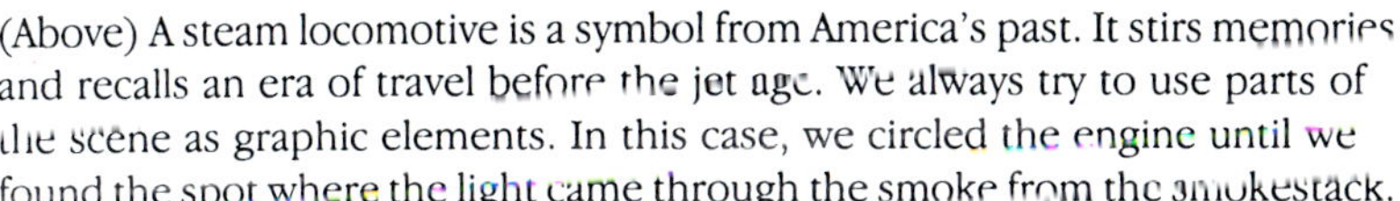

(Above) A steam locomotive is a symbol from America's past. It stirs memories and recalls an era of travel before the jet age. We always try to use parts of the scene as graphic elements. In this case, we circled the engine until we found the spot where the light came through the smoke from the smokestack.

(Right) Commuter traffic in and out of major cities is a good subject to shoot. Traffic congestion is a problem many people must contend with daily. We are frequently asked for photos of a busy highway. Many environmental-awareness articles also are illustrated with just such a picture.

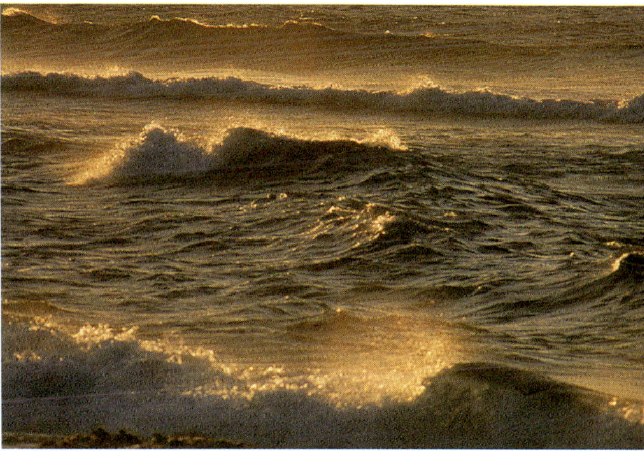

The ocean in its many moods is an ideal subject for the stock photographer. This picture of waves breaking depicts a restless ocean and has proven to be successful for stock purposes. A music cassette company used this photo on a cassette sleeve as the background for an inset picture and it was used as a postcard in France.

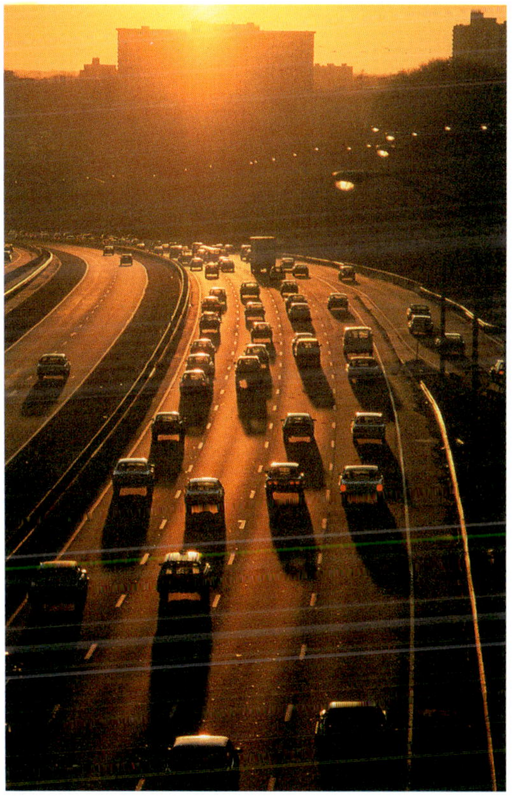

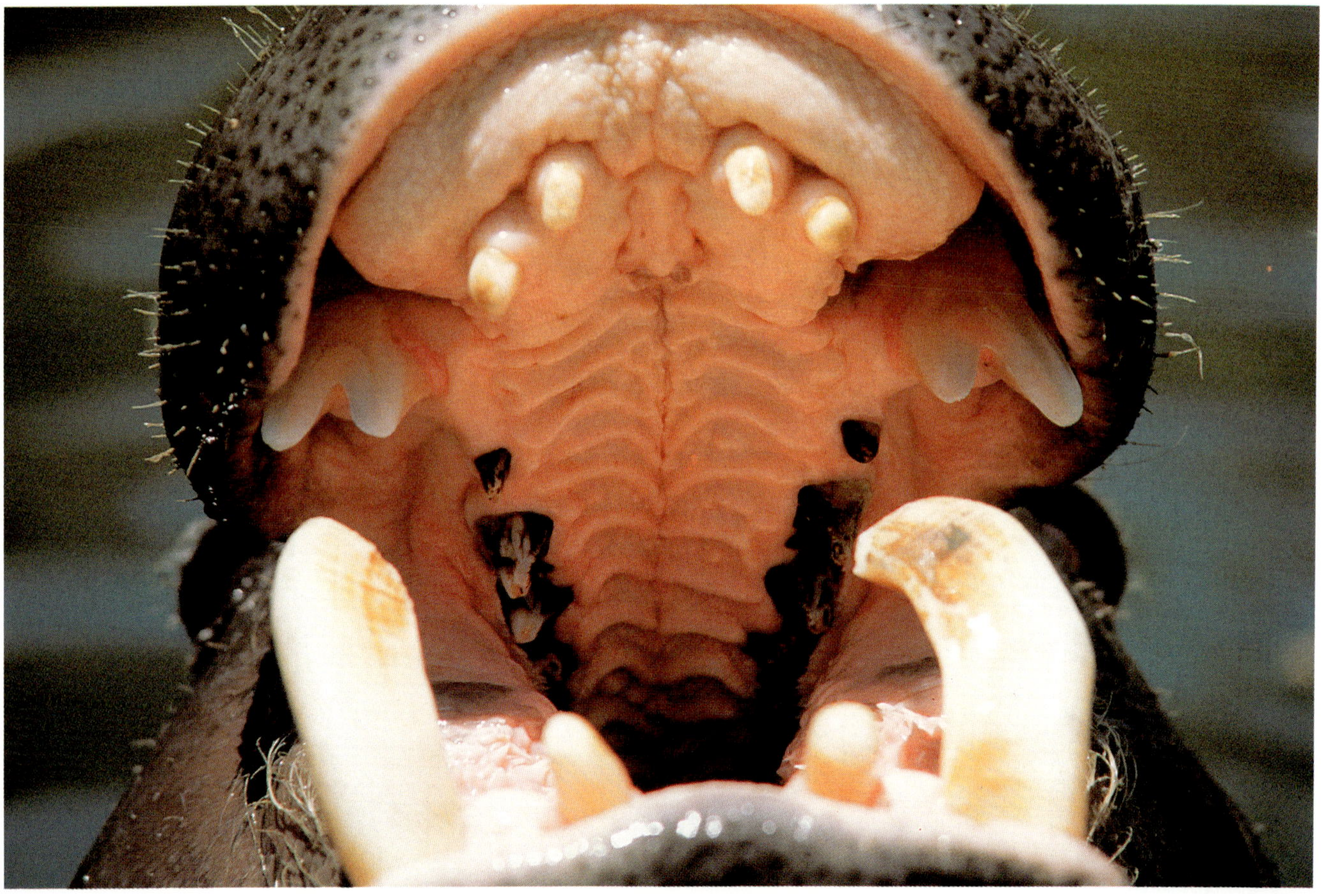

The open mouth of a hippopotamus might be used as an advertisement for diet pills or dental surgery. Such an image has many possibilities for stock sales. "Look Mom! No cavities!"

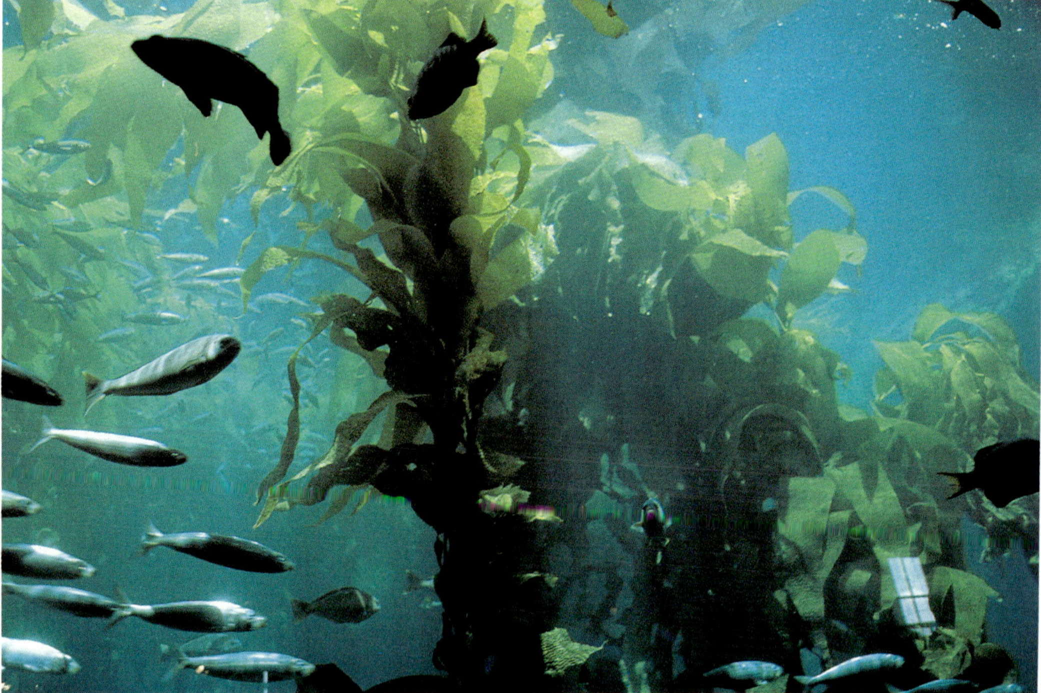

The Monterey Aquarium offers a land-bound photographer a chance to take pictures of an underwater kelp forest. This picture sold as a menu cover for a seafood restaurant.

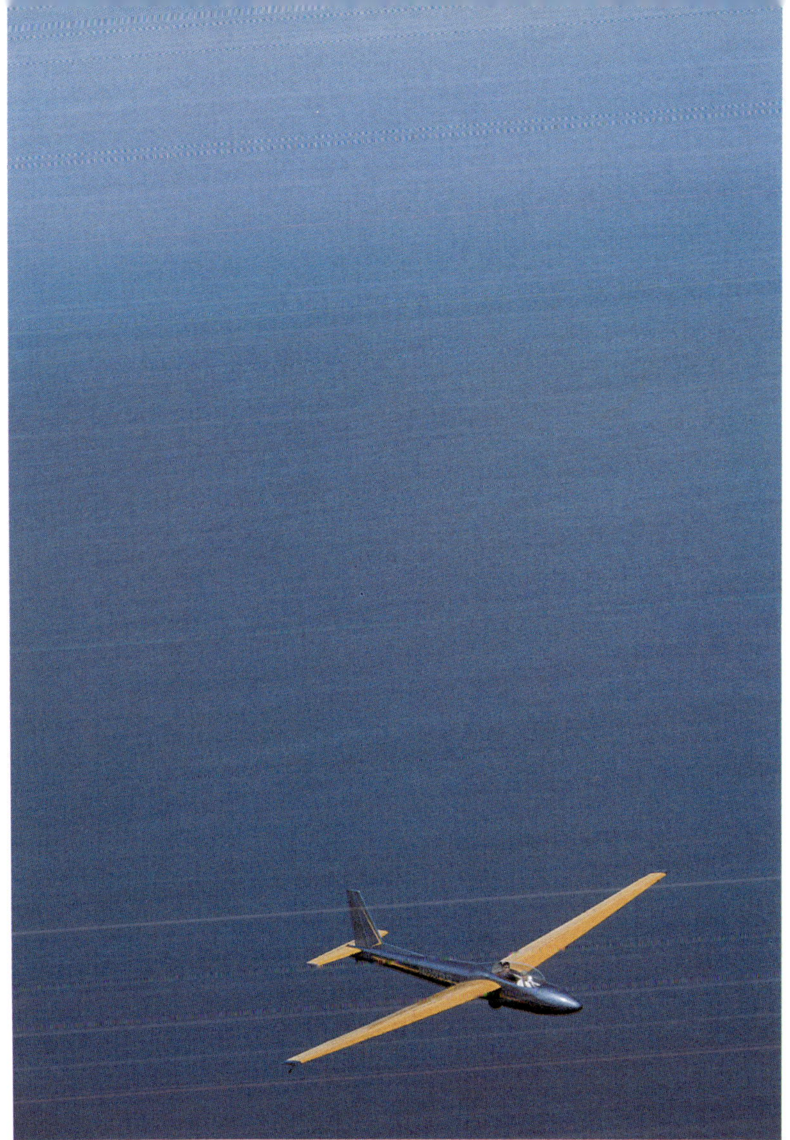

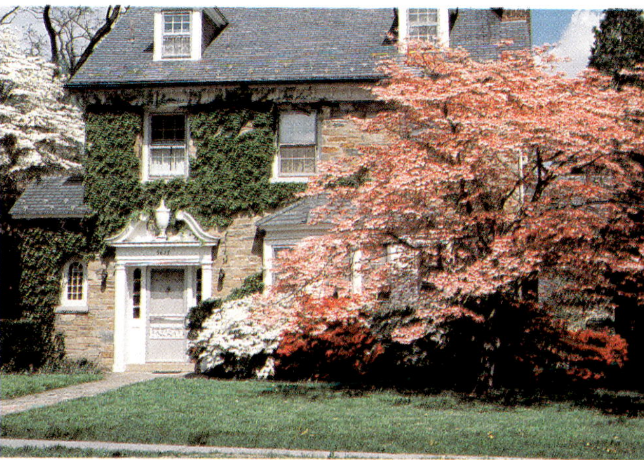

Homes are worthwhile subjects for stock if you get property releases from the owners. A property release is necessary if a picture of the house is to be used for advertising or any other commercial purpose. Try to take the photographs of homes in an attractive season. If the background is not very good, the alternative is to take the house at night, with all the windows lit up from inside.

(Below) People, especially Americans, dote on their pets. Cats and dogs with their owners are very popular subjects.

This picture of a glider or sailplane in Hawaii could meet a variety of needs. It might illustrate the concept of soaring freedom. Notice that we left ample space in the composition for reverse type or a magazine logo.

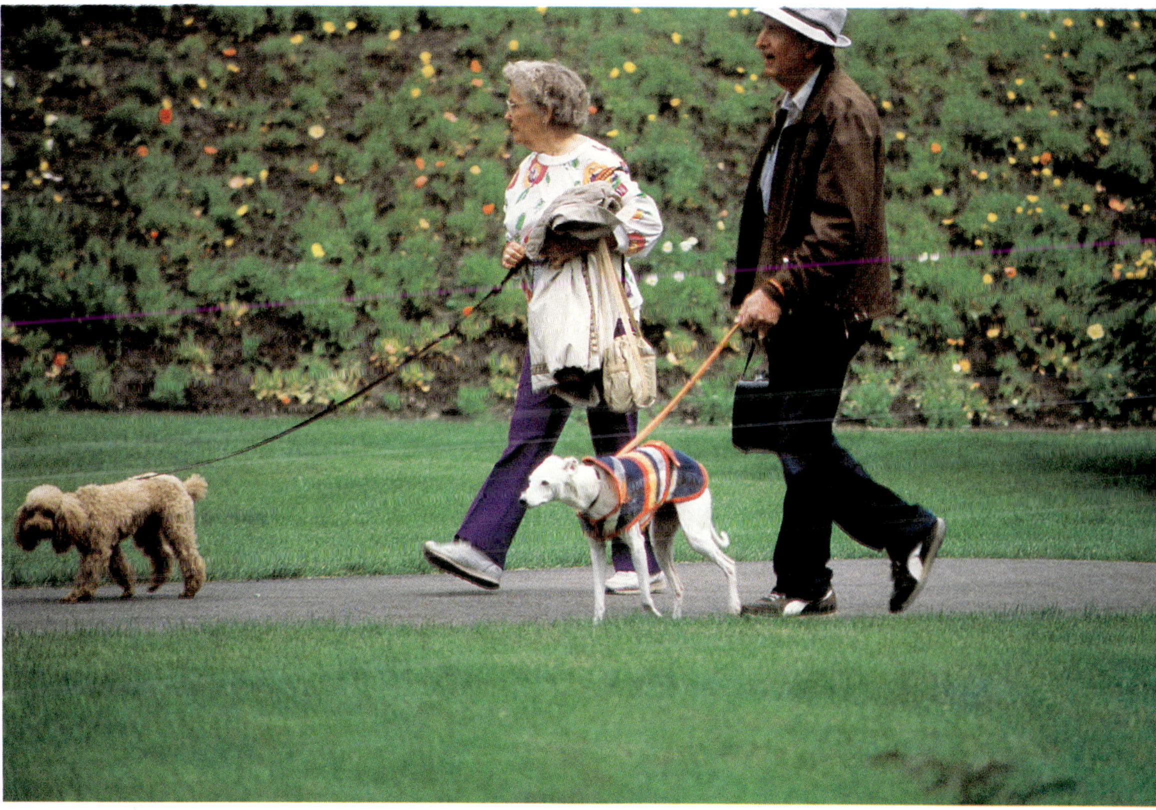

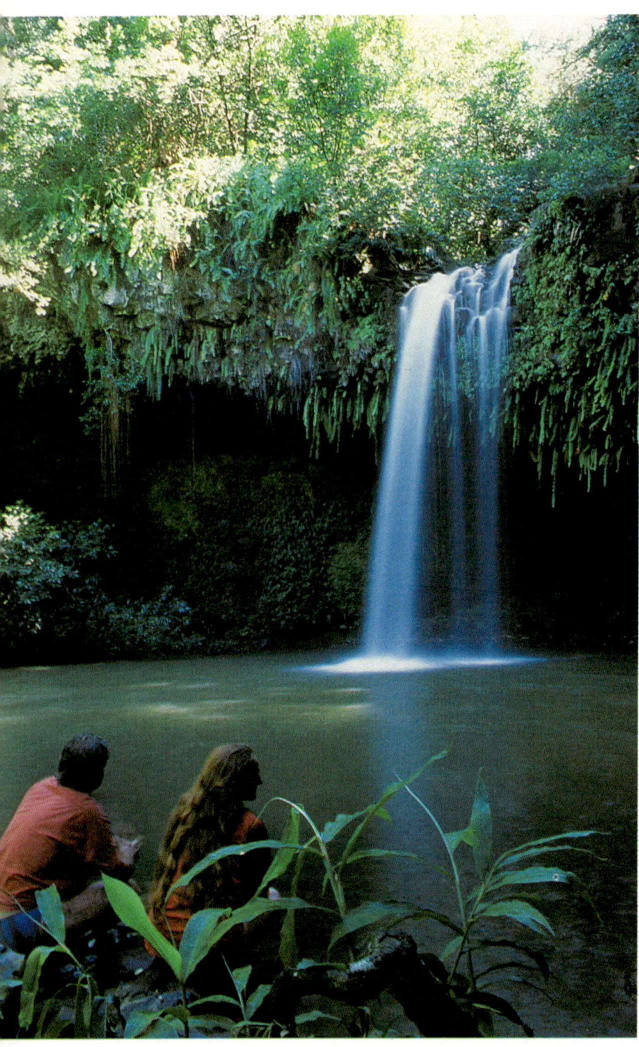

For travelers there is always a secret, dream paradise, a perfect place they hold in their hearts and minds. We try to create such travel images when we find ideal locations on our travels. This requires an awareness of light and a careful study of composition. This hidden waterfall on the island of Maui is typical of the dream images we try to create. In this instance, we set up a tripod and posed the couple in the foreground. The ten-second time exposure transformed the waterfall into a veil of flowing silk.

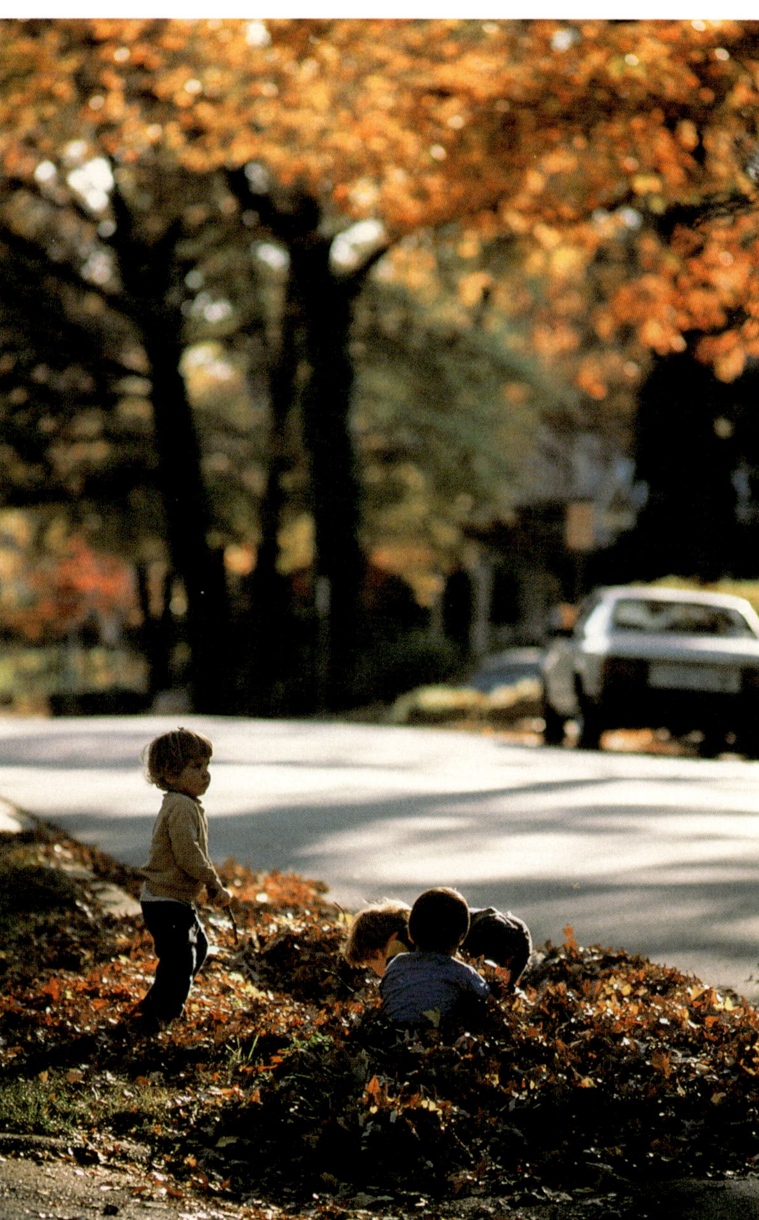

We caught this picture of children playing among fall leaves on a sunny afternoon in September. The light filtering through the trees enhanced the mood. It is the type of image that can be sold again and again for stock.

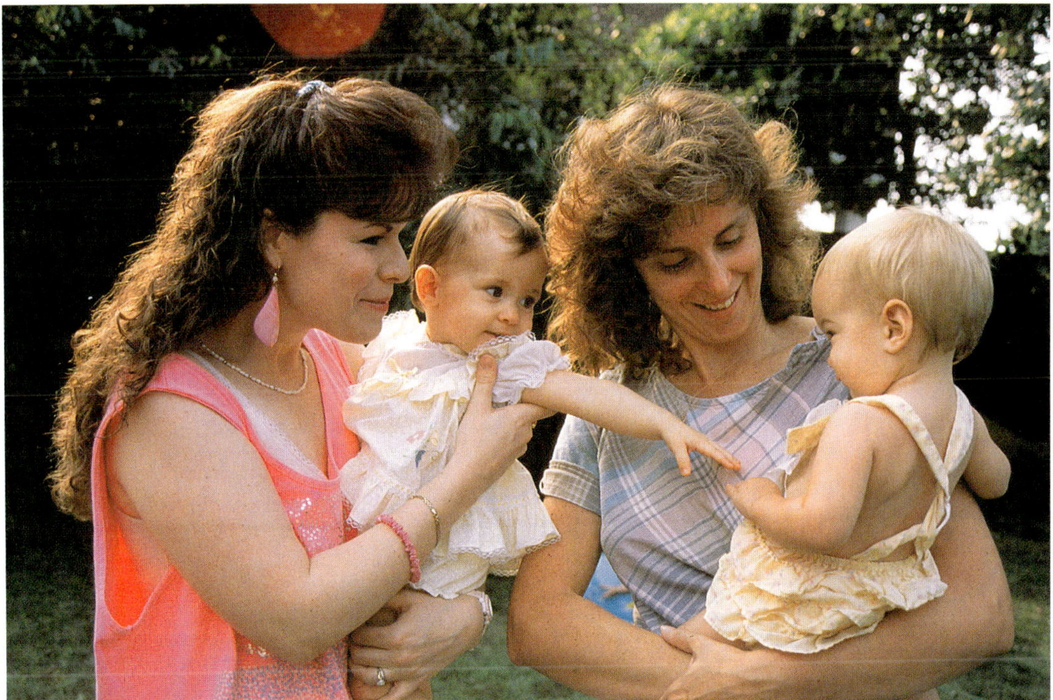

We took this picture of two young mothers with their babies when we attended a neighborhood picnic. Such shots are easy to get and make excellent stock pictures. We later gave the women color prints of the picture and asked them to sign model releases.

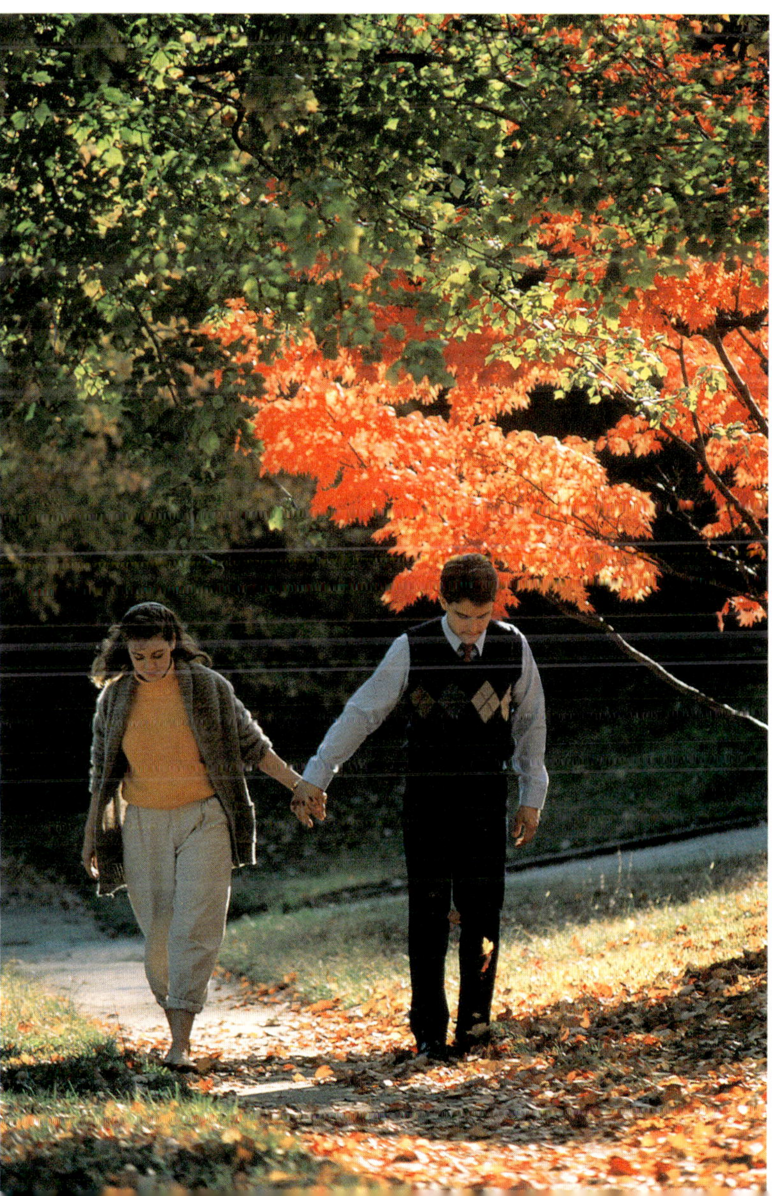

A young couple walk hand-in-hand along a leaf-covered sidewalk on a fall day. Actually, the couple is our son and daughter who agreed to pose for us. We often use our family for stock pictures.

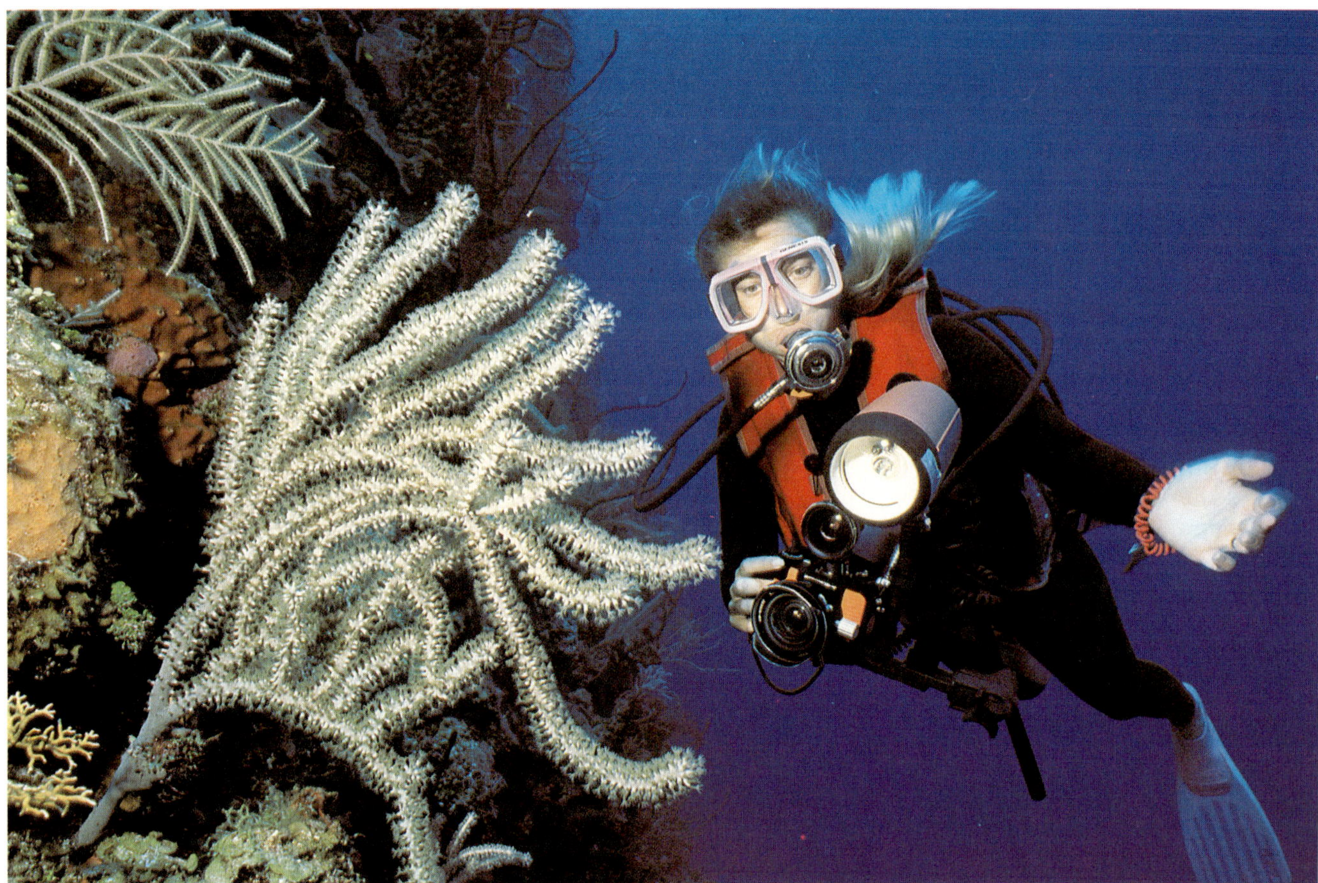

Diver and underwater photographer Donna MacLaughlin pauses in front of a Gorgonian sea fan on the Great Wall off the coast of Little Cayman in the Caribbean. This wall is reputed to be one of the three best diving sites in the world. Underwater photography is one of our specialties, but it requires underwater cameras and electronic flash to bring out colors. Some photographers devote their professional lives to shooting underwater pictures.

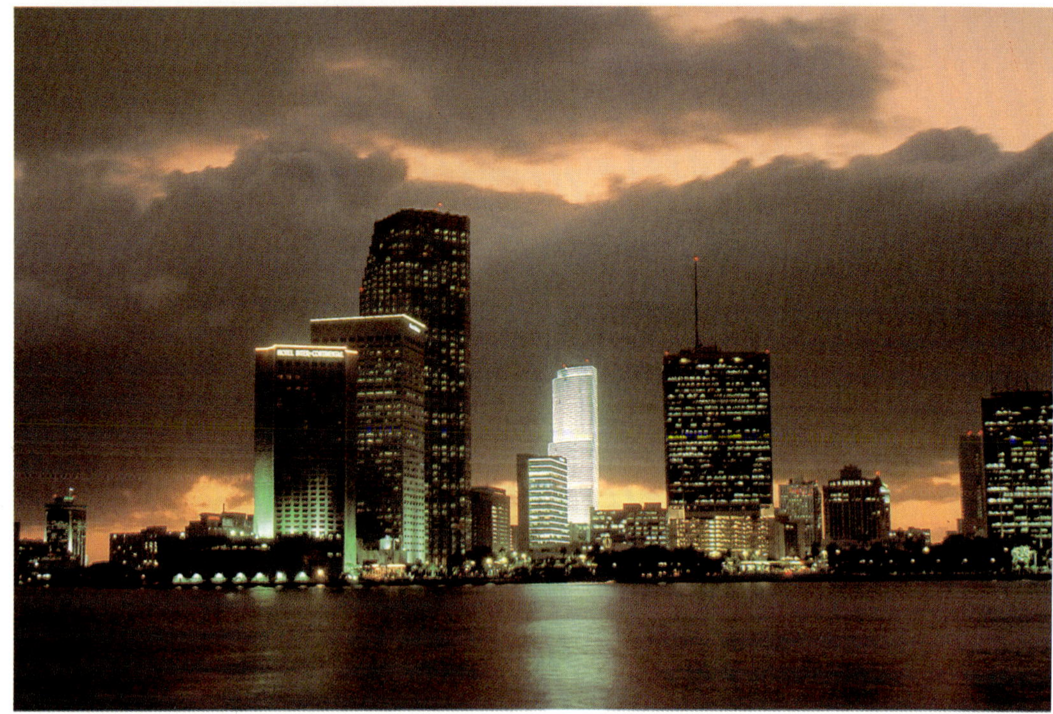

Major city skylines are always in demand, but remember that skylines change every time a new major building is erected. We shoot Miami from a choice location across Biscayne Bay whenever we are in southern Florida, as we do when visiting other major cities like New York City. We shoot these skylines during the day, at sunset and shortly after dark. The night shots are ideally done while there is still a touch of ambient light left in the sky.

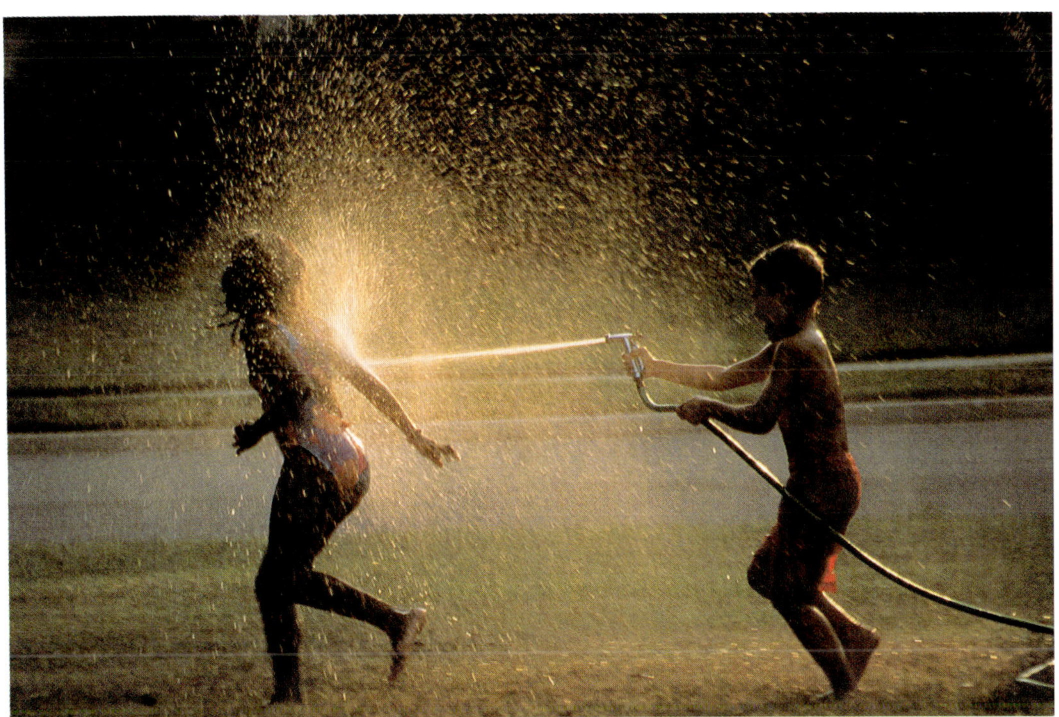

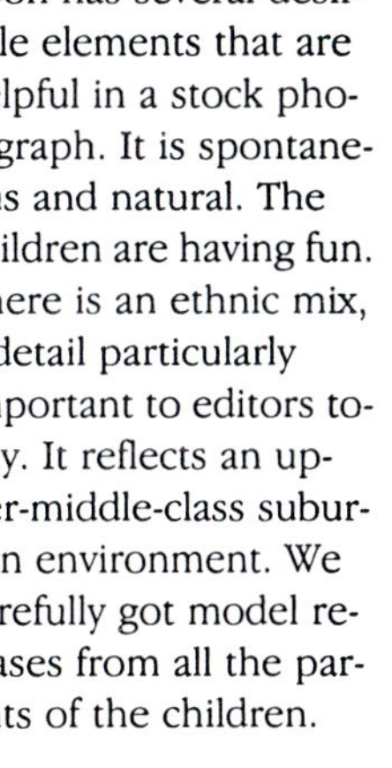

This picture of children playing with a hose on a hot summer afternoon has several desirable elements that are helpful in a stock photograph. It is spontaneous and natural. The children are having fun. There is an ethnic mix, a detail particularly important to editors today. It reflects an upper-middle-class suburban environment. We carefully got model releases from all the parents of the children.

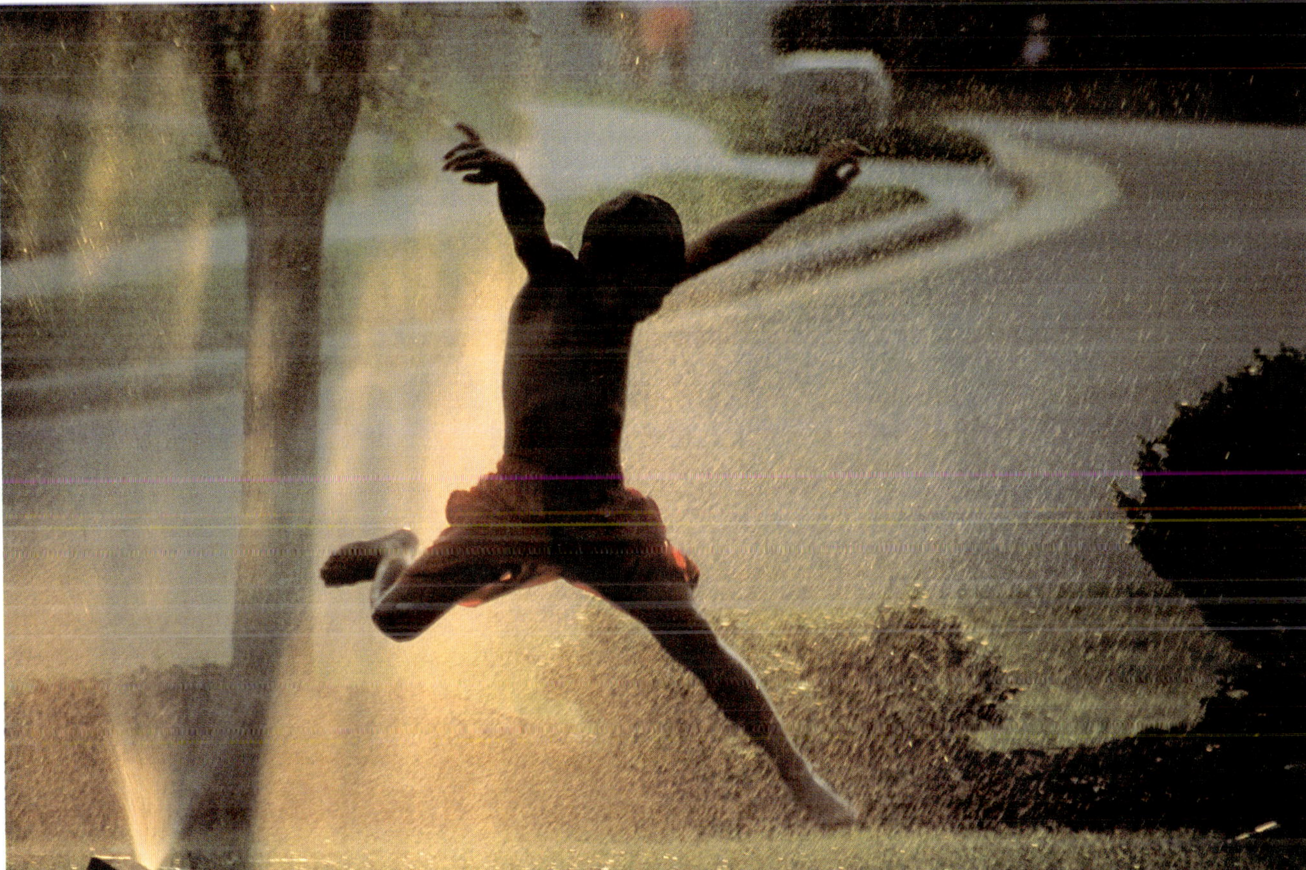

A young boy leaps in the spray of a sprinkler on a late summer afternoon, the droplets of water frozen in golden sunlight. This picture, taken just a few days before we finished this book, is an image in search of a market. It is one of our favorites and we feel it epitomizes the joy of childhood and the exuberance of youth. Unlike many stock pictures, we feel it captures a fleeting moment in time. This image may never be the kind that sells over and over again, but when the right art director sees and appreciates the picture, we feel confident it will be used in some sort of upscale institutional advertisement.

The perfect girl, the perfect beach, the perfect palm tree and the perfect sunset is a generic image of tropical paradise that sells again and again. We enhanced this sunset with the perfect graduated orange filter from Cokin. Let one pocket of your camera bag be your filter pocket. Filters are an inexpensive investment for richly enhanced photos.

This picture of two zebras in Kenya sold through one of our agencies for $10,000. The image appeared in the agency catalog. Non-exclusive rights were purchased for two years to promote McGraw Hill's multimedia encyclopedia. This allowed multiple use in the *New York Times*, *Investors Business Daily* and *Business Week*. With such a sale, the agency takes 50 percent and we receive 50 percent. Advertising sales are not unusual through stock photo agencies. We made a previous sale to the Nissan Motor Company through our Tokyo picture agency for $9,000.

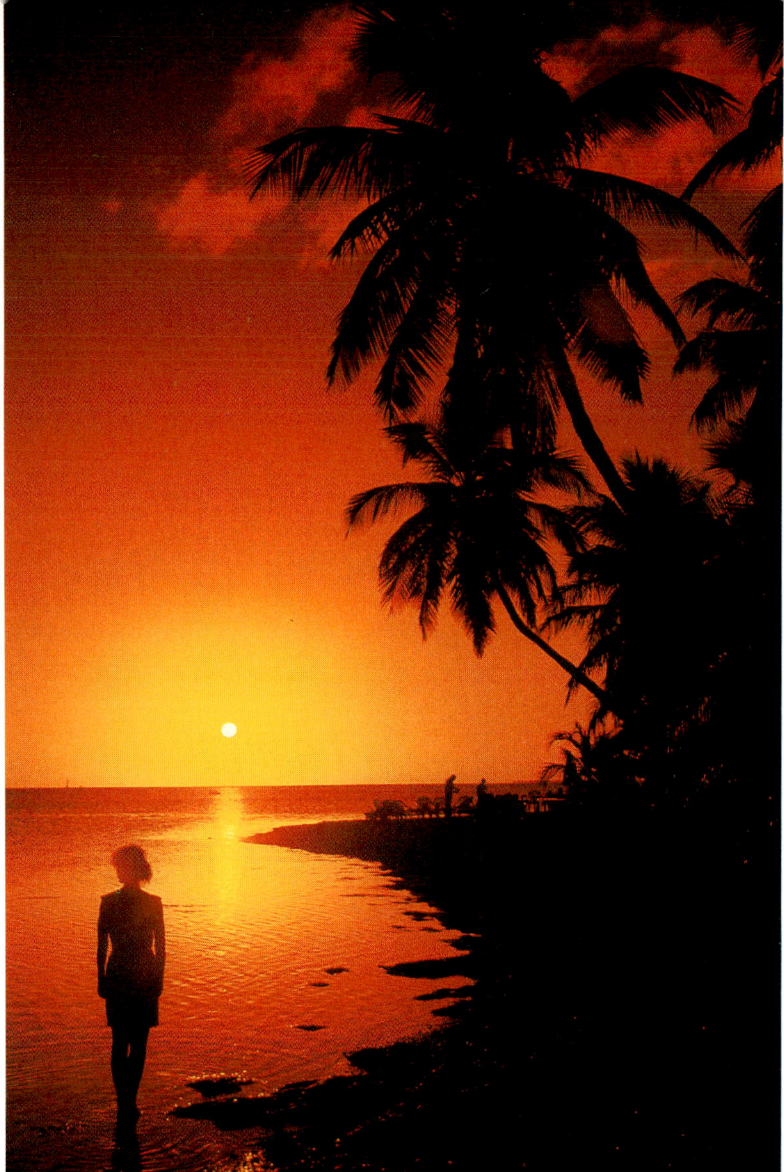

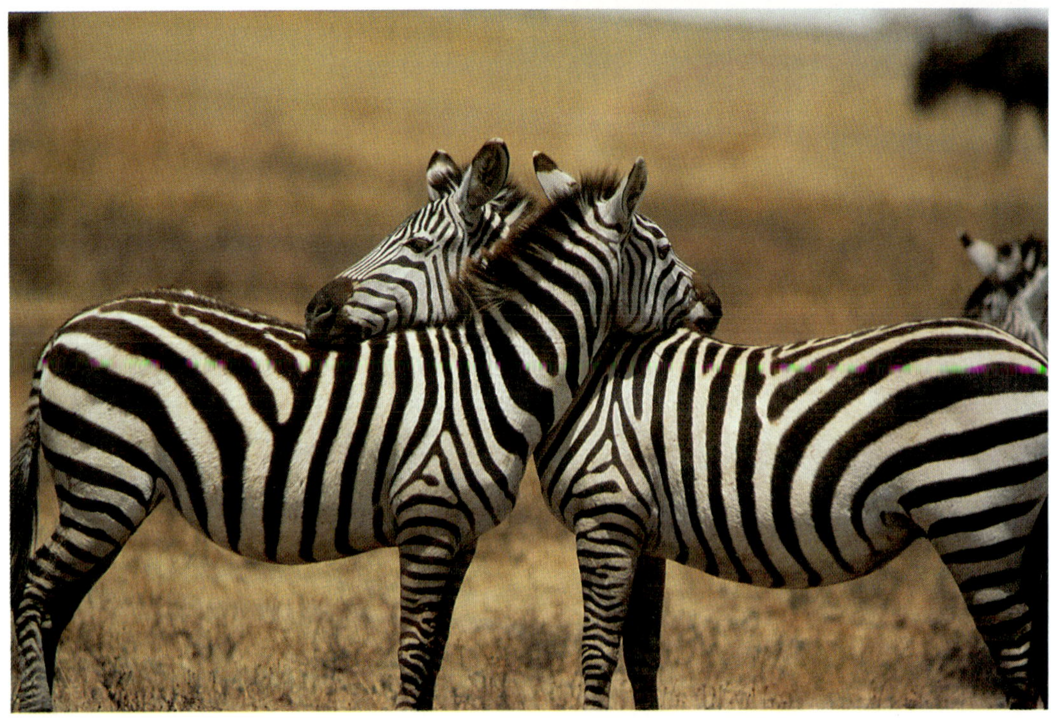

*Chapter 6*

# MARKETING AND SELLING YOUR OWN STOCK PHOTOS

We covered how to shoot stock pictures and how to file them. The next step is marketing those great images you have in your files. The first decision you must make is whether to sell stock yourself, to sell through a picture agency or a combination of both. We recommend the last option. Picture agencies will be covered in the next chapter, so here we will deal with self-marketing.

## THE STOCK LIST OR CATALOG

Whether you're selling widgets or stock pictures, the first job is to let potential customers know about your product. You will need a stock list or catalog of your picture subjects, which might include:

1. People
   a. Men
   b. Women
   c. Children
2. Animals
   a. Wild
   b. Domestic
3. Countries
   a. England
   b. France
   c. Germany

The easiest way to create a stock list is to type your subjects on your letterhead and make a number of photocopies. Actually, a stock list or catalog can be much more elaborate, even to the point of including four-color reproductions of samples of your photography.

We created our catalog with our Macintosh computer and a desktop publishing program. (The same can be done on an IBM or IBM-compatible computer.) The software allowed us to design the publication and illustrate it with clever drawings. For reasons of economy, we chose not to use four-color examples of our pictures in the catalog, but inserted a color sheet example of our pictures, which was printed for another purpose. This is mailed to clients and potential clients. We update our catalog at least once a year. (See pages 66-67 in chapter four.)

## PHOTOGRAPHIC STYLE

Most photographers, intentionally or unintentionally, develop their own style. Some well-known names such as Richard Avedon, Pete Turner and Cartier Bresson have such distinctive styles that picture editors can identify their work at a glance. To some degree, we all have our own style, but it is important to remember that the primary purpose in stock photography is to produce good, useable pictures with a broad appeal. If such pictures happen to embody your style, that is well and good. The most versatile photographers can adopt a style to meet their needs and suit their subject. For instance, you can shoot for strong graphic color and design when you have the right subject. On the other hand, other subjects might call for a straight photojournalistic approach.

## SPECIALIZING

There is some value in specializing. If you are an outstanding food photographer, hopefully you will get numerous stock requests for table settings and kitchen scenes of food preparation. If your name becomes known because you specialize in a specific area, this can be very beneficial. Just remember that it is up to you to get the word around to the right picture editors and art directors about your specialization. Here are just a few other areas in which photographers specialize:

- Wildlife
- Antiques
- Boating
- Water Sports
- Skiing
- Aircraft
- Computers
- Automobiles
- Trains
- Underwater

The list is potentially endless. Some photographers already have a special interest or expertise in a particular subject and have existing pictures on this subject in their files. It is to their advantage to expand their coverage on this subject. Other photographers choose a subject in which to specialize and methodically go about taking the necessary pictures to build their file in the chosen area.

Our colleague, Kjell Sandved with the Smithsonian Institution, is a photographer who has become very well known for his pictures of wildlife. His files contain striking images of penguins, eagles, white tigers, seals, lions and gorillas. He has produced and marketed a number of striking posters. One of the most memorable is a series of close-ups of butterfly wings, each with a design that simulates a letter of the alphabet. These colorful pictures spell out the entire alphabet from A to Z. They are sold in zoo and nature center gift shops.

Another colleague, Len Kaufmann of Florida, has specialized in Brazil and Central America. Editors have learned to call him when they need strong images from these countries.

While we encourage photographers to specialize, we do not think they should do this to the exclusion of general coverage. We specialize in travel, and this is such a broad subject that we pick up hundreds of generic shots on every trip. It was a wise choice. We have been able to fill specialized needs and wide-spectrum photo requests from our stock files. Our choice of travel photography also has let us do what we like to do best, travel together, while in the guise of doing work and earning a living.

## THE NEEDS OF THE MARKETPLACE

A major key to success in stock photography is understanding the needs of the market. The best way to do this is to study

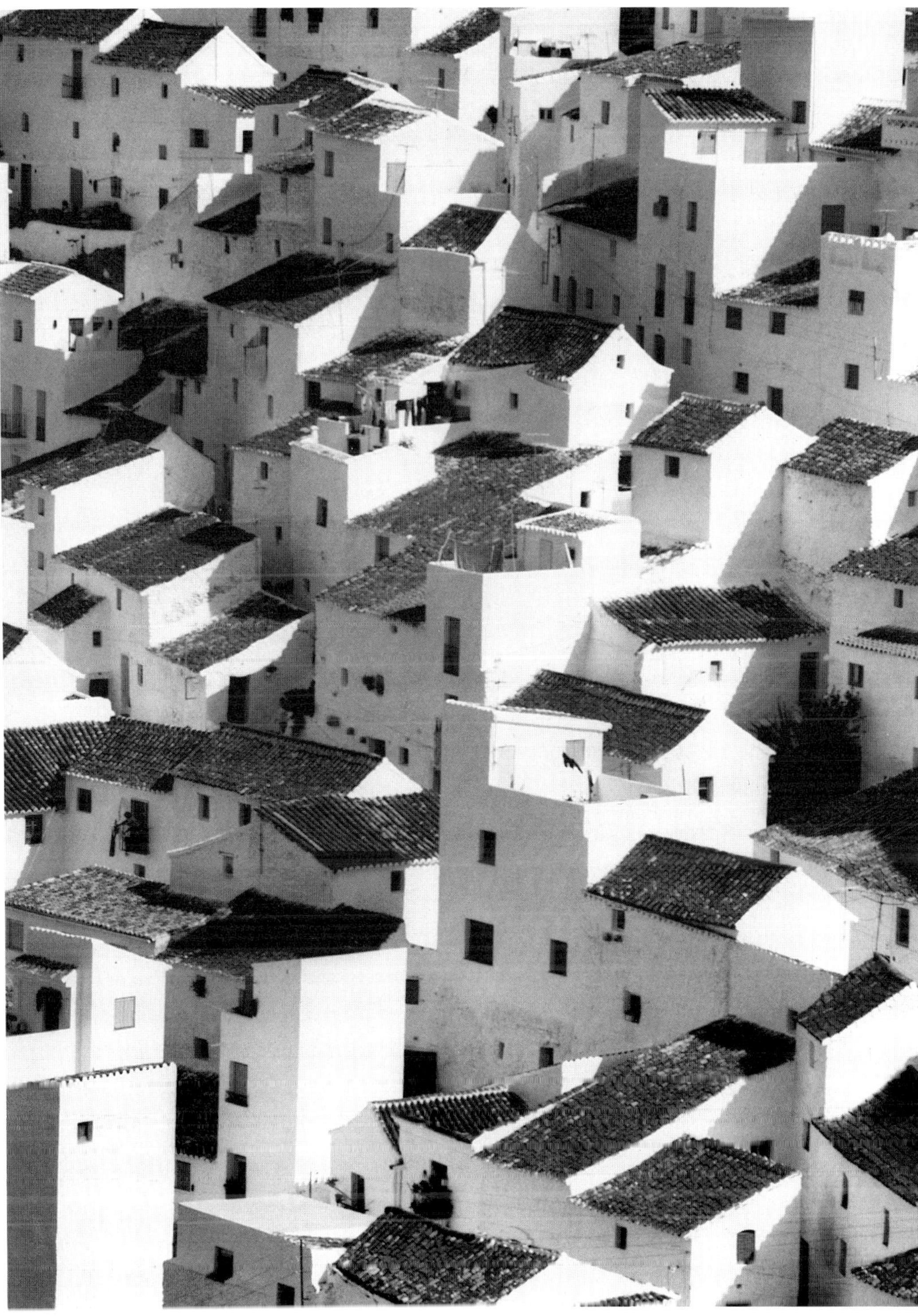

The mountain town of Caesares is typical of the white-walled villages of Spain. This shot has been used frequently to illustrate travel articles on the Iberian Peninsula.

the major magazines, both their editorial photographs and their advertising pictures. This will give you a good sense of what sells.

Look at textbooks and other types of publications. This knowledge is vital when it comes to shooting and when you make pulls for a submission. Picture researchers know the difference in the style of pictures they would submit to *National Geographic* as opposed to *Conde Nast Traveler*. As a stock photographer, it is important for you to have an understanding of different styles as well as the subject matter sought by specific magazines. For instance, it would be inappropriate to submit pictures of hunters to *National Wildlife*.

The major picture agencies make a careful study of what sells and if they don't have a hot subject in their files, they ask their photographers to shoot it. They do this by periodically sending out want lists to their photographers. As a stock photographer, you're actually a one-person agency and you should analyze which subjects sell well and which of these is not in your current file. As you look at the magazines and even TV still shots, remember that these are the images that sell certain concepts. Then go out and shoot them. To some extent, this requires foresight. For example, we went to Spain in advance of the 1992 Olympics and Expo, the World's Fair in Seville held that same year. We thought Spain would be hot in 1992 and we were right.

## SELF-PROMOTION BY ADVERTISING

### Sourcebooks

You have a product to sell and every business needs promotion and advertising. There are various places to advertise your stock file. The most common is called a "sourcebook." These were originally published in New York under such names as the *Red Book*, the *Black Book* and the *ASMP Sourcebook*. More recently other sourcebooks have come out in major cities throughout the country, some contending to be national and others specifying regional distribution. Most often photographers advertise in these books to seek assignment work, but stock sources also advertise with varying degrees of success. Space in these books is expensive, ranging from about $1,000 a page to as much as $10,000. Naturally the picture or pictures you use and the accompanying words are crucial to the success of the advertisement. The other important factor is the distribution of the book. Normally sourcebooks are given free to major picture buyers. If your work is mostly editorial in nature, it would not be useful to advertise in a sourcebook that goes mainly to art directors of advertising agencies. We have used sourcebooks with moderate success.

In making a decision on a sourcebook, it is wise to get a sample book published the previous year and an unbiased opinion. Don't rely on the book publisher to provide names, but call several photographers, taking their names at random from the book, and ask what kind of results they got from their advertisement and if they were pleased. Be sure that you talk to stock sources as opposed to photographers seeking assignment work.

Sourcebooks usually provide an advertiser with a certain number of printed sheets, often on slightly heavier stock than used in the book. Additional sheets can be ordered at a nominal cost. You can use these as direct mail promotion. We also insert them in our color slide catalog to show the quality of our color photography.

There are two other publications designed specifically for photo researchers and picture editors. These are the *Stock Photo and Assignment Source Book*, edited by Fred W. McDarrah at 127 E. 59th

St., New York, NY 10022, (212) 838-8640, and the *Stock Workbook*, published by Scott & Daughters Publishing, 940 N. Highland Ave., Los Angeles, CA 90038, (213) 856-0008 or (800) 547-2688.

The *Stock Workbook* is a massive and glossy book in full color that mostly features spreads by picture agencies, but it does include advertisements by a few individual photographers. Space rates are high compared to the smaller *Stock Photo and Assignment Source Book*, which is in black and white.

A newcomer on the scene is *Direct Stock*, a stock photography catalog designed specifically to accept the work of individual photographers and puts those photographers in direct contact with buyers. The minimum space you can buy in this book is one page for $1,995 plus $75 for each separation. The telephone number for *Direct Stock* is (212) 979-6560.

### Agency Catalogs

Although stock agencies will be discussed in detail in chapter seven, the agency catalogs should also be mentioned here. If you have started working with an agency that puts out color catalogs, and the agency wishes to use some of your photographs in the catalog, you will often be asked to bear some of the catalog production cost. This fee is usually deducted, slowly over the space of several months, from the income that your photos have generated over the billing period. Generally, the pictures chosen for an agency catalog tend to earn money quite well. The expense of having your photos included in the catalog can sometimes be paid off with just one or two good sales.

## SELF-PROMOTION BY MAIL

### Signatures

The very best advertising you can get is absolutely free. This is the publication of some of your best work in a national magazine. Quite a few years ago we had a major spread of pictures (six pages) in *Popular Photography*. Many top picture editors saw and admired that spread. As a result, we received several important assignments and sold many of our stock pictures, including images that had appeared in the magazine. We had the foresight to ask the editor to print an overrun of that particular signature. The cost of about $300 was very reasonable compared to what it would have cost to have several thousand full-color brochures printed from scratch. We used these in a direct mail campaign to our clients and to a target mailing list we purchased. After all, we reasoned, not all of our potential clients had seen the original article in *Popular Photography*. In some cases, it may be necessary to purchase the whole magazine, but this can usually be done at a substantial discount when you deal directly with the editor or publisher.

We also had a two-page color signature printed from our book, *A Guide to Travel Writing & Photography*, also published by Writer's Digest. It was a fold-over sheet, blank on the front and the back. We chose two of our favorite pictures to be used on the blank pages. Our names, address and phone number were printed along with the picture on the last page. The cost was $800 for 2,000 copies, a bargain in these days of high-cost printing.

The alternative to advertising or signature overruns is to work with a commer-

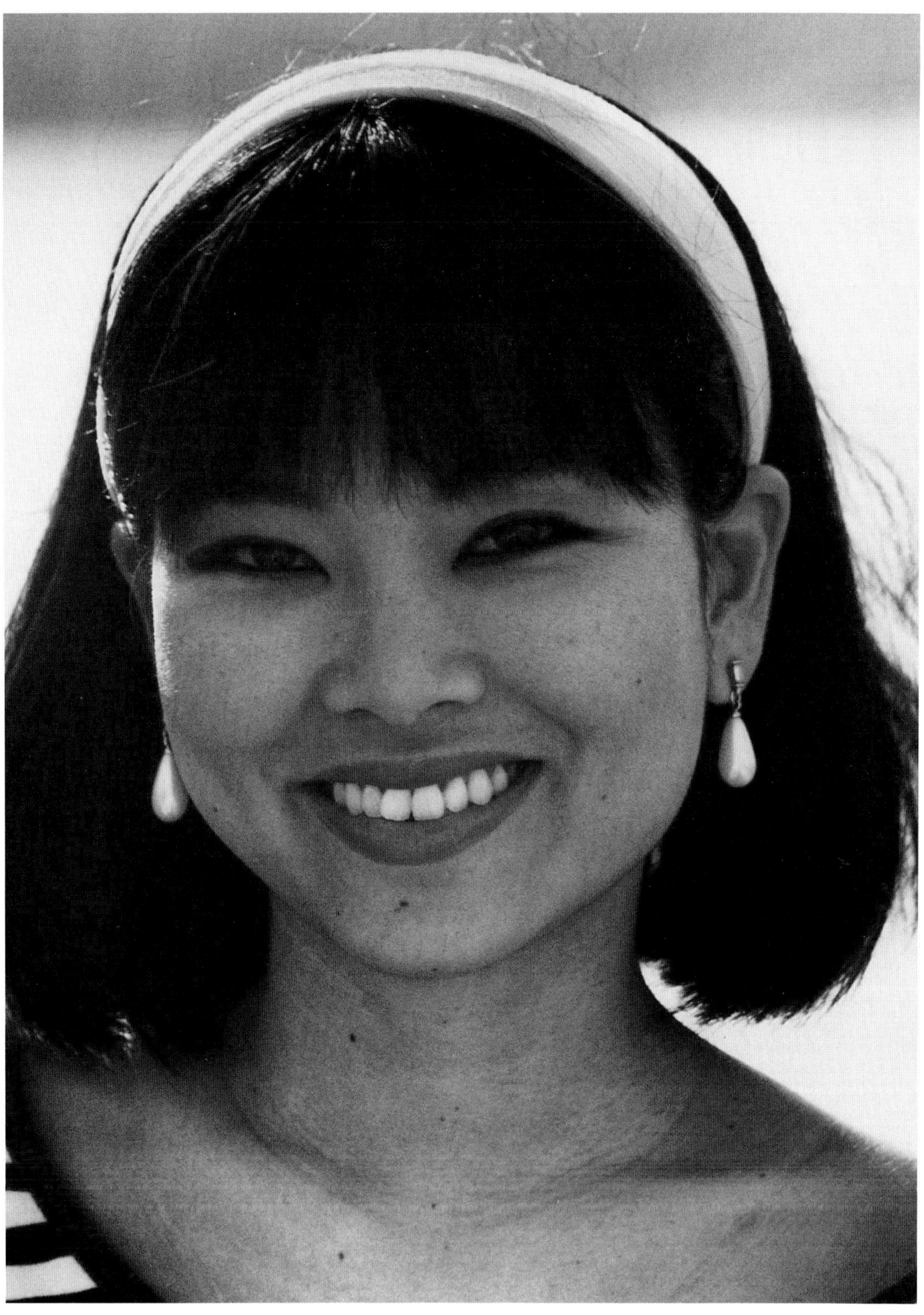

As we travel, we are always on the lookout for attractive faces. This young woman works in public relations in Honolulu and was glad to give us a model release. When you are photographing people, never forget to take a few close-up shots. These are usually the best-sellers.

cial printer and produce your own brochure. As mentioned earlier, this can be expensive, but the major advantage is that the brochure can be designed for your specific needs. You can expect to pay about $5,000 for a high-quality, four-page brochure (8½-by-11 inches) on glossy paper. While some stock photographers opt to design their own brochure, there are advantages to hiring a competent designer to lay out the pictures and choose the fonts for the text. It is extremely important that your brochure look professional, and the few hundred dollars for the services of a designer is money well spent.

## Desktop Publishing

If you happen to have the computer, the necessary programs for desktop publishing and some talent in design, it is possible to do your own brochure for a fraction of the cost of going to a designer and working with a leading printer. (We cover desktop publishing in more detail later in this chapter.)

Adobe PageMaker and Adobe Photoshop used with a slide scanner and a Macintosh or IBM with 16 to 20MB of RAM, will give you the tools needed to design your own brochure and make color separations that can be delivered directly to a printer on a floppy disk. This will allow you to negotiate a much better price with the printer, especially if you agree to accept the results on the first run. This sounds risky, but we know photographers who have done this with great success and saved thousands of dollars. See chapter eight for more desktop publishing possibilities.

## 70mm Duplicates

There is a way to show examples of your color work without doing an expensive four-color printing job, especially if your mailing list is relatively small. Suppose you have taken a toe-curling, prize-winning picture that is sure to catch the eye of any picture editor. It is possible to have a 35mm slide duplicated up to a 70mm transparency and put into a 4-by-5-inch mount.

These duplicates cost as little as $2.50 each, depending on quantity. If you want the picture editors of *Life*, *National Geographic*, *Travel & Leisure* and *Travel Holiday* to see a particular picture, this is a practical solution. The format is large enough that it will not be ignored and it can be mailed along with your stock list or catalog. We have found that editors who do not have a light table really like the 70mm duplicates because they can hold them up to a window or room light to see the details of the photograph with ease.

The 70mm has not only become a useful marketing tool for us; we also use it when publishers do not want the responsibility of handling many original slides. For instance, all the color pictures in our last Writer's Digest book, *A Guide to Travel Writing & Photography*, and the book you are holding now came solely from 70mm slides. There are not many companies in the United States who can make sharp, rich true-color 70mm dupes. The best 70mm duplicate slides are made by Repro Images, 243 Church St, N.W., Vienna, VA 22180, (800) 998-3873 or (703) 938-2604. Repro Images also makes reproduction quality 35mm duplicate slides that can actually be better than the original! (If it is necessary, they have developed a liquid gate that they use to eliminate scratches when copying the original.)

## Using Your Promotional Tools

After you have a brochure, overrun of a signature or extra sheets from a sourcebook, you have a promotional tool that demonstrates the quality of your work. The next step is to see that your clients and potential clients receive your stock photography list and color samples. You already have a list of your current clients. Where can you get the names and addresses of other picture editors and art directors who might be interested in using your work? One of the best sources is an annual publication called *Photographer's Market* published by Writer's Digest Books and available in many bookstores. The entries in this detailed book tell what each picture buyer is looking for and approximately what rates they pay. Go through the book carefully and compile a list of potential clients. We do this on a computer, adding crucial information such as specialties about that market, in addition to names and addresses.

Another valuable source of markets is a firm called Creative Access based in Chicago. For a fee they will provide you with an up-to-date set of mailing labels of all picture buyers in any special category. For instance, they can send you a list of all buyers who purchase travel pictures. If you can narrow your field down, acquiring such a list can be a good investment.

In addition to a direct mail campaign, enclose your picture catalog and brochure in each new picture submission you make. Leave these promotional materials with every picture editor and art director you call on. If you meet a potential client in a social situation, ask for his or her business card and send them your promotional package by mail. You can never tell when these efforts will result in a big stock sale. Often it will be months or even years later.

The new computer technology can be very helpful in creating professional-looking business cards, personalized letterheads and invoices, not to mention that indispensable stock catalog. Programs such as Aldus PageMaker, QuarkXPress, Publish It and Aldus Personal Press allow you to lay out any printed product from a one-page brochure to a complete book. A desktop publishing program allows you to create banner headlines, set columns, choose from a variety of fonts and even import clip art. It may take a few days to learn the ropes for using one of these programs, but the money you save is well worth the investment, the time and the effort. Desktop publishing programs are available for both Macintosh and IBM systems. For the best results you will need a laser printer, but if you do not have one, it is possible to take your disk to computer print shops and have the necessary pages printed out for a nominal cost, often less than a dollar a page. These can be copied on a copy machine or taken to a local printing shop for reproduction in the quantity needed.

## The Important Last Step of Promotional Mailing

It is a fruitless exercise for you to get all your material together for a fantastic mailing, blitz the country with your packages, and then sit back waiting for the results. Without follow-up, your material will end up in the wastebasket and your name will be forgotten. You need to set up a cast-in-concrete schedule for your marketing.

For example, you can decide that every Monday morning, you will mail out twenty promotional packages. Ten days later you should follow-up with twenty calls to the recipients of that Monday's mailing. Some of your packages will have been thrown away without perusal by secretaries or mail room clerks. You can offer to send another, marked "Personal Attention." You should ask if you can help with any projects that are coming up. Over the period of one or two months, you can refine your new "promotional list" to potential clients who have shown an interest and a need for your work. For this list, repeat your mailing/telephoning exercise with new material every few months.

## SELF-PROMOTION BY IN-PERSON PRESENTATIONS

### Looking Professional

What we covered in chapter four and in this chapter has been designed to help you look professional. You may still be an amateur photographer, hoping to sell some of your pictures, but no matter what your status, it is important to look professional in terms of your business cards, stationery, stock list, brochures and picture submissions. If you look and act professional, you'll be treated accordingly.

### Meeting a Potential Client

When you send a mailing to someone within driving distance, it is a good idea to try to set an appointment, during your follow-up telephone call, so that you can come personally to show examples of your work. It is harder to say "no" to a warm body than to throw mail into the trash can. Some of your most important contacts will be made when you meet editors and art directors in person.

Although you may normally wear Docker's jeans and a photographer's vest when you are taking photographs, you should dress appropriately to go to someone's office. Most art buyers work in suit-and-tie offices. If you come into the office looking like a dusty Indiana Jones, you will not be projecting an image of efficiency and quality.

You should bring some examples of your work, preferably a portfolio and some slides, a catalog or color slide index, a notepad and a pocket calendar. Keep careful notes, later to be transcribed on your computer Rolodex, of the kinds of projects this company does, preferences if any are stated (such as types of film preferred), who to contact to ask about future projects, and how often you should call for updates. The calendar will be invaluable if assignments or future appointments are discussed. Sometimes the person you are seeing will want to refer you to another, more appropriate, department or person, and you can make the appointment before you leave the office.

### Creating a Portfolio

The most important tool in such meetings is your portfolio. This is a collection of color prints and/or tear sheets put into a ringed notebook with clear acetate or Mylar sheets with black paper inserts. Some photographers use a large artist's portfolio, capable of holding a full newspaper page; we prefer a slightly smaller one, which can be packed inside a suitcase when we are traveling. Pick only your strongest work to put in your portfolio. When getting started in the business, you may include mainly high-quality color prints made from your slides. As you have more and more pictures published it is helpful to show examples of your published work. We will often include the logo of the magazine next to a picture, especially if it is a prestigious magazine

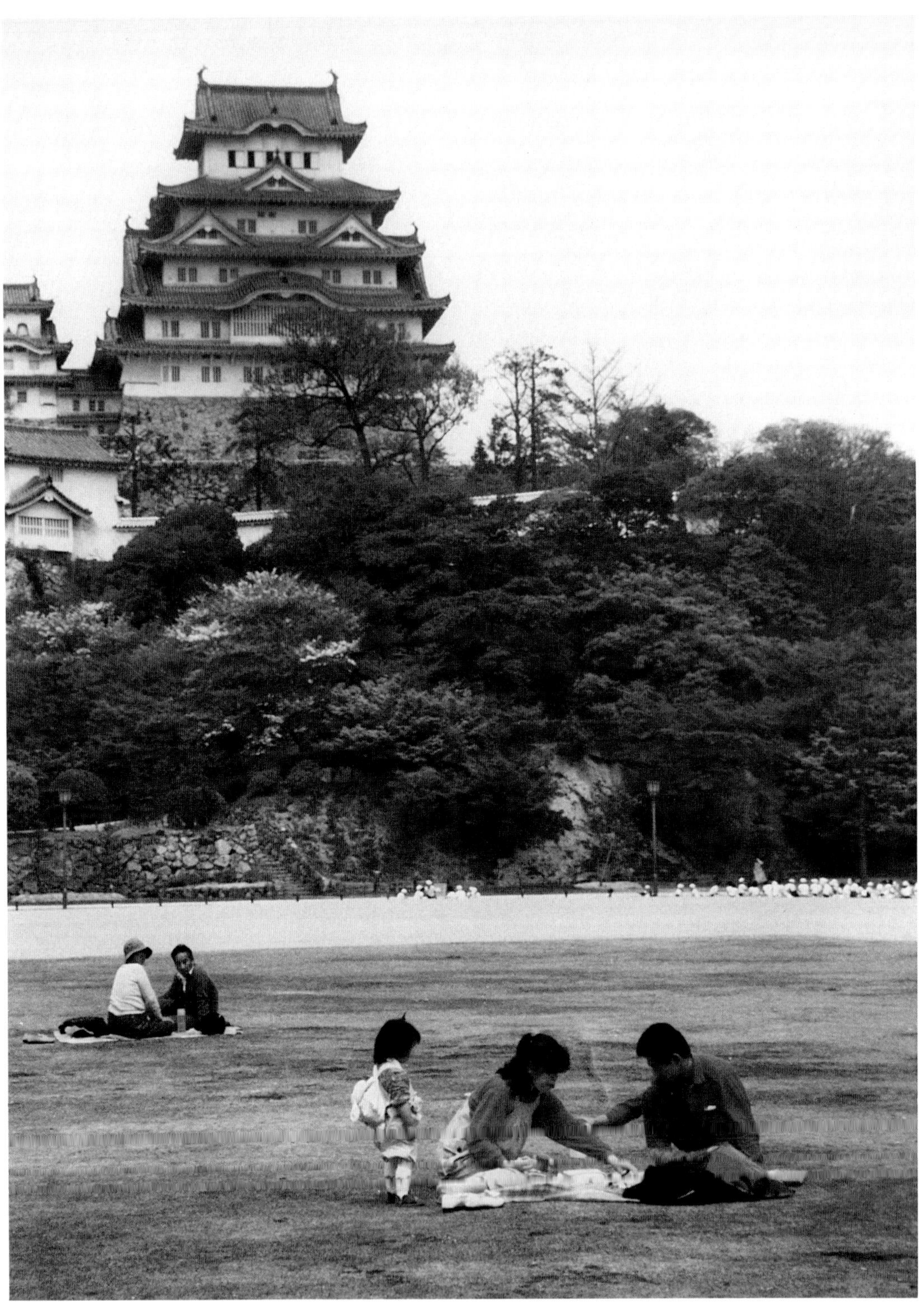

This scene of a family picnic in Japan combines not only the people and the distinctive architecture of this Asian country, but it also is a study of family relationships in Japan. Whenever you can get several generations together, you are creating a stock shot that will make you money.

such as *Life* or *National Geographic*.

Care should be taken in arranging the pictures on a portfolio page. Caption and supplementary information can be done on white cards with a laser printer or by hand with India ink. The exterior of your portfolio, like your pictures, should be attractive and eye appealing. Many portfolios are leather, with edge zippers and a handle. Remember that your portfolio is a presentation of your very best work, virtually an extension of yourself. Some photographers make mini-portfolios, color prints of their very best pictures and tear sheets in a smaller size, like 8-by-10 inches. These can be mailed to editors and art directors outside of your immediate city with return postage.

## Projecting Your Slides

Often the most effective tool for selling your photography during in-person presentations is a Kodak Carousel tray. These trays come in both 80 and 120 capacity. We urge that you use the 80-slide tray. If you can't convince a picture editor of your talent in 80 slides, you won't do any better with 120. Not all picture editors and art directors have the equipment or space to project slides. Ask about this when making your appointment. If they can't project, show the slides in plastic sleeves.

A few photographers, including ourselves, put together elaborate slide shows with narration, music, word frames and more than one projector. These are great for events such as meetings of your local art director's club or a convention of picture editors. A really good show can do much to enhance your reputation. The main problem is finding the appropriate place and audience for an elaborate slide presentation. We do not recommend such a show for individual editors. They are interested in the quality of your work and are not seeking to be entertained.

## Thank You Alexander Graham Bell

The final important tool for selling yourself and your work is the telephone. There are a number of long-distance services such as AT&T, MCI and Sprint. In all likelihood, you're already using one of these. If you have not already done so, it is worth making a careful comparison of the different services available and see which one is most economical for your calling pattern and business needs. Look carefully at the details of their literature. Do not be influenced by the hype of their television commercials.

Telephone manners are essential to selling yourself and your product. Call a client or potential client only when you have something of importance to say. For instance, a conversation might go like this:

"Hello, this is picture editor, John Doe."

"This is photographer Mary Jones. You may recall receiving my stock list and color brochure."

"Yes, I think I have it on file."

"I just got back from three weeks of shooting on the French Riviera. I wanted you to know that I have excellent coverage on Marseille, Cannes, Nice and Monte Carlo. If you need anything from these areas, I'll be glad to send in a submission."

If you're talking to the picture editor of a major travel magazine, their stories are scheduled about six months in advance. If, by chance, the Riviera is on that schedule, the editor will probably invite you to submit. If not, he may ask if you have coverage of the unified Berlin, Holland at tulip time, or possibly pictures of your own hometown. (Don't forget that all places are travel destinations to someone.) You may make a stock sale on a totally different subject. Keep the call short. Be pleasant and courteous.

You can also use the phone (or mail) to let editors know where you will be going on your next assignment. If that happens to be San Francisco and the editor is familiar with your work, you may find yourself with a second assignment.

Getting through to some editors on the telephone can be difficult. If you have contributed to the magazine before, be sure to let the secretary or receptionist know that when asking to speak to the picture editor. If not, just give your name, say that you're a professional photographer from such and such a city, and ask for the picture editor by name. Some of our best stock sales and assignments have come from telephone calls we have initiated. Don't hesitate because of the cost. The results will invariably pay for any long-distance charges.

We have crammed a lot of information on marketing your stock photography into this chapter. Apply it to your specific situation and you will hopefully make many sales and lots of money.

*Chapter 7*

# STOCK PHOTO AGENCIES

Most professional photographers, with the possible exception of those specializing in weddings and portraits, consider placing at least some of their images with a picture agency. While agencies take about 50 percent of any sale, they can often more than make up for their commission by the volume of sales they generate. Many photographers simply do not have the time or inclination to do the marketing necessary to make stock sales on a regular basis. It is necessary to have someone available in your home or office to fill picture requests. That means you have to be there yourself or have the help of an employee or spouse. A stock photographer's time is better spent in taking pictures than in sitting in an office and waiting for the phone to ring. These factors make a strong argument for putting your slides with an agency.

## HOW WE DO IT

We do both direct marketing and work with over ten picture agencies throughout the world. We have two long-time employees, Marlene Lane and Ludwine Hall, who fill up to ten extensive picture requests every day. Over a period of time they have become very familiar with our files and, in most instances, can immediately tell a client if we have a particular subject. If you decide to sell stock directly, there are compelling reasons to have office help.

In choosing an employee for a stock business, there are several important qualities. Besides having an eye for good photography, a candidate should be well organized, neat, able to type, and have a pleasant and courteous telephone manner. It will take a person about six months to learn your files and be able to handle all business matters when you are on location or traveling on assignment, so it is important to find an individual who will stick with the job for at least two years.

Our methods of selling stock have evolved over a number of years, but what works for us may not be the best solution for you. We do, however, suggest that you make at least some direct sales. Dealing directly with a client will give you a feeling for what picture editors want and need.

## HOW PICTURE AGENCIES WORK

Picture agencies work on contract with a number of photographers, reviewing their submissions on a regular basis. Over time, an agency accumulates a collection of marketable slides and submits them to fill client requests. When a sale is made, the agency records this and sends out a statement and payment on a quarterly or monthly basis. The usual split is 50 percent, but this can vary, depending on the agreement with the photographer.

Agencies will always try to get new photographers to sign an exclusive agreement with them. We were even approached by an agency who wanted us to give up the right of selling our own stock from our office. The arguments sound great. If the agency knows that it has exclusivity on your work, it can supposedly make more sales for a higher price, being able to guarantee that there are no similars or duplicates being sold for the same use elsewhere. In reality, it is a totally one-sided argument. The agency, representing perhaps another 150 photographers, is certainly not giving you, the individual photographer, exclusivity. To illustrate this in hard figures, even our five most productive agencies do not make as much money for us as the stock business that we run from our house. The reason seems evident. We are the sole photographers showcased and submitting slides from our own stock business. If an agency wanted to give us that kind of exclusivity, we might be willing to sign our first exclusive contract. Later in this chapter, you'll see a further discussion of contracts.

Agencies prefer to have original slides, although we have found a few who will take duplicates. In fact, we feel that there are advantages in having the agencies work with originals and we will explain that later. The agency will hold the slides for the duration of your contract, usually three years with a renewable option.

All agencies are slightly different and are run according to the temperament of the owners or management. We resisted, for example, joining with one agency that played "favorites." Their number one photographer just happened to be a powerful member of the agency's staff. Other photographers' work was used only when his work couldn't fill the order. The lesson learned here was that the contract should stipulate that no owner or employee of the agency can be represented by that agency.

Sometimes your income from an agency is altered drastically when the agency management is changed. One European agency, for example, used to consider itself very high fashion and arty. Until the management changed, we had a very poor acceptance rate for the slides that we submitted. Now, under new management, the same agency is looking for more natural, unposed photos from a broader spread of destinations. As a result, the acceptance rate for our slides has gone up and so has our income from the agency. We also find it helpful to be established with multiple agencies in various countries so that, while the agency working with one country's economy might be faltering, the agency under another country's economy might be thriving.

## GETTING MARRIED TO AN AGENCY

Affiliating with a picture agency is a very important step in a photographer's career. It can be compared to marriage, a union that both parties hope will last forever, but often ends in divorce. Like marriage, choosing the right partner among picture agencies is crucial to your future happiness. The first step is finding a list of picture agencies, and one of the most comprehensive lists is in the annual *Photographer's Market*, available in most bookstores and at your local library. This book, published by Writer's Digest Books, provides the names and addresses

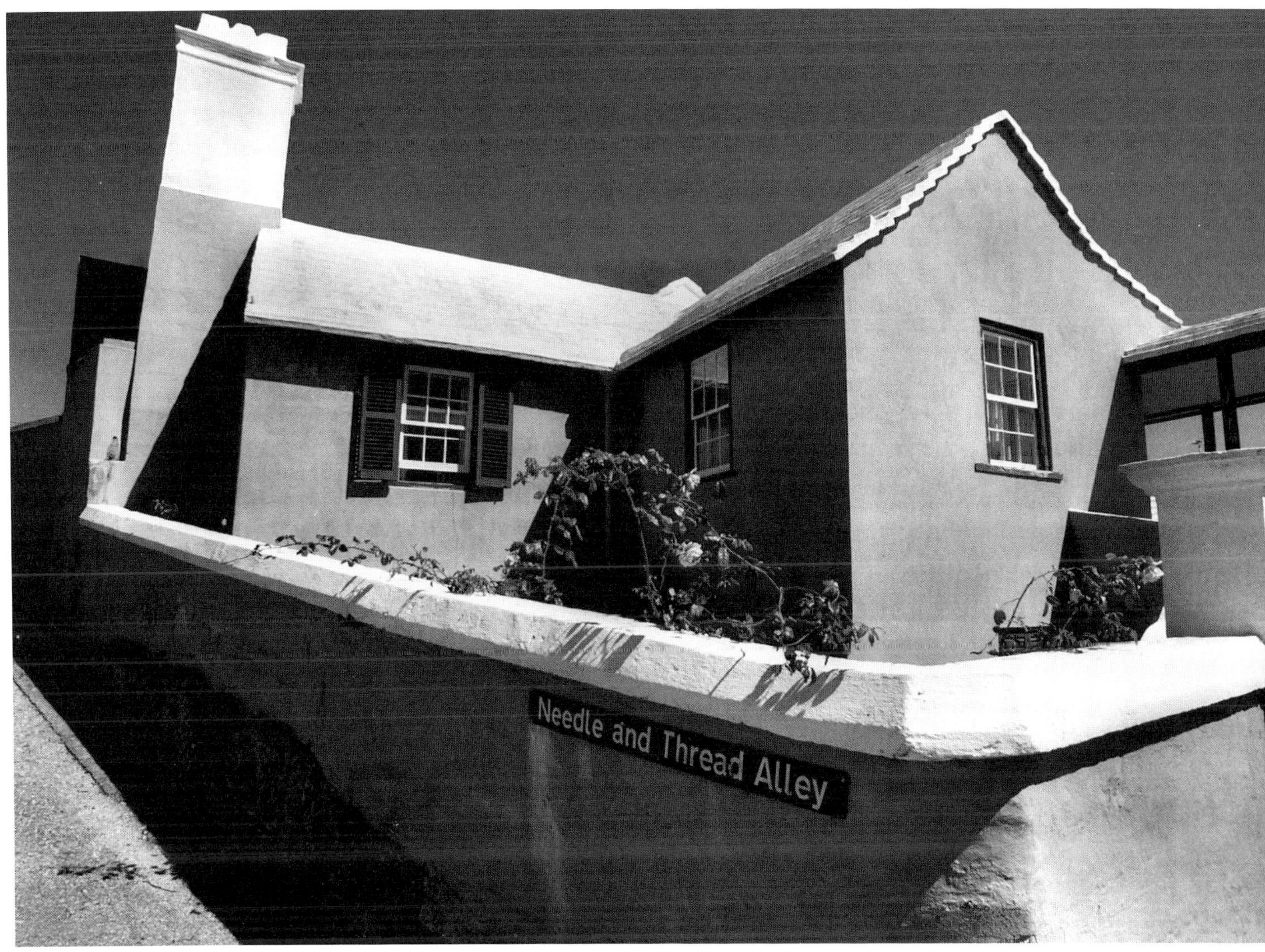


The architecture of Bermuda is unique. This picture of an old house on Needle and Thread Alley in St. George's shows the typical style that has prevailed for generations. We took it for a guidebook on the island. A wide-angle lens gave us the name of the street in the foreground, while keeping the house in the background in focus.

of major agencies and a brief description of their needs and specialties. Most agencies are looking for broad general subjects with universal appeal. A few specialize in areas such as wildlife or personalities, but unless you specialize, you should choose an agency that carries general subjects. You certainly will be concerned with the reputation of a picture agency, and you can learn a great deal from your photographic colleagues, especially those who are affiliated with the picture agency you are interested in joining.

Before you sign a contract, it is quite acceptable for you to ask to see a list, with telephone numbers, of the agency's photographers. If the agency does not wish to share a full list with you, and only provides two or three names, you can be sure that those two or three are making good money and are happy with the agency. We insist on seeing the entire list and explain that if we see a familiar name on the list, we will be contacting that friend to learn if they enjoy working with this agency. Even if you don't know anyone on the list, choose someone at random and call. Other photographers are always glad to "network," to share their experiences with you before you sign the contract. We will discuss the questions you need to be asking later on in this chapter.

## Putting Your Best Foot Forward

The ideal approach is to make an appointment to visit the agency of your choice with a broad selection of your best pictures. Come as a suitor and make the best possible impression. We suggest wearing business attire without overdressing. Don't try to look like a working photographer by wearing a photo vest and an Indiana Jones felt hat. Do come bearing gifts, but forget the flowers and chocolates. What the agency wants most are your best pictures. We suggest about 300 to 400 top-notch slides in plastic sleeves. The alternative is to call or write the agency with the proposal that you make your initial submission by mail. If they are taking on new photographers, they will probably ask you to send a submission by UPS, Federal Express or insured mail.

## The Courtship

Any marriage is a two-way street. As the eager suitor, you must make a good impression. The best way to make a favorable impression is to submit stunning pictures, but there are other factors. You must convince the agency that you are a producer, a photographer who will continue to take outstanding stock pictures in future years and on a regular basis. If they like your photographic style, they want to see a good selection of it coming across their desks every few months. Of course, they cannot know ahead of time if you will produce this volume of work, so you must convince them that you will.

The agency network is probably just as active as the photographers'. After you have a proven reputation, you may find yourself courted by agencies. This has happened to us nearly a dozen times, and sometimes we were visited by agency talent scouts from as far away as Europe. At least four of the agencies we have joined were results of their approaching us.

The agency will also be interested in seeing that most of your pictures are model released. Releases are not normally needed for editorial use, but they are invariably required for promotion and advertising. It is a tiresome chore, but be sure to get releases whenever possible. It will make your work more attractive to an agency, and more important, it can pay off in lucrative advertising sales.

## Checking References

You want to be assured that you are selecting a reputable agency, one that will look out for your interests as diligently as you would yourself. The inevitable question is how can you make such an important decision before you put your name on the dotted line? There is a simple and straightforward solution, which we mentioned briefly at the beginning of this chapter. Ask the agency to provide you with a complete list of the photographers they represent. You do not want a limited list that includes only those photographers who make the most money. Call about five or ten at random and ask them if they have been satisfied with their relationship with the agency. Most photographers will be honest and candid in their answers. You should realize that most photographers will always feel that an agency should be selling more than they are, but the most important points include:

1. **Honesty.** There are several ways an agency can be dishonest. One way is to "forget" to include the photographer's name on a remount and then let the house take all the income from subsequent sales of that slide. Another is to charge loss or holding fees separately from the use fee, and then report only the use fee to the photographer. If an agency is having trouble paying their overhead, they sometimes pay only partial income to the photographers, keeping the rest in a sort of "carry over." There are also some agencies who do not send your payments until you ask. Not only does this give the agency the use of your money; your money also can get "lost" in the shuffle.

2. **Complete and prompt sales reports.** The sales report should give the gross amount invoiced (research, holding and use fees), the type of sale, the name of client or publication and, finally, your share of the fees. It is best to ask for monthly sales reports.

3. **Prompt payment.** We usually ask for monthly payments, although many agencies prefer to pay on a quarterly basis. If we don't have our check by the 15th of the month, we consider that payment to be late.

4. **Reasonable turnaround time on submissions.** When you send a large number of slides to an agency, you want a quick edit and all the rejects returned to you promptly so that the slides can start to earn money for your home business. Slow turnaround can cost you a great deal if the slides are not in your files when the photo requests come in.

5. **Reasonable withholding for dupes and catalogs.** Most agencies have foreign affiliates and make duplicate slides for the affiliates' files. (For sales made by foreign affiliates of U.S. agencies, photographers are usually only reimbursed 25 percent of the gross sale.)

Today, an increasing number of agencies put out glossy catalogs for picture buyers. The photographers are usually asked to pay for one-half the cost of the duplicate slides and a portion of the cost of the catalog production. This amount is withheld from your agency income in small increments each month and usually paid in full over a one-year period. As you will read later in this chapter, it is important that you know the actual price charged to your agency for the duplicate slides.

## THE EXCLUSIVE CONTRACT

Once both parties are convinced that this will be a marriage of both passion and convenience, the agency will usually request total fidelity, or what is known as an exclusive contract. While we agree that fidelity is highly desirable in a marriage between a man and a woman, we consider it undesirable between a photographer and an agency. Obviously an agency is going to have relationships with other photographers. Why should you devote all your creative efforts to one agency? This point is open to negotiation. We recommend that you offer to give an agency an exclusive for their region or their part of the country, but reserve the right to work directly with agencies outside of their immediate area and certainly reserve the right to market your own work. If they really want your work in their files, most agencies will agree to such an arrangement. It is very important that you read and understand all the conditions in any contract that you sign with an agency. We strongly recommend that you take any offered contract home with you and read it in detail. It is also wise to have your lawyer go over it with you and pencil in any changes you both feel will be desirable. Picture agencies expect photographers to make changes in the basic contract and most of them are willing to negotiate differences. Here are a few points you should be concerned with:

1. Be sure your contract is non-exclusive. You might agree not to be represented by another agency in the immediate region, but you do not want any exclusivity strings tied to your work.

2. What is the duration of your contract?

3. How is it renewed? (We do not suggest roll-over contracts, which are automatically renewed unless personally canceled by the photographer on a specific date.)

4. What percentage does the agency receive? (It should never be more than 50 percent.)

5. The contract should specify monthly sales reports showing both the total amount invoiced, the percentage you are to receive, type of sale and the name of client or publication.

6. Your contract should limit the number of previously accepted slides that can be returned to you annually. Each year, most agencies do a "spring cleaning" and return to you the slides they feel cannot be used anymore. Up to a point, this makes good sense. What you want to prevent is receiving great amounts of returned slides just because the agency signed with too many photographers and now has space problems.

7. Payment should be made automatically on a quarterly or monthly basis.

8. The contract should specify what happens to your pictures and the income from them in case of your death. You will want to assure that payment is received by your heirs.

9. Look for hidden administration fees or duping costs. Do not let any agency charge you more than 50 percent for duping costs of your slides to be sent to subagents. We were shocked when we learned that one well-known agency was having duplicates made for fifteen cents each, but charging their photographers thirty cents as "their 50 percent share."

10. Your contract should spell out the cost of participating in the agency's catalog and how and when payment will be made. The most desirable way, from your standpoint, is to have the charge deducted in small increments from your earnings.

11. Be sure to include a clause allowing you or your accountant access to the agency's books for auditing purposes in case of a financial dispute. An agency that won't agree to this just might have something to hide.

12. You may want to set a lower end limit, below which reproduction right for a single slide cannot be sold. Some agencies will sell images for very low prices, especially when making a bulk sale, and this undercuts the market for everyone.

13. We strongly urge that you do not allow your images to be included on a

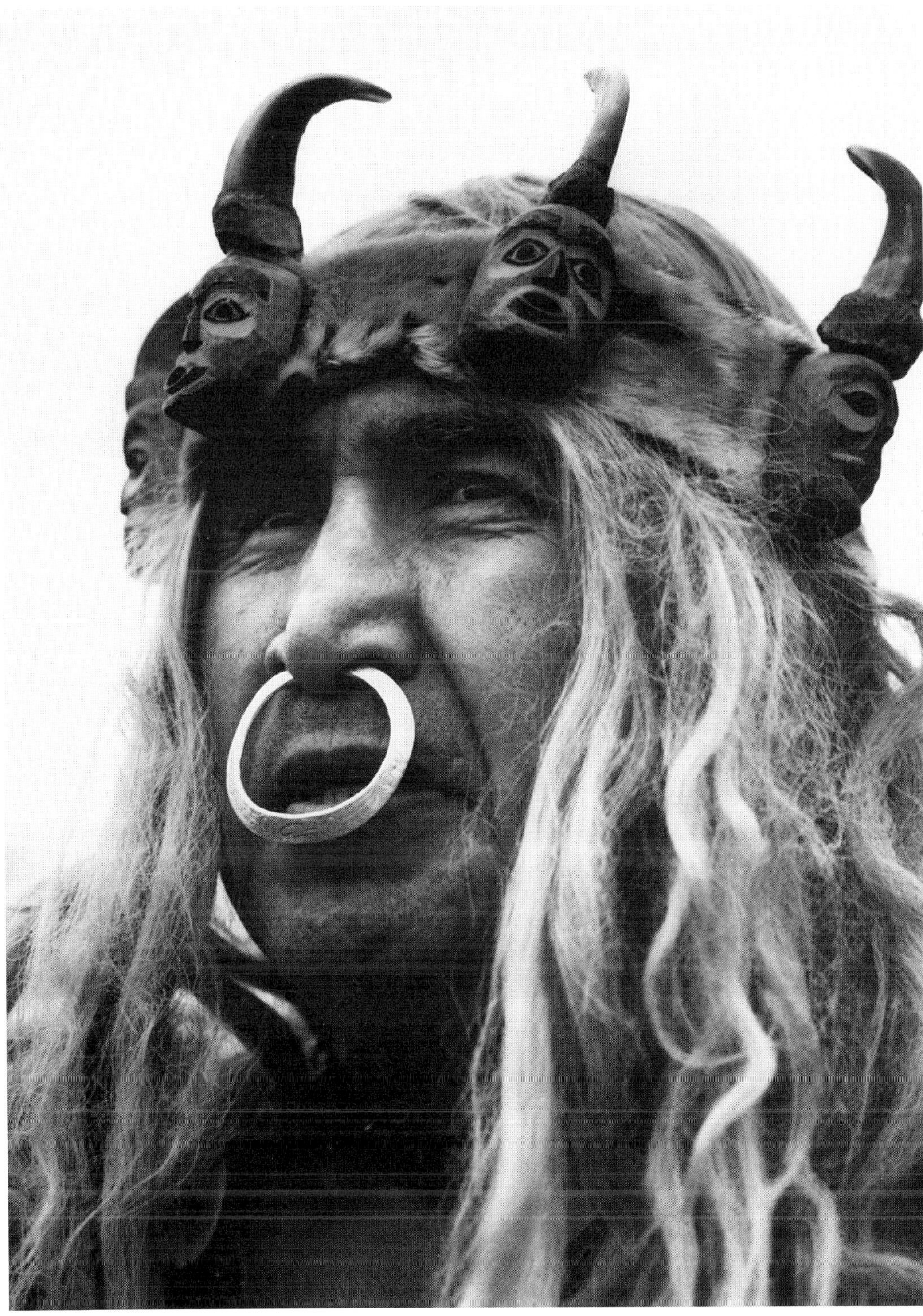

The headgear and nose ring this Indian in Alaska wears during a ceremonial dance makes him a striking subject for a stock picture. When taking such a picture, be sure to get a model release and the name of his tribe for your caption. When the background around your subject is busy or cluttered, drop down and let the sky make a clean background.

CD-ROM disk of photographic clip art put out by the agency. Although the agency might make a good deal of money from a CD-ROM disk, the individual photographer will not have any control over the rights allowed, nor will his income be very high. This will be addressed in more detail in chapter eight.

## THE BEST FORMAT

We have mentioned earlier that the most acceptable film format for an agency is

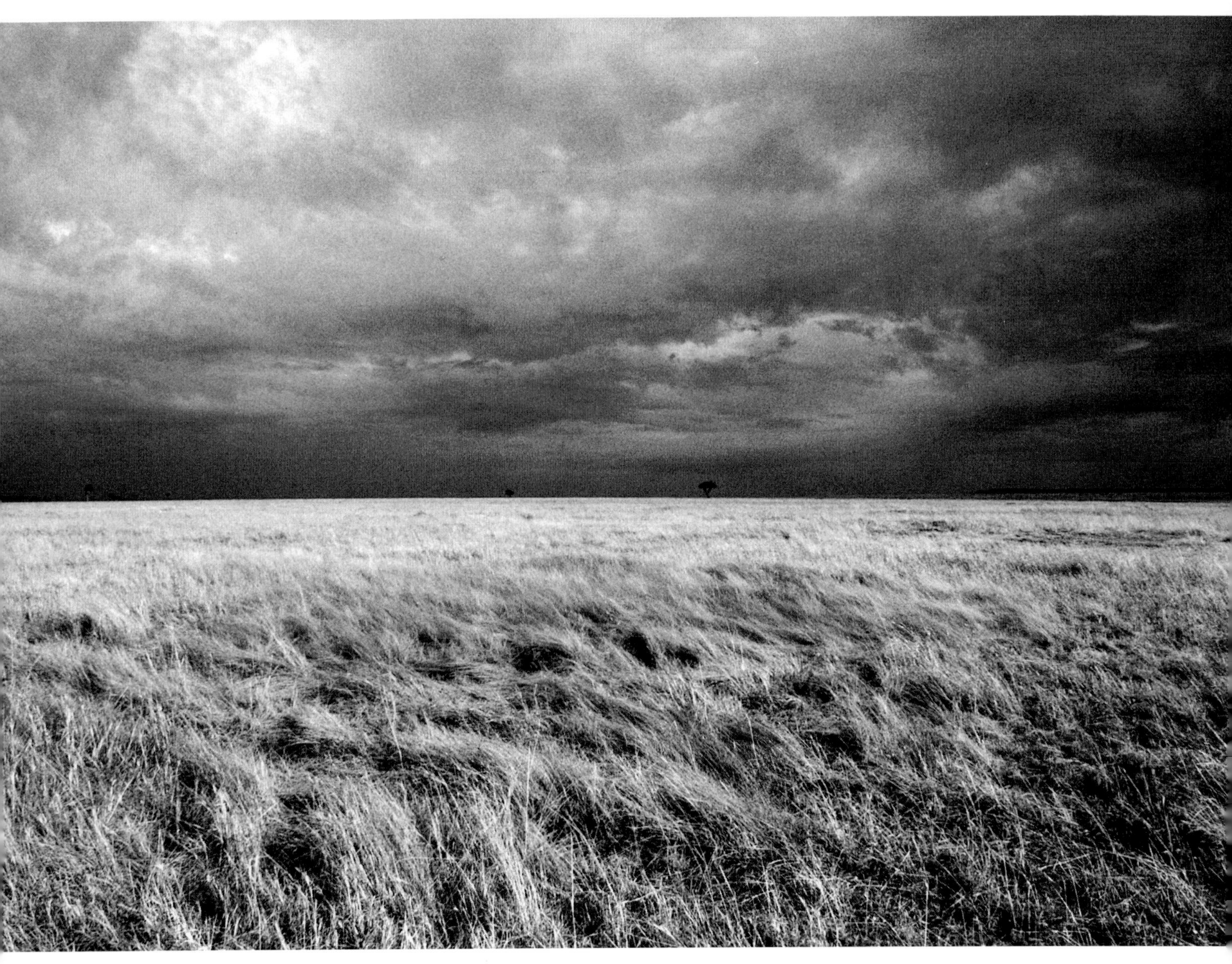

The empty savannah of the Masai Mara in Kenya is a strong image for stock. This picture is a perfect background photo. It could be used with a headline and type set on the plain or in the sky. It would also be relatively simple to superimpose a giraffe, an elephant or a safari vehicle on the plain with computer imagery.

35mm slides. This format for publication was originally pioneered by *National Geographic* and Kodachrome film. In the early years, most publications and printers preferred to use larger film formats such as 4-by-5 inches, or 2¼-by-2¼ inches. It was the *Geographic* that proved top-quality color reproduction was possible from the tiny 35mm slide. *Life* magazine staff photographers started to use 35mm German and Japanese cameras, originally with high-speed, black-and-white film and later with color. Gradually, more publications accepted, and finally preferred, the spontaneous, candid pictures taken with 35mm cameras. Picture agencies shifted from the larger format pictures, which tended to be static and posed, to the more journalistic images possible with smaller cameras. Today only a few agencies work only in the large formats. Aside from photographic style, one of the major advantages of 35mm slides is that they can be stored in relatively small space, often in convenient metal file cabinets. Large submissions can be shipped in plastic sleeves at a moderate cost. The whole photographic industry has shifted toward 35mm, both in terms of camera equipment and the storage and filing of photographic images. Obviously a few agencies still accept larger-size transparencies and one or two even specialize in the larger formats.

## BLACK AND WHITE

One cannot ignore the market for black-and-white photographs. It does exist and for certain market outlets it is flourishing. Some of the most fashionable magazines are rediscovering black and white, and use monotone images to evoke the twenties, thirties, forties and fifties. Other low-budget publications use black-and-white pictures for economy, but expect to pay lower prices for black-and-white prints. Two agencies, the Betman Archives in New York and H. Armstrong Roberts in Philadelphia, specialize in historical photographs, many of them in black and white.

Another viable outlet for black-and-white photography is the museum and gallery field. The chemistry of black-and-white emulsions is more stable than the dyes used in color prints and that archival quality has made black and white prints a better investment for the collector. The personally made prints of such masters as Ansel Adams and Edward Weston command very high prices in today's market. There is a great deal of personal and creative satisfaction in shooting black-and-white film, developing the film, and making a custom print of your best image. However, as satisfying as this is, we do not consider the black-and-white medium a good one for making money in the stock photography business.

We often need good quality black-and-white prints to illustrate our newspaper travel articles. For a number of years we struggled to take both color slides and black-and-white negative film during our shoots. It required carrying more equipment and taking twice as much time to shoot a subject. Our final solution has been to shoot nothing but color slide film and convert a few key shots to black and white. This can easily be done by a good custom lab and should cost about $10 for each transfer negative. Then you can have as many prints made as you need. When done properly, the quality is excellent and equals the results of shooting the same picture with standard black-and-white film.

## THE UNIVERSAL FILM

In many ways we consider color slide film to be universal film. The primary or first generation image is a positive color transparency or color slide, the product that is a printer's first choice for reproduction. This slide can be used for making a transfer negative for black and white or for making high quality color prints. It can also be used for making repro-quality color duplicate slides or larger format color transparencies. Both Kodachrome and the E-6 color transparency film such as Ektachrome and Fujichrome can be push processed for higher speed ratings. For instance, Fujichrome 100 can be pushed to 200 or 400 with little loss of image quality and sharpness. Ask your local film lab about the availability and cost of push processing. You may want to shoot one or two test rolls to try it out and evaluate the results.

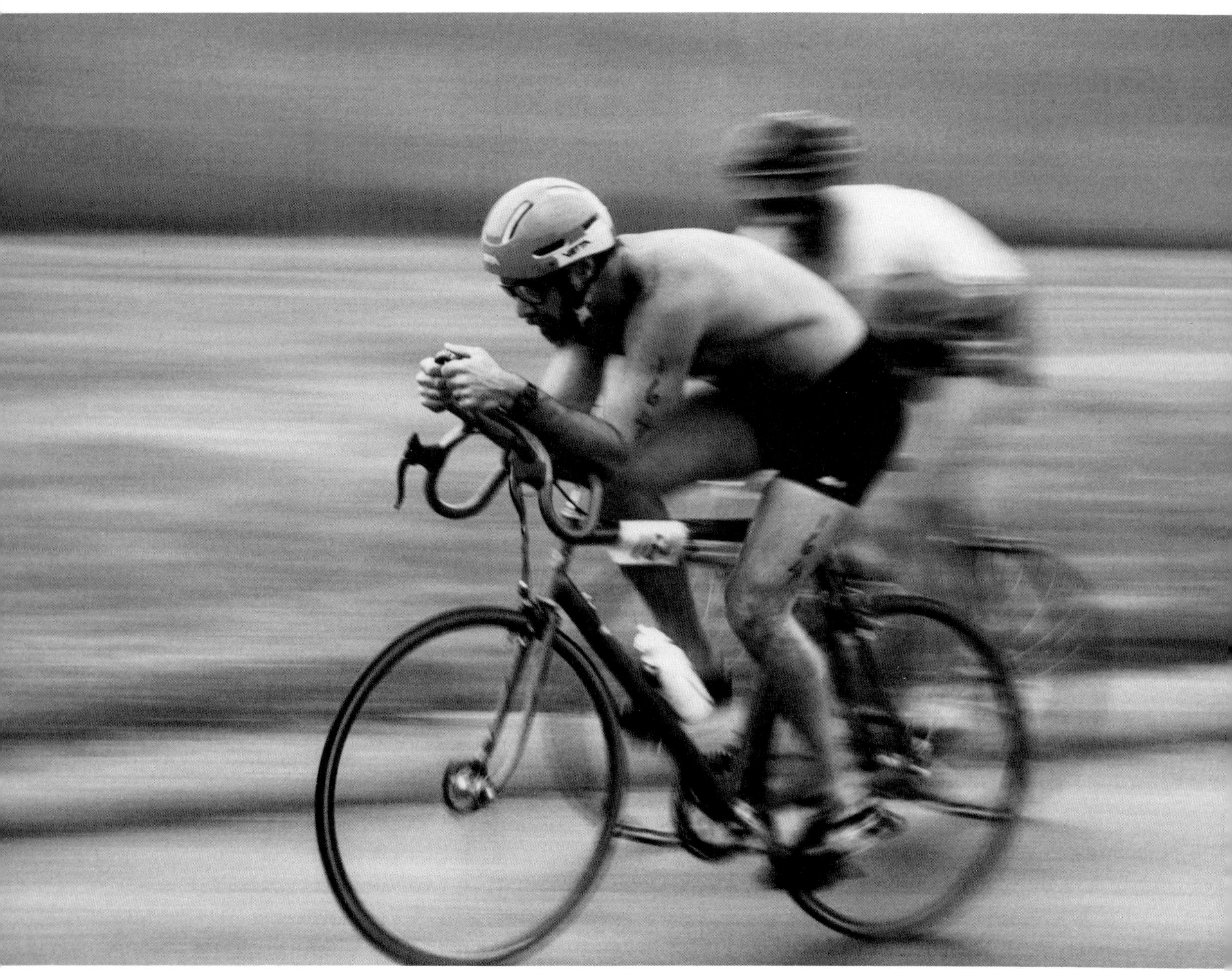

Pan with a moving subject (at a relatively slow shutter speed) to convey a feeling of movement in a picture. These cyclists were shot at 1/60th of a second while panning the camera in the direction they were moving.

## HAPPILY EVER AFTER

If you sign a contract with an agency, you owe it to your photos to accept that this will be a long-term relationship. It will take almost a year from the time the agency first accepts a slide until that slide starts to generate income. The agency has to document the slide into a database, put an identification label on each slide, have duplicates made, and perhaps even have color separations made for a catalog. Then the slide must be filed and wait until a photo request comes in.

We have found that as a very safe ballpark figure, you can count on each slide with agencies to make an average of $1 per slide per year. This may sound like very little, but over the years you may get up to 6,000 slides into an agency and $6,000 would be a steady, if unremarkable, income from them. In actuality, our slides with some agencies are earning $5 or more a year, particularly if that agency has a lot of advertising clients. One or two good sales can make a difference. For example, last month one of our agencies sold a shot for $10,000. It was good for them and good for us.

## LEAVING AN AGENCY

If, for any reason, you and the agency decide to sever your ties, you should be aware that it is a lengthy process. To weed your slides out of a massive slide file and return them to you may take up to three years, unless you wish to personally pay the salary for a researcher to do it more quickly. We have always felt that the hurry would not benefit us. The agency will continue to pay your share of income from the slides (or the duplicates in their subagents' files). For example, we are still receiving quarterly checks from an agency we left nine years ago, an agency that, according to our figures, has returned all but five slides.

## DON'T STOP SHOOTING

Although your choice of agency may have been made with great care and you may be convinced that this will be a perfect marriage of both passion and convenience, it is important that you remember that good marriages require constant attention. Keep shooting and submitting your slides to your agency on a regular basis. We have noticed that our income always rises after frequent submissions. Though we trust our agencies to be impartial, we do recognize that it helps if agency employees are familiar with our work. If a researcher has just looked at one of our slides, which would perfectly fit a client's needs, it is only human and practical that the researcher would pull out our slide to submit to that client.

Your marriage with your agencies is important. It will bring in additional income throughout your life and may still be giving your children gifts from you when you are no longer alive. Work at it. Keep this marriage vibrant!

*Chapter 8*

# THE NEW TECHNOLOGY

## THE RISE OF PHOTOGRAPHIC TECHNOLOGY

Marvelous new inventions, which start out impossibly cumbersome and expensive, are refined until even the average person can afford to have a version at home. The computer, which started out as two rooms filled with equipment, can now be held in the palm of your hand. Early software programs were custom designed by computer programmers. Soon, you could go to a store and, for a reasonable price, buy a disk that would load the most sophisticated and incredible programs directly onto your computer. These amazing machines made it possible to keep your finances straight, do spreadsheets, keep client records and track individual sales. Merge mail allowed you to write a personal letter to hundreds of people using just ten minutes of your time. You could do sort and select searches simultaneously and pull out a specific type of information for a specific date from massive collections of data.

Then, desktop publishing became the rage. It was suddenly possible to sit at your computer, compose your own business forms, newsletters or even brochures, and make them look highly professional. Clip art became available. You could buy disks full of clever drawings in all conceivable styles. You could lift pieces of the art from the disk and use them to illustrate your own publications. You could combine, enlarge or shrink, or even alter drawings to meet your needs. The computer enabled you to blow up a drawing as much as 400 percent, making possible the alteration of minute details. Drawing programs, such as Aldus FreeHand and Adobe Illustrator, permitted you to do your own drawings and illustrations from scratch. Laser printers were so good that they could reproduce the drawings with even the most delicate shading.

Somewhere in this sequence of events the computer designers developed a device called a scanner, which is shaking the very foundation of the photographic industry. A flat-bed or hand-held scanner reads a visual image, such as a drawing or cartoon, and translates it into digital information that can be saved on a hard (or floppy) disk and printed on a laser printer. It is even possible to scan type from a book.

The next steps were inevitable. If you can "scan" type and drawings and transmit them to a computer, why not scan a photograph? If you can have a disk full of clever drawings for your desktop publishing, why not a disk full of stunning, full-color photography? If you can have a laser printer capable of reproducing a black-and-white photograph, why not connect a computer to a color laser printer, a color copier or even directly to a printing press?

## CD-ROM

Compact disks (or "CD"s) have been used in the music world to render a precise, distinct and accurate sound. When it was time to start scanning photographs onto a disk, CDs were the logical choice. The resulting disk, which can be filled with photographs, text, video film and even sound, is called CD-ROM, which stands for "Compact Disk—Read-Only Memory."

Photographs on CD-ROMs can be either low resolution or high resolution. Low-resolution images use less memory than high-resolution images because less information about each picture is stored per square millimeter. The low-resolution picture looks fine onscreen. It is a good illustration for reading purposes, but is not acceptable for high-quality printing. Because low resolution uses less memory, more information can be put on each disk. For example, a low-resolution disk can hold an entire illustrated encyclopedia or the complete works of Shakespeare.

High resolution uses much more memory because it stores more information about each picture per square millimeter. Such an image allows the end user to make color separations for printing on a conventional press. These high-resolution computer images also can be printed, with fine results, on special printers that use photographic paper or on high-quality color copiers. Results vary, depending on the quality and resolution of the scan, but it is possible to get results equal to that achieved in the finest glossy magazines. One CD-ROM disk can hold up to 300 high-resolution images and still have room for text.

## IMAGE MANIPULATION

A few years ago we heard disturbing rumors about new developments in computers that would allow for electronic manipulation and alteration of images. This raised an ethical question, as it seemed to open the door for the dishonest use of photography and confusion about copyrights. If it was possible to transplant palm trees onto a deserted beach or show a political leader in the company of scantily clad show girls, the very integrity of photography was at stake. If the photograph of a little girl (enter one photographer) could be integrated (enter one computer expert) with a luxuriant background (enter the second photographer) and a beautiful butterfly could be posed on her hand (enter the third photographer), to whom does the copyright belong?

We were amazed that technicians at *National Geographic* were able, purely as a technical exercise, to eliminate a Coke bottle from the grass in a picture of a park, to literally clean up a scene and make the world a perfect place. We've even heard that an editor used a computer to move the Egyptian pyramids around to suit the layout needs in a cover picture. His artistic license was somewhat controversial.

We read an article in *Photo District News* which announced that hundreds of high resolution color images could be stored on a CD-ROM disk and that these images could be retrieved directly from the disk, displayed on a computer screen and reproduced in a magazine or newspaper. We didn't get much sleep that night, concerned that this technology could flood the market with low-cost stock images and destroy an important segment of our business. The following morning we telephoned David Walker, author of the article, and asked some pointed questions about CD-ROMs and their potential application in the field of publishing. He confirmed that this technology will have an impact on stock photography and publishing, but said it had not reached the point where the resolution could compete with use of an original color transparency. It was obvious, however, that it was only a matter of time until such quality could be achieved.

Eastman Kodak has launched a massive effort to place itself in the forefront of electronic imagery. The Kodak Photo CD, a slightly different format from CD-ROM, was initially introduced as a device to play back amateur snapshots on a home television screen, but it has evolved into a sophisticated tool for professional photographers and stock agencies. While slightly different, the Photo CD has been designed to be compatible with existing CD-ROM technology. (Both types of disks can be played on either system.)

Obviously the Kodak player can also be attached to a high-resolution color computer. It is faster than CD-ROM for scanning color slides or negatives into a computer, and, like CD-ROM, the level of resolution can be determined when the image is scanned. The computer of choice for working with photographic images seems to be a color Macintosh with a software called Adobe Photoshop, but IBM and IBM-compatible computers can also handle this type of task. Working with photographic images requires prodigious amounts of RAM (about 20 megabytes for convenient speed of operation) and huge hard disk storage capacity. The Syquest hard drive with removable cartridges works extremely well to store and access images for short-term use. An optical write-once (WORM) storage drive is another, but more expensive, option. The ultimate storage device for long-term, read-only storage is the CD-ROM or the Kodak Compact Disk.

Setting aside the ethical questions concerning image alteration or manipulation, this new technology offers exciting creative possibilities for putting together the best elements of several color pictures to come up with a prizewinning stock image. For instance, it is possible to take a sunset from one scene, the silhouette of a sailing vessel from another, a flying sea gull from a third picture and combine them all into one. We recently sat down with two of our colleagues, Jim Pickerell and Fred Ward, in front of Fred's Quadra Macintosh computer with Adobe Photoshop software and played around with our images, which were on a CD-ROM disk being marketed by Educorp. It was an eye-opening experience. We were able to take a picture of the Grand Canal in Venice and change the sky from lackluster gray to Kodachrome blue. We were able to change that vivid sky to a glowing sunset and then tone the overall picture to a golden tone to match the setting sun.

Such image manipulation takes time and patience. The rough edges between the buildings and the sky have to be touched up, but the overall image can be enlarged to the degree where the operator can change, at will, the color and density of each individual pixel. When combining different images, the problem is, if the pictures were taken by three different

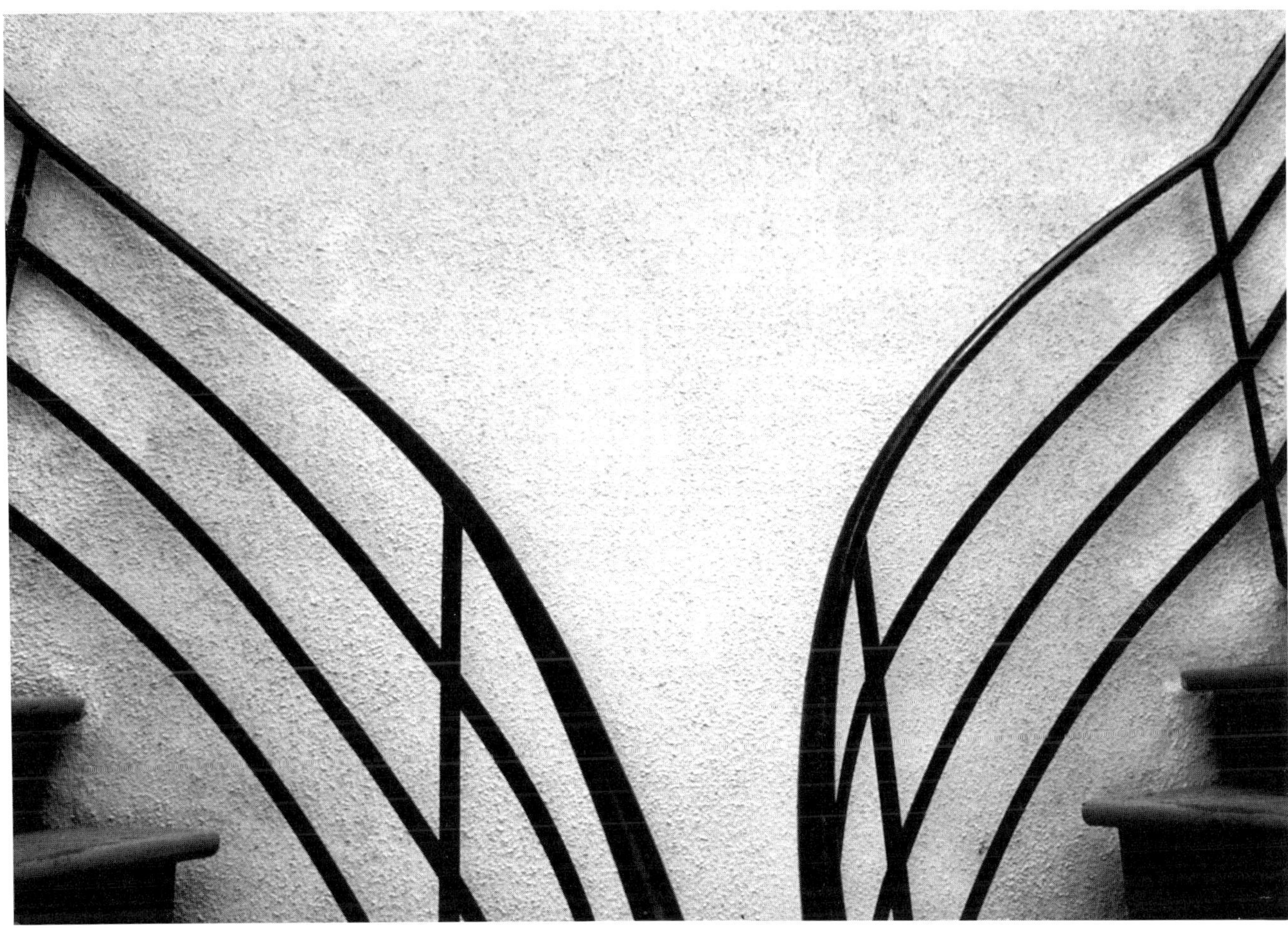

These stair banisters in Montreal made an interesting, almost abstract, composition. Always look for graphic details in your surroundings. Isolate the details and they often become an artistic composition.

photographers and combined by a fourth person, who gets paid for the final picture and who gets the credit line? These are legal copyright problems that must be resolved in the future, but combined image photographs are already being created. Some art directors and picture editors are working without any set copyright guidelines.

Fortunately, the American Society of Magazine Photographers is getting involved in an attempt to act as a clearinghouse for interested photographers, trying to clarify the issues and police copyright protection for its members in the manner that ASCAP does for the music industry.

The reaction of some photographers to this new technology is to bury their heads in the sand and pretend it doesn't exist. The reality is that it does exist and it will forever change the way we market and distribute pictures. Critics of the technology protest that an end user can purchase a disk of 200 color images for around $200 and then has the right to use any of these pictures for publication at no additional cost. That is about $1 per picture and such a low price flies in the face of traditional stock marketing. In spite of the low cost, some picture agencies are starting to put their images on disk, but the return to an individual photographer is negligible. Some individual photographers with large files are doing the same, most often through CD-ROM publishers and, if a disk is highly successful, that photographer could do very well. If a photographer has only his or her images on a disk, the potential, as the market continues to grow, could be very promising.

Our analysis of this new technology is that it will initially exert a downward pressure on stock prices, but that it will offer new and exciting opportunities for creating images to meet specific needs. It will also generate a voracious demand for new and up-to-date photographic images as innovative leaders in the public relations field recognize the potential it offers for fast and inexpensive distribution of photographs featuring their products or travel destinations. If a company, such as a Visitors and Convention Bureau, a resort complex or a tourist office, has a photo file with top-quality images, they can convert the file to CD-ROM and distribute 500 to 1,000 of their best pictures to picture editors at less than $3 per disk.

## NEGOTIATING FOR ELECTRONIC RIGHTS

The major question a stock photographer needs to ask himself is whether or not he wants to get involved with CD-ROMs or to make his pictures available in an electronic form. While there has been an understandable negative reaction within the photographic profession to the Pandora's box that has been opened by this technology, we personally feel that photographers need to accept the fact that this technology is here and will not go away. We recommend that photographers proceed with caution and, if they decide to license electronic rights to their images, that they evaluate it like any other business proposition.

As we mentioned, the American Society of Media Photographers (ASMP) is currently planning to set up an office that will establish guidelines and standards in this new area of photography and hopefully police the use of images through the electronic medium. At the moment, ASMP is our most powerful protection against abuse of our images. We personally urge all stock photographers to join this professional organization, which over the years has done and is doing so much to protect the rights of individual practitioners.

The fact that photographs can now be manipulated, combined and re-touched on a computer has forever changed one of the basic concepts about the medium of photography. We can no longer presume that a photograph is an honest statement. It is like an illustration or a painting. The image can be anything the artist wants it to be. While this may change the way we perceive photography, it allows for new dimensions of creativity in this visual medium. We think that stock photographers need to fully understand both the problems and potential in this new field. We predict it will bring drastic changes to the way we all do business.

Because of all the problems we mentioned in the first part of this chapter, CD-ROM companies are trying to get as many rights as they can from photographers who are still fairly inexperienced with copyright ramifications. You may get a call tomorrow from someone who wants to put 500 of your photos on CD-ROM. You should be even more careful about signing an electronic rights contract than you were when you signed an agency contract. The agency contract can be canceled at the end of three or five years.

Once your photos are on CD-ROM, the purchasers of the CD-ROM disks, or end users, will have access to your images as long as they have the hardware to read them.

To be able to lawfully license rights to the end user, the CD-ROM publisher will have to get worldwide, perpetual and irrevocable rights from you. We insist that limits be written into the end user license agreement about use of our images, such as:

> Unlimited editorial and advertising rights are granted for national distribution of less than 10,000 copies. All pictures must include photographer's credit. The pictures may not be used for commercial sales outside the U.S., T-shirts, posters, calendars, billboards and postcards. The images may not be reused in any computer digital media or included in any software product for resale without the express permission of (the CD-ROM publisher). Copyrights will be strictly enforced. For distribution other than explained above, please contact Carl and Ann Purcell at (703) 845-1104 or fax (703) 845-1103.

It is very important that your name and telephone number are on the end user licensing agreement. If an advertising agency decides that they want your photograph for a really large ad campaign, they must be able to reach you so that a financial agreement can be reached and, if necessary, they can use the original slide.

We feel that the 10,000 press run limit will allow a publisher to use one of our photos for a brochure or a textbook, but it would not cover a widely read national magazine with a circulation of several million. If, for example, *Time* magazine or *U.S. News & World Report* wanted to use one of our photos for a cover, they would have to negotiate directly with us.

We have also stipulated that use can only be national and not international. It is almost impossible to police all European magazines, especially from the United States.

It is also important that under the section headed "Warranties," the end user license should state:

> If End User abuses or misuses a photograph or the subject of a photograph in this Product, the End User will be held solely responsible for all legal costs arising from such misuse, including any court proceedings involving the CD-ROM publisher or the Photographers.

Although you will probably have model releases for most of the people pictures on your CD-ROM disk, it is still conceivable that the end user might misuse the photo in a way that would slander the subject. You don't want to pay lawyer fees to defend yourself. Refer to chapter four for a discussion on liability insurance. Be careful to retain the right to continue sales of your photos in other mediums and even use up to 20 percent of the pictures scanned for this disk on other CD-ROM disks. Finally, protect yourself by letting a lawyer go over the contract with you before you sign it.

In this brave new world of the future, we will probably submit pictures via telephone lines, and picture editors and art

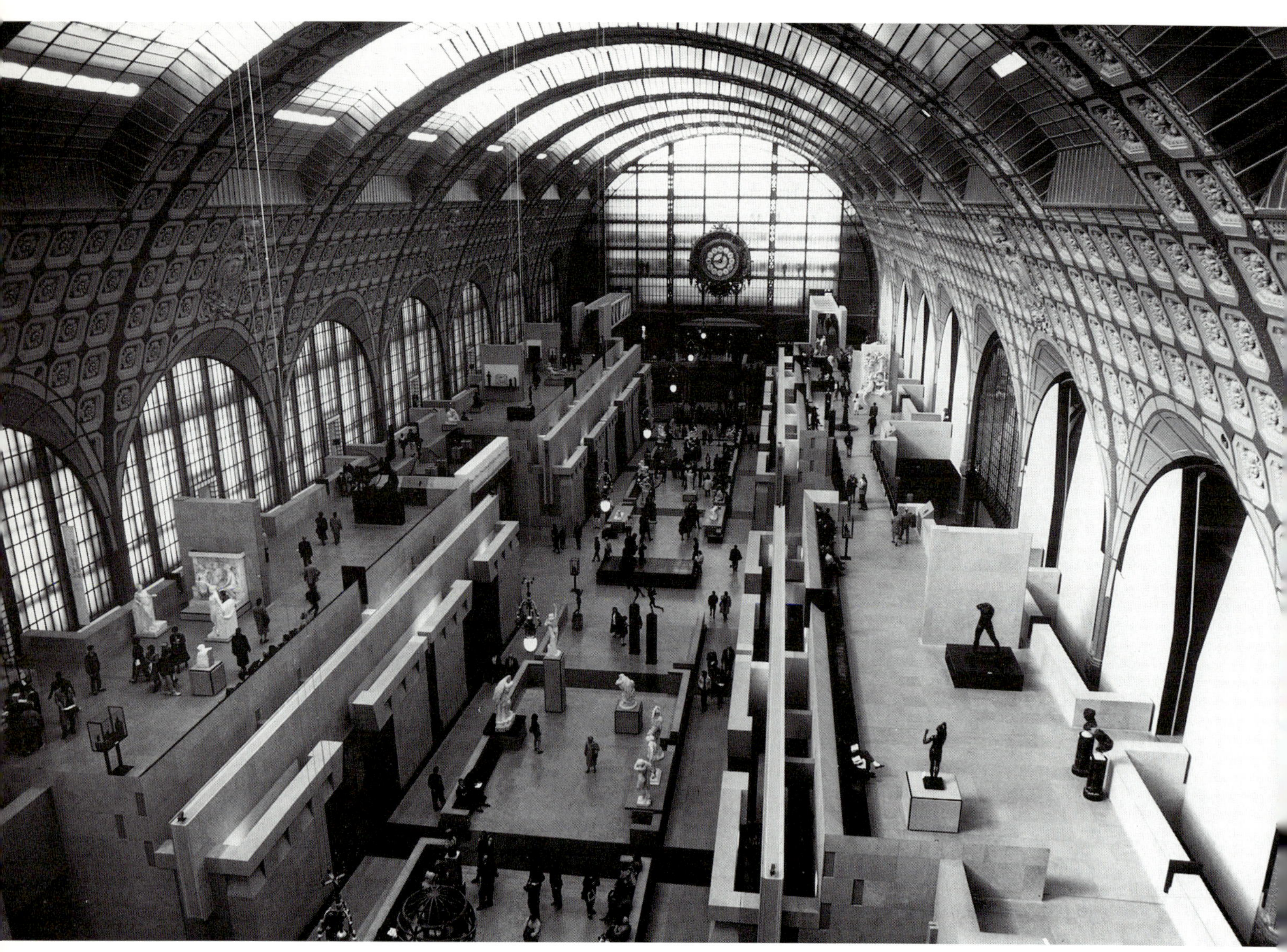

The Musee D'Orsay in Paris was originally a train station. Today it is a stunning art museum. Most guidebooks on Paris or France would need such a picture as an illustration.

directors will look at images on computer screens instead of light tables. Who could have predicted twenty-five years ago that cameras would operate with auto-focus and automatic exposure?

As a successful stock photographer, you must be flexible enough to accept new technology and make it work to your advantage. It is the way to make sure that your stock business will thrive, not just to make a fortune for you today, but also to ensure a steady income for you after you retire.

Great shooting, good luck and best wishes from both of us!

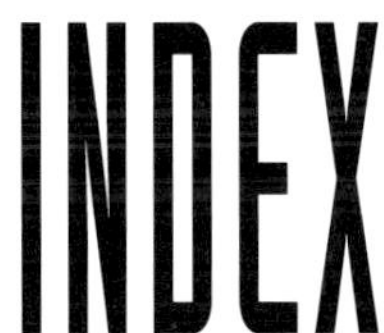